VERA

"FIRST LADY OF MARIN"

A biography of Vera Lucille Smith Schultz

EVELYN M. RADFORD

1998

Printed in the United States of America

First printing 1998

ISBN   0-912133-14-7: Hilltop Publishing Company,
          Sonoma, Ca.

Library of Congress Catalog Card Number: 98-72848

Publishers: Vera Schultz Biography Fund
Printed by McNaughton & Gunn,
          960 Woodland Drive
          Saline, MI. 48176
Distributed by the Gift Shop, Marin County Civic Center,
          3501 Civic Center Drive, San Rafael, California.,
                              94903

TABLE OF CONTENTS

AUTHOR'S NOTE

In May of 1994, Vera asked me to assist her in writing the story of her life. I would record as she dictated, then transform her oral story into written prose. When my time became free to pursue the project in the fall of that year, her deteriorating health prevented us from doing more than record 44 hours of scrambled memories over a period of four months. After the first session it was apparent to us both that autobiography must necessarily become biography. I was able to write no more than rough drafts of a few minor passages dealing with her childhood, before she became too ill to even be involved in plotting the scope or direction of the book. Memory becomes fallible within hours of any event, and when she left for Texas we were relying on memory alone. Though Vera's mind remained clear, penetrating and youthful until the end, more thorough explication of the events of her political life was cut off by her death. I have had to rely on the unexamined data of the tapes we made and the memories of people who were participants in the events covered by this work. Fortunately, I had a wealth of materials saved from 1971-1972 when we spent hours and hours together as I gathered material for my doctoral dissertation that became *THE BRIDGE AND THE BUILDING*.

Some of the personal information included herein came from 25 years of being her confidante. I didn't live in Marin. I didn't know her friends. I was a safe depository for tales not to be told. For a quarter of a century she used me as a sounding board for all the anguish of her life not included in this book.

I entered Vera's life in 1970 when I began the research for my doctoral dissertation and met Vera for the first time. From then on, I attended almost every major event that focused on her. Because of my personal experience of the woman reflected in these pages, my presentation of Vera may be coated with a patina of the friendship we shared. I hope not. I hope that what I've written measures up to her standards of realistic appraisal and accurate reporting, thereby fulfilling the purpose of this book. Vera would have wanted absolute accuracy. I have tried to authenticate the material in this work by submitting sections of the book to various people for verification, but only she could determine how faithfully I have recounted the events of her life as she remembered them. How extensively I elaborated on material that did not come from her memories was determined by space limitations imposed by publication costs. I wanted to present Vera three-dimensionally: the fullness of her public life, the fecundity of her mind, and the richness of her generous personality. I hope I succeeded.

Vera protected those she loved, and cherished them. If the reader wonders at the paucity of information about her personal life in these pages, I shook hands with her daughter to seal a promise that, in-so-far as possible, I would keep her father out of the book. Ray had to appear at times in order to tell Vera's story, but this book is not about him. The story of Ray's life is yet to be written. Additionally, her daughter desired that neither she nor her children would appear in this narration of her mother's life. We made that bargain in Vera's presence, recording it on tape to make it as binding as a person's word could be. To the best of my ability I have honored that pledge. This book is about Vera, and only Vera.

ACKNOWLEDGMENTS

I want to thank all the people who graciously shared pertinent materials with me, and allowed me to play Vera's memories against their own. There were gaps to be filled. Sincerely, my thanks to the seven women who became the "Friends of Vera Schultz" committee to raise funds for this book: Jody Anne Becker, Kathleen Foote, Sally Hauser, Kathleen Hill, Jacquelyn Mollenkopf, Trubee Schock, and Ailene Taylor. Their success is evident in the listing of donors at the end of the book.

Kathleen Hill, of Hilltop Publishers, contributed one of her ISBN numbers and oversaw the publication process. Trubee Schock created the solicitation letter, loaned me materials, and contributed a large number of the pictures. Further, she clarified for me the sequence of events that led to the establishment of the AAUW Fellowship. Jody Anne Becker provided insights about many things, most importantly, information about New Horizons Savings & Loan Association, and the Marincello project. Josette Gavin let me browse through scrapbooks the Southern Marin AAUW Branch, and provided the name of the first Vera Schultz Fellow. Margaret Azevedo read the Marin City material and corrected it. Ed Ryken gave me invaluable information about Manny Charnow, and the creation of Whistlestop. Sally Hauser and Dorothy Killion talked to me about what it meant to be a reader for Vera after she became blind. Jacquelyn Mollenkopf spent hours explaining the months Vera spent working on the Save Our County Libraries Committee, and even more hours creating the Index for this book. Ailene Taylor, historian of the League of Women Voters of Marin County, served as an insightful critic of my handling of The Woman Suffrage Movement. As the project struggled to take form, without portfolio, she became ex-officio chairman of the committee to drive it forward, and to oversee the editing done by the committee.

Leland Jordan, Doug Dawson and Kathleen Foote met with me in the City Manager's office in Mill Valley to reminisce about Vera, and in doing so they rounded out the Mill Valley material. Beth Ashley read the manuscript and reviewed it for the Marin Independent Journal, April 2, 1998. Many of the above named people read and corrected excerpts from this work, filling in additional information in the process.

The Marin Senior Coordinating Council became the non-profit fiscal agent for the Committee, renamed the "Vera Schultz Biography Fund." Kathleen Vote spent countless hours recording gifts received, paying bills, and rendering the necessary accounts. Phyllis Evans came on board as Marketing Assistant for the book once it is in the hands of the Gift Shop at the Civic Center. Happily, Grace Holley, Manager of the Marin County Civic Center Gift Shop, was willing to take on the warehousing and distribution of the book, an invaluable, and major undertaking. Due to the advocacy of Supervisor Annette Rose, a most generous gift came from the Board of Supervisors, a gift that doubled the funds already accumulated. Following the generosity of the Supervisors, the Marin Community Foundation swelled the coffers with an equally generous grant, matching the contribution of the Supervisors. Therewith, we were at last fully funded and could push forward toward publication and marketing.

Kathleen Foote, attorney, took the chair and steered us through the contractual phases of the process. Under her oversight, it all came together at last. No greater tribute could the people of Marin have made to Vera than to underwrite the publication of her last benediction to her beloved county. Referring to her desire that her story, whole or in part, be written, she said, "I want it all." Marin is open-handedly giving themselves, and her, what she wanted.

Also, I want to acknowledge my husband, Barney Rubin, who applied his skill with computers to format this book camera ready for publication. He also scanned, enlarged or reduced, and otherwise adapted the pictures herein. Finally, the three professionals who took the book in hand: Paul Erhlich, thanks for your finely honed skill in editing. I learned a lot; proofreader Nancy Keiffer, thanks for your red pencil which was mercifully merciless; and Graphic Artist, Heather Brook Graef, thanks for creating the beautiful book cover.

Most of all, I want to thank Vera for entrusting me with her memories, and the honor of being her biographer. E.R

PREFACE

May 9, 1995, a day almost as wet and rainy as the day she left Marin for Texas, more than 70 people braved the weather to meet in the Supervisors' chamber of the Marin County Civic Center to remember Vera Lucille Schultz. A proposal was made that the Marin County Civic Center be renamed to honor her. "There were two geniuses at work on that building," the speaker said, "Frank Lloyd Wright who designed the building, and Vera Schultz who had had the vision necessary to bring such a building to Marin County in the first place."

On the preceding Friday, May 5, an editorial headline in the *Marin Independent Journal* read, "Vera Schultz Saw Forever." The last paragraph of that editorial was particularly insightful into what made Vera the "First Lady of Marin." "So relentlessly did Vera Schultz dare to dream—and so lasting is her legacy—that it's hard to believe she's gone now, at 92. Marin is richer today because Vera Schultz never stopped believing in tomorrow—and in herself."

Vera Lucille (Klingen)Smith Schultz belonged to that body of women who were inheritors of the suffragist (the American term for suffragette) ethos. Born near the turn of the 20th century, they came of age too late to join their "genteel" older sisters' crusade for the right to vote. These "New Women," as they were tagged by the press, became torchbearers for the right of women to go beyond voting. They wanted to enter areas of public life rarely open to their gender. Single-minded, dedicated, competent, they ignored society's chiding about a "woman's place" in the world. Some achieved national fame as pace-setters and change-makers. A larger number of them were little known outside their regional sphere of influence.

In any comprehensive list of national female leaders and reformers, the names of Eleanor Roosevelt, Helen Gahagan Douglas, and Margaret Mead, can be found. All were contemporaries of Vera Schultz and she knew two of them personally. The third, Margaret Mead, she admired for her independence and courage. These "New Women" pursued different objectives but each shared some of the same attributes and/or circumstances as the others. One of their common denominators was that each had a female mentor, or mentors, who supported and encouraged her as she launched into her chosen field of action.

For Eleanor Roosevelt (born 1884), her mentor was Marie Souvestre, head of the Allenwood School for girls in London. The shy, orphaned, lonely child was sent to Allenwood at age 14. For Helen Gahagan Douglas (born 1900) there was her teacher-mother, Lillian. Because of her husband's adamant opposition, Lillian Gahagan was denied the joy of pursuing her own dream to sing with opera companies in the New York area. When Helen wanted a career on the stage, Lillian Gahagan fought for her child as she had not been able to fight for herself. Margaret Mead (born 1901) was championed by both her mother and her grandmother. Grandmother Mead attended college in a day when less than two percent of her generation of females matriculated. Margaret's mother, ardent feminist Emily Fogg Mead, pursued a Ph.D. in sociology while raising five children. When Margaret wanted to pursue a career in anthropology, these two formidable women allowed nothing to stand in her way, not even a financial crisis in the family. None of the three women cited above were rebels. None needed to march in unison with other women or carry placards. None required a man's blessing to do what she did.

In the process of bringing about change in local or regional communities, the women who come face-to-face with their male detractors are more influential on the future status of women than the stars of the national stage. Reconstruction of the local social order is the more difficult endeavor. To bring about major changes, these women have to butt heads with the men they know--and sometimes the traditionalist women around them. Vera Schultz was one of the most meritorious female local and regional leaders of the 20th century.

Born in 1902, Vera spent her childhood on the frontier of the mining West. In that culture, a man's word was as good as his bond, and women had more social equality than in older, settled communities. Vera's widowed mother, Elizabeth Ann Mathews Smith, ran a boarding house in Tonopah, Nevada. She transmitted a pattern of work and self-reliance to her tagalong child. "Miss Patty," Vera's school teacher sister, 18 years older than she, was Vera's model for persistence in pursuing a goal. Miss Sullivan, her first grade teacher, taught her more than the three r's. She taught her to love books. Margery Brown, the librarian in Tonopah, introduced Vera to great music through recordings brought back from Milan before World War I, and when Margery discovered that Vera had read every book in the Tonopah Library, she ordered books especially for the gifted child who read to entertain herself. These women recognized Vera's exceptional intelligence, and they encouraged, taught, and appreciated her.

As a neophyte politician running for office at the University of Nevada, Vera read the writings of women like Alice Paul. Paul, who had become famous for her militant suffrage work, wrote the Equal Rights Amendment in 1923 that still lies crumpled in the Congressional dust bin of unresolved social issues. Carrie Chapman Catt, the founder of the League of Women Voters, was perhaps the most important icon in Vera's gallery of heroines. As a result of her tutelage by such a stellar group of mentors, Vera entered adulthood with a conviction that women should take stock of the world around them and carve out a niche for themselves. They should refuse the roles assigned to them by tradition.

Vera said, "I had been born independent and I had been encouraged by my family to make my own choices, to make my own decisions, to do things my way."

If the values learned in the bosom of one's family are immutable, Vera's life reflected the wholesome impact her dynamic, moral siblings made on her character. Unquestionably, she was a product of their survival instincts. With no inherited wealth to see them through and no Father to create the wealth needed to support them, every Smith had to make it on her/his own. By the time Vera was ten she was earning money to pay for her piano lessons, since the older members of the family were providing the family's basic necessities. Vera blossomed in Tonopah, Nevada, before World War I, and belied then-current beliefs in the need to cushion a child's contacts with a hostile environment.

Did the solitariness of her childhood lead to her creating the world according to her best insights without fear of criticism or censure? Probably. Vera's mother opened her first boarding house when Vera was five, and after that, Vera had to create her own world and put together her own agenda. Left to while away long hours alone, the child Vera developed a keen imagination with which to create would-be companions and the settings for their fancied adventures. Out of her voracious reading came ideas not then circulating in Tonopah, Nevada. Her conversion to Christian Science when she was fourteen gave her a lifelong belief in the power of the mind, though her faith in Christian Science did not survive a major episode of poison oak when she was twenty-two.

"I'm a feminist," she said after that term came into vogue. "I believe that women should go into politics. They represent more than half the population. They should not leave the fate of the nation in the hands of a minority, a very small minority at that when you consider that most men in public life are white."

On another occasion she said, "You could sit out in front til the cows come home but if you wanted to make change you had to have power. I hate the word 'power' but that's what it is. If people think you are trying to aggrandize yourself, they will turn away. But if they know you are working for the best interests of the people, they'll stay with you!"

Vera was not yet awake to her latent desire to hold public office when she became a resident of Marin County in 1928. As a citizen volunteer, Vera led a major assault on the life and government of Mill Valley. Energetically she set to work to expand and enrich the town's intellectual climate by establishing chapters of the American Association of University Women and the League of Women Voters. She joined forces with Maude Faye, Marin's resident opera star, and founded The Marin Music Chest. As the assistant to the Superintendent of Schools, she broadened the curriculum of the public schools to meet the needs of a rapidly expanding student population. She created a parks and recreation department in Mill Valley. After being appointed to the new Parks and Recreation Board, she set up neighborhood playgrounds throughout the town. After a major epidemic forced the closure of the Marin schools in 1938, Vera determined to create a county public health department. A citizen activist for 74 of her 92 years, Vera held public office for only 12. In those 12 years, she routed an entrenched oligarchy and revamped the government, leaving her fingerprints everywhere.

In 1946 she ran for office and became the first woman to sit on the Mill Valley City Council. During her term on the council, the town's government was completely overhauled. Her Mill Valley Council experience became a springboard in 1952 from which to plunge into the race for Supervisor in Marin County. She would be the first woman elected to the Board of Supervisors in Marin and the first woman Supervisor in Northern California. She became the first woman to sit on the Northern California Association of Supervisors, the first woman to take a leading role in flood control in Northern California, and the first woman to zealously stump for water quality standards in the Bay Area. Vera garnered many "firsts," all of which paved the way for other women to follow.

The chronology of the changes Vera wrought in Marin County unfolds in the pages of this book, but the pinnacle of her achievements was bringing Frank Lloyd Wright to Marin County to design the world-famous Marin County Civic Center. In spite of a mounting fury from a conservative rural Courthouse Gang who saw the county as their fiefdom and resented her intrusion into their affairs, she gave Marin a building to be cherished forever. The opening of the Golden Gate Bridge in 1937 brought a great "in-migration" of people employed in San Francisco. Their arrival did little to dispel the parochialism of southern Marin. Little changed until Vera Lucille Smith Schultz broke the gender barrier to political office, and reconstructed everything she touched.

What made Vera such a superb political animal? She was extraordinarily gifted with the ability to see the impact of the present on the future, a visionary of keen perception and sound judgment. Perhaps, the most significant of her attributes was her unquenchable belief that if something needed to be done, she could and should do it. She never waited until an organization was in place to grapple with an issue. If an organization was needed, she created it. She never paused to consider whether her femininity was a help or a hindrance. Gender had nothing to do with the task before her. If men in power had a problem with her sex, that was their dilemma, not hers. She took on men in high places if she thought they were wrong and ardently supported them if she thought they were right.

This story of Vera's life and work is not a brief on her psychological development, nor on her triumphal emergence from the backwaters of a Nevada mining frontier. It is the personal story of one woman who rose to preeminence as an activist and a politician in Marin County, California. Second to Orange County, Marin is the most affluent county in California, and was the second most Republican during Vera's politically active years. Vera was an ardent Democrat. All politicians are actors, and Vera was no exception. They play many roles and jostle for as much of center stage as they can command. Vera's stage was Marin County, and her dressing room was Mill Valley.

At the end of World War II, high up on the slopes of Mount Tamalpais, the Schultzes built their long, stone-faced rambler, their aerie. From the living room, the verandah, the dining room and the corner windows of the master bedroom, Vera could see one of the most magnificent panoramas in the San Francisco Bay Area. She reveled in the wonder of Richardson Bay lying in the immediate foreground of her "Corot painting" with glorious San Francisco Bay and fabled "Cable Car Town" filling out the rest of the canvas. Sometimes, "the city" lay hidden in shrouds of foamy white fog which sinuously snaked its way from the Pacific Ocean through the Golden Gate to lace its fingers around the hills of Tiburon. Sometimes, sunlight made the waters of the bays sparkle as they danced, and reflected whitely off the Mediterranean-style housing that graced the hills of the city in the distance. As long as she could see it, her spectacular view lifted her spirits and renewed her love for her adopted corner of God's earth. Twenty-Six Ralston Avenue was home from 1949 to 1995. She always hoped she'd die in that house and she almost did.

IN THE BEGINNING

Eleanor Roosevelt was born rich. Helen Gahagan Douglas was born wealthy. Margaret Mead was born into a family of professors. Vera Lucille Smith was born with a tin spoon in her mouth on a desert ranch at Dutch Flats, Nevada. Not hungry poor, just plain-folks poor as were most of the sturdy families who built the West, the Smiths knew they would prosper by hard work and sensible living. At the time of Vera's birth there was no reason to expect the baby to make a name for herself in a place like Mill Valley, California. Vera and her siblings were born under a dark shadow cast by their paternal grandfather, Mormon Bishop Philip Klingensmith. Their paternal grandmother shortened the surname to Smith when she walked out of her husband's life taking her children with her.

Nicknamed "Tina," Vera was the last child of Elizabeth Ann Mathews Smith, whose child-bearing spread over 20 years and produced eight living children. Tina, or Bobbie as she became later on, was cherished by four tall brothers, three short sisters and her mother. John Henry Smith, father of the brood, did not live long enough to see his three youngest children out of childhood. With only one vague memory of wrapping herself around his legs and standing on his boots, Vera had to create her father from her mother's memories and the episodic tales told by her siblings. Unfettered by reality, she wove his shadowy figure into a towering man of unassailable integrity. Stories about her father became part of the habilitation in which she cloaked her ancestors, reverential renderings of someone else's remembered fragments.

One of her favorite stories about her father, which was passed on to her by her mother, left a lifelong indignation burning in Vera. It had to do with a black couple, ex-slaves, who had a place just south of the Smith ranch on the Big Muddy River. One winter day when Jimmy, the child next above Vera in birth order, was a baby, their mother slipped on ice, fell and broke her arm. Since John Henry, Vera's father, was away, a plea went out to their neighbor, Uncle Ike, for help. Uncle Ike hitched his team to his buckboard and, leaving his wife to tend

1

to their chores, took Vera's mother and her nursing baby, Jimmy, to Panaca where the nearest doctor had his offices. Mae, the oldest of the eight, went along to help. Fourteen miles by buckboard over frozen rutted roads in the middle of winter was at minimum a three-hour journey. By the time the doctor splinted Elizabeth Ann's arm it was too late to start back that day. They found rooms for the night but the family with whom they stayed would not allow "the nigger" to sleep in the house. They made a place for Uncle Ike in one of the outbuildings.

Not long after the trip to Panaca, Ike dropped by the Smiths for some reason lost in memory and John Henry invited him to stay to supper. Many people sat down to eat at the Smiths' table: neighbors, tramps, prospectors—whoever happened by when the vittles were ready. Everyone was welcome and everyone was treated as a friend. The school teacher who boarded with the Smiths, a southern lady with the usual baggage of southern prejudices, came into the room to take her place at the table and saw Ike seated beside John Henry.

"Oooh!" She gasped. "I can't sit down at that table. I've never eaten with a 'darkie' before."

John Henry looked up calmly, his fork poised in mid air, and said quietly, "I'm sorry, but you'll just have to have your supper in your room, I guess." He went on eating without any further fuss while the red-faced teacher flounced out of the room.

"I love that story about my father," Vera said. "It made me proud when mother told me about it." Years later her ardor for integrating Marin City had its roots in Uncle Ike and the southern schoolteacher.

Having created ancestors larger than life, Vera could not be reconciled to the fact that her grandfather had been accused of, and tried in federal court for, the cold-blooded murder of 126 men, women and children. (See Appendix for the story of Philip Klingensmith and the Mountain Meadow Massacre.) Neither could she forgive her grandmother for having shortened the family name to such a pedestrian name as Smith. Vera's grandmother severed her ties to the Mormon church and her bishop husband in the 1860s, then homesteaded a semi-arid piece of land at Dutch Flats, Nevada. All of the Smith children were born on that ranch.

Vera's grandparents, Hannah Henry Creemer and Philip Klingensmith, married enroute to Utah from Pennsylvania. The prophet, Brigham Young, sent for Klingensmith, a skilled worker in explosives. He ordered him to move to Utah to help develop an arms industry. Philip so energetically entered into the Mormon community he became a bishop within four years of arrival. Some years later, Young ordered every Bishop in the church to take a second wife in defiance of the United States Government. (Polygamy was to be defended by being expanded.) The Klingensmiths already had 15 children and the idea of Philip taking a second wife was an insult to Hannah, a fiery little woman, independent and proud. Hannah chose to take her fifteen children and go it alone. She had no intention of being senior wife to a younger woman, nor of being a nursemaid to the new wife's children.

Among Hannah's host of children were two sets of twins: a pair of girls, and a pair of boys. The boy twins were John Henry, Vera's father, and Philip. The twin girls and John Henry all married children of a strongly Mormon family named Mathews. John Henry Smith was as strong-willed as either of his parents. When he fell in love with Elizabeth Ann Mathews, it delighted him to learn that she'd be excommunicated for marrying a gentile. John Henry's identical twin, Philip, had already married Clara Mae Logan who had no religious ties to cut. For both women the bonds that bound the twins to each other's fate determined the course of their lives.

The twins built identical houses close to each other on the Dutch Flats ranch. Together, the brothers ran cattle, operated a sawmill supplying railroad ties to the two railroads being constructed nearby, did some freighting, and worked hard. But, their ideas of the good life went beyond "getting ahead." A man had to have time for laughter, for conviviality, for camaraderie, as well as for work. Each of the twins fathered eight living children—seven sons and one daughter for Philip; four surviving sons and four daughters for John Henry.

Together they had enough children to make up the student body of a rural one-room school.

When the Smith twins petitioned Lincoln County for a school, they were notified that their two families would run out of students in time. Thus, they did not merit county funds for a private school. If they wanted education at Dutch Flats, they'd have to build a schoolhouse themselves, and hire their own teacher. Hiring their own teacher was not easy. A young woman could not expect to carve out a career for herself or find a husband in Dutch Flats. When a new teacher heard of a school being built in a nearby railroad town, or near a mining camp, she turned in her resignation. The Dutch Flats School would again be in recess. Furthermore, no teacher could be lured to such an out-of-the-way place unless she was assured she'd have her own quarters. Since Clara Mae was not as keen on education for her children as Elizabeth Ann was, John Henry's boys always had to sleep in a shed out behind the house in order to make a room available for the teacher.

The Smith children, in descending order, were Effie Mae, called Mae, born in 1883; Elizabeth, called Patty, born in 1885; John Henry Smith Jr., called Jack, the most driven of the Smith children, born in 1887; Eugene, called Gene, born 1889; Charles Philip, the only Smith son who never married, born 1891; Muzetta Viola, called Zetta or Zet, born 1894; James Jay, called Jimmy, born 1897; Rilla, a girl, stillborn, 1901; and last of all, Vera Lucille, the future Politician.

Vera was born August 31, 1902, the year Jeannette Rankin, the first female to be elected to the U.S. Congress, graduated from the University of Montana. Jeannette Rankin took her seat in Congress in 1917 and immediately introduced the 19th Amendment that gave women the right to vote. That amendment had been placed before the congress every congressional session since 1869, but never before by a woman. Also, in 1902, the nation was riveted on the great anthracite coal miners' strike in western Pennsylvania. The first "progressive" president, Theodore Roosevelt, made 1902 a propitious year for the birth of a future champion of "Good Government." Roosevelt, the great phrase maker, avowed that his intention was to give the laboring man, i.e., the miners, "A square deal." In the years ahead, Vera's brothers would all rise from the rank of miners to become men of modest wealth. The plight of the "little man" in a capitalist world gone greedy who did not get a square deal constantly rang in Vera's ears as she was first learning words and their meanings.

Not everything she heard made sense to little Tina. One thing that went over her head was that her father and his twin brother had a serious problem, one they shared and one that would cost her father his life. The Smith brothers were too popular for their own good. In raw places like Caliente, Dutch Flats' market town and the county seat, male sociability centered on saloons. There wasn't much of any other place where men could gather to swap yarns, bet on the prowess of a horse or a man, tell jokes, share laughter. Hard-driving, hard-drinking, hardpan living was the way of life. In the mellow lantern light of saloons, men "bellied up to the bar" and bought each other "snorts." The Smith brothers were good company -- gregarious, easy-going, good-natured, good-looking, good story-tellers, competent horsemen, successful businessmen. Everyone wanted to buy them drinks.

Other men might stagger home long before they became falling-down drunk, but not the Smith twins. Especially not Philip. They'd drink until they couldn't get home without help. Such excesses are never kept secret, even in anonymous cities, certainly not in a place the size of Caliente. In that community the townsfolk knew and the community gossiped. Vera learned about her father's alcoholism from the stories her sister Patty told years later. Her mother never mentioned it. Eleanor Roosevelt learned about her adored father's alcoholism first hand. Like Vera, Eleanor wrapped her father in robes of nobility that diluted the shame of his drunkenness. Because of alcoholism, both their fathers died when Eleanor and Vera were children.

In 1906, after Philip left the ranch, John Henry decided to move to Cedar City where he had an opportunity to invest in the sheep business. He had a dream of establishing an estate near the town where his father, the Mormon bishop, had been Lord High Potentate. Cedar City had an established school system including a high school. Even a normal school was located there. As soon as they settled in, Patty and Charles could begin attending teachers' college. Jack and Gene had already taken flight to seek their fortunes when the ranch sold. Philip and his family moved to Caliente, forcing the sale of the ranch. With cash money from the sale, all things came together for John Henry. Vera's father went into the sheep business in Cedar City, and Patty and Charles enrolled in the teachers' college. Mae, now 23 years old, went off to Los Angeles to live with relatives and attend business college.

Everyone hoped that the separation of the twins would be the end of their drinking, the major reason for the two families' uprooting. Patty knew intuitively, what many refuse to accept even now: an alcoholic cannot be removed from temptation, nor will a mere change of address alter anything. John Henry promised to leave his drinking behind to keep the peace but his daughter didn't trust a promise made to appease. Cedar City was a dry town but dry towns always have hidden spigots. John Henry began his usual convivial tippling and Charles had to make the rounds of all the watering holes to drag him home. Patty was outraged. One day when she found him in his cups she called her father outside beyond earshot of her mother and mercilessly upbraided him.

"We're sick of your drinking," she stormed. "We've moved to a new town where we could be somebody if you stopped drinking but you don't! Your promises don't mean anything! It's not fair. We couldn't hold up our heads in Caliente and if this keeps up we won't be able to hold our heads up here either. If you ever get drunk again I'm going to the sheriff. I'll tell him where you're getting the liquor. I know. And I'll tell."

John Henry glared down at his diminutive daughter. "Don't threaten me, girl," he huffed from his great height. 'You'll do nothing of the kind."

"Oh yes I will," she said defiantly, stretching to her full five feet to let him know she was not afraid. "I'll do it and you know I'll do it."
"If you do, I'll kill you," he snarled, raising his hand as if to strike her.

Patty didn't flinch. "I know that too," she retorted, "but I'll do it anyway."

John Henry stared down into the stony eyes coldly looking up at him. After a long silent contest of wills, John Henry turned on his heel and walked off, too furious to speak. But the drinking stopped. At 21, Patty was already a force to be dealt with.

At the time John Henry moved to Cedar City, Philip was elected sheriff of Caliente. Being a sheriff and living in town meant Philip spent even more time in saloons where even more people wanted to buy him a drink. A short time after their arrival in Cedar City, the telegraph boy began making regular visits to John Henry bringing cries for help from his sister-in-law. Usually, a second telegram followed the first saying the crisis had passed. Phil had been found. One night John Henry received a final telegram from Clara Mae that sent him riding off into the night toward Caliente. He would not come back from that rescue mission.

Every man wore a gun in those days, and every man rode horseback. It was late when John Henry reached Caliente. Most of the houses were already dark. John Henry rode around the little town going from one saloon to the next inquiring for the sheriff. At last he found Philip lying at the end of a broad beam of dim light coming from the open door of a barroom across the street. Intending to throw Philip over his own horse to lead him home to Clara, John dismounted and stooped over his brother to lift him. When he slipped one arm under Philip's shoulder, disaster struck. Addled, fearing he was being robbed, Philip drew his gun and shot his twin. John Henry died three weeks later. Elizabeth Ann and the five younger children were left stranded in Cedar City with no means of support, and very little insurance money. Stunned, Elizabeth Ann was immobilized. What was she to do? Who was there to rescue them?

BOOMTOWN AND BOARDING HOUSES

When Jack left the ranch at Dutch Flats, two years before the rest of the family, he headed for the site of the biggest gold strike in Nevada's history. On the slopes of Mount Brougher, in the San Antonio Mountains, gold and silver were discovered in 1900. Instantly, the land containing the great deposits was swallowed up by Eastern investors. The little town of Tonopah, a tent city springing up out of the desert in a narrow valley between Mount Brougher and Mount Oddie, was home to the prospectors and miners who descended on this latest bonanza. This was no fizzle with much light at the beginning and only dead ash at the end. The gold was there. Tonopah had a future. When that was certain, the Tonopah Railroad came to town on July 25, 1904. The railroads of the West tied the towns they spawned or served to the rest of the nation. They brought in additional population, extensive commerce, and the pot pourri of American civilization. Merchants received ice cream from Reno by refrigerated car; laundry was sent to Reno and returned; and, miners shipped ore through the railroads to smelters in California.

Jack, with Gene hot on his heels, cast his lot with the wave of miners and prospectors pouring into Tonopah. All the boys' letters home were filled with the excitement of hunting for gold in the shafts of mines owned by other men. When Mae finished her course in Los Angeles, Jack urged her to come to Tonopah rather than go to Cedar City. Two new mercantile companies had opened and were doing landslide business supplying the needs of the miners pouring in. Big merchants needed bookkeepers.

As Elizabeth Ann grappled with the dilemma John Henry's death had created for her, Jack ran a foot race on the Fourth of July, 1907. He won $1,000! With his sudden windfall in hand, he wired his mother to pack up the family and come to Tonopah. It made good sense to have all the Smiths in the same town. Patty could find a "teaching" in a country school nearby and spend her weekends at home. Charles could go down in the mines with his older brothers and make more money than he would being a schoolmaster. Zetta and Jimmy could enter the new school system, and everybody could help out. Eagerly,

11

Elizabeth Ann closed up life in Cedar City and bought the tickets. When the snorting little train crept down the narrow valley between Mount Oddie and Mount Brougher and pulled into the little Tonopah depot on Main Street, Jack was waiting on the platform. From the train window Vera's mother pointed out a slender dark-haired man with her father's blue eyes, waving his hat and grinning from ear to ear. Vera didn't remember him.

Jack swept his mother into his arms as brother Gene swept Zetta into a crushing embrace to show off his new muscles. Both boys had become men. The West did not coddle the young, it aged them. Gene and Zetta went off arm in arm, laughing and talking as Jack set his mother on her feet, then bent down to smile into the serious little face staring up at him. He tumbled Tina's hair with his big rough paw, then reached down for her hand and led her up the dusty main street. Men spoke to him, tipped their hats to her mother, and Vera swelled with pride.

In such a helter-skelter place, where half the dwellings were still canvass, Jack had been unable to find a house large enough for them all. He rented two houses side by side that, together, provided enough room for all the women and Jimmy. He and Gene and Charles would board elsewhere. Elizabeth Ann sized up the situation and decided she'd go house hunting on her own. There had to be a roof big enough to shelter them all somewhere in town. Meanwhile there was supper to fix. Tired but happy, they ate by lamplight while sounds of mining operations shattered the quiet of the desert night. The "whumps" of ore being dumped into rail cars, the rackety clatter of elevator cages going up and down, the staccato of mining drills—faint sometimes, booming at others depending on wind direction—all the cacophony of the sounds of mining kept up day and night. When Vera clamped her hands over her ears Jack laughed. He assured her she'd get used to it.

Men with no place to stay were swarming into Tonopah. Tents had to serve as shelter during the freezing cold of winter as well as the sweltering heat of summer until freight wagons brought in lumber to build housing. In among the tents along Main Street were weather-beaten old houses brought in from the ghost towns of past strikes. A new discovery of gold or silver caused a stampede of would-be millionaires to swarm over the newly discovered field until the ore ran out. Then the miners left and their abandoned houses stared vacantly at each other across empty, dusty streets until dismantled and carried off to the next bonanza.

When the Smiths arrived, Tonopah was just beginning to shed its tatters. New buildings housed the two emporiums where one could buy five-and-dime stuff as well as shovels and tools, grub stake supplies, miners' boots and owners' suits. The first time Vera saw a clerk take her mother's money, put it in an open work basket hanging from a wire strung across the room just below the ceiling, then pull a handle that sent the basket zinging across the ceiling of the store, she was dumbfounded. The noise level in the stores assaulted her. Cash register bells ringing, singing wires going every which way, little baskets zipping back and forth, boot heels hitting wood floors, people's voices rising above the din: the clash and clatter indicated that progress and technology were alive and well in Tonopah. Such a confusion of sound was nerve-wracking to a child newly arrived from a place where only the wind's song broke the silence. By shutting the world out and focusing inward, Vera could find a quiet place to think. For the rest of her life, amid numerous conflicting demands on her time, Vera was always able to concentrate on the one thing currently demanding her attention to the exclusion of all else.

Elizabeth Ann made up her mind to find a house where she could take in roomers. Before World War I, widows ran boarding houses all across America and in small midwest and western towns long after that. It was a respectable enterprise where widows could keep their families around them as they sheltered and fed others. Boarding houses, catering to whole families as well as to solitary figures a long way from home, existed in every major city in America. They were about the only source of meals and shelter in the lonely places like Tonopah that civilization had scarcely reached.

The term "boarding house" erroneously conjures up images of tight houses reeking of cooking odors situated in congested areas where single men lived monotonous lives. Such images accurately describe only one type of boarding house.

Beautifully appointed boarding houses, whose clienteles were the wealthy "wintering in town" or enjoying their "month by the lake," lined the streets of resort towns. In big cities, elegant boarding houses substituted for hotels. Usually these boarding houses were the dwellings of people who opened their homes to the prominent, whether in town for the season or just passing through. They could be found all the way from San Francisco to New York City.

While she could not hope for elegance, Elizabeth Ann did not intend to open a boarding house of the first type mentioned above. She resolved that her boarders would be part of her family. Just as winter gave way to spring she found what she was looking for, a tall three-story, raw, unpainted house beside the main road. Eighteen men quickly signed up to take their meals at her table and six of them came to live under the Smith roof as well. They paid by the month for three meals a day, two at her table, and one in a pail for noon. Vera's mother was an excellent cook and quickly Mrs. Smith had the reputation of setting a fine table and packing smacking good dinners. While her mother cooked, Vera set the table. Once the men were seated, she and Zet served.

Table talk of mines and shafts and danger and politics fascinated little Tina as she hurried to and fro. "I cut my teeth on Democratic Party politics at my mother's table," Vera declared. "I learned that the rich squeeze the poor, and the wage-earner has nowhere to turn but to the government. Those were the years when workers were crushed, and the little man was helpless unless he had a union or a government to give him a chance."

As Vera carried away the dishes, men lingered over the table, smoking and shouting each other down as ideas were tossed out, batted about, examined and embraced, or discarded. One night they might talk about the amazing pace of change being brought about by industry, and the next night denounce the men who were exploiting the workers to bring about that change. With Zetta and Patty in on the arguments, they derided and glorified the proposed suffrage amendment with equal vehemence on both sides of the issue. Newspapers from the East were quoted like holy writ. More intrigued by women voting than by other issues, Vera imagined the possibilities such an amendment could open up for her someday. She was for it before she understood it.

"THE CHILD IS FATHER TO THE MAN."
(Wordsworth, taken from Milton)

"I had a happy childhood." Vera always began her reminiscing with those words. Time enhances the joys of our childhood and downplays the anguish of those years. One of Vera's earliest memories was of forlornly hanging around the school yard at Dutch Flats waiting for her sister Zetta and her brother Jimmy, along with her cousins, to come out to play at recess. Zetta was eight years older than Vera and Jimmy five years older so the little tag-a-long spent a great deal of her childhood hanging around the lives of others, soaking up ideas, opinions, and attitudes.

When school began in Tonopah in the fall of 1907, Vera was too young to enter the 1st grade because of her August 31 birthday. She was left to meander about alone, creating imaginary companions and situations. She followed one path after another up the mountains to see what lay hidden near the top, or what a person could see from the other side of the hill. One day as she made her way along a faint trace that wound around Mount Brougher she came upon an abandoned, rusty old iron cook stove. One leg had fallen off. It looked as if it had been abandoned because it was crippled. Vera tried to right the behemoth but it was too heavy. The pioneer lore Miss Patty constantly read to her contained stories about pioneers headed West plodding along beside covered wagons, weary, dirty, thirsty and hungry. In some stories, the oxen grew so gaunt from lack of forage they could hardly pull the conestogas. People had to lighten their loads by leaving heavy household items behind along the trail. Vera wove a story around this old stove. Perhaps, it had fallen off the back of a wagon when the owners were too tired to notice they'd lost it. Maybe...? Before she got on with her fanciful scenario she stopped trying to solve the mystery. She had another idea.

Next morning when Elizabeth Ann went to feed the chickens Vera slipped into the kitchen for supplies. She was headed for a big adventure as a pioneer cook. She took a fry pan out of the cupboard and a paring knife from the drawer, she copped two eggs from the egg basket and two potatoes from the potato bin. She slipped the knife into one apron pocket and the eggs and

17

potatoes into the other. Then she climbed on a chair and stole a sulfur match out of the iron match holder hanging behind the stove. Equipped with what she needed, she tiptoed out the front door and headed off around the mountain. It took her thirty minutes to find her way back to the old iron range, and another five minutes to scour up enough dry sticks to build a fire.

She laid her sticks on top of some dry sage, then lit her match. As the little blaze began to crackle, she put the fry pan over the uncovered hole and broke her two eggs into the skillet. Fascinated, she watched as the golden egg yolks became firm, and the gooey milky whites congealed. Once, she tried to take hold of the handle so she could flip the eggs over as she'd seen Lottie Nay do down at Stimler's Restaurant. The handle was too hot to touch. Since there was no fat in the pan to make the edges crinkle as they did at home, it wasn't even possible to shove the eggs around with her knife. All she could do was sorrowfully watch her culinary masterpiece begin to smoke, then burn, and at last become a blackened charred mass. Knocking the pan off the stove with a stick, she waited until it cooled enough to pick it up. She got the egg debris loose by pounding the edge of the pan on a rock. Then she scraped out the charred residue with the knife until she was satisfied the pan was clean enough to use again.

Diligently she set to work to peel the remaining breakfast contraband in her pocket. When she held the smudged potatoes, skinless, coated with dirt from her hands and apron front, over the pan and began to slice them, she realized that without fat for the frying she was only going to repeat her first debacle. She slipped the potatoes back into her apron pocket, and set to work to clean up the remainder of her mess by scouring the inside of the frying pan with sand. Satisfied that her mother would never suspect that the fry pan had left her kitchen, Vera took the potatoes from her pocket, wiped them off on her sleeves and began to eat them raw as she dispiritedly trudged her way back around Mount Brougher. When was she going to have someone to play with? Everything she did by herself was unsatisfying.

Within months of their arrival, Jack announced that now that they were all together, he was going to get married. Elizabeth

Ann and the girls were stunned. There had been no hint that Jack was about to take a wife when he urged them all to come to Tonopah. The bride-to-be was a waitress in the restaurant where Jack had taken his meals. Her name was Helen and she was an orphan. Since she had no mother around to arrange a wedding it fell to Jack and Elizabeth Ann to plan a wedding in the two little houses. They moved beds out of one house into the other and set up tables in every room but the kitchen of the emptied house. Jack had made a lot of friends among the mining engineers and owners. Every man in town knew Helen. She'd served them all. With great excitement the family went to work to do Jack proud. That wedding was the only traditional wedding anyone in the entire Smith family ever had.

Jack's wedding preparations were exciting for only a week. Then Vera was back to wandering here and there with her imaginary friends or heroes. On the lower slopes of Mount Brougher stood a big wooden water tank that glistened in the sun. A little puddle had formed at its base. One day Vera decided to visit the shiny water tower. The ugly little puddle triggered her overly-active imagination. The shallow dirty-brown water became the clear cold depths of a sparkling blue lake amid white birch and pine forests. Patty had read aloud "The Song of Hiawatha," and Vera's head was filled with images of Indians and waterfalls and lakes covered with birch bark canoes. Every day she returned as an Indian princess, living on the banks of her private woodland waterway, floating about in a canoe all alone.

On the make-believe shores of her lake she created a miniature Indian village with teepees made of cardboard and sticks that she brought to the site in her apron pocket. As she unpocketed her prefabs, she arranged them as she thought an Indian village would appear. She made stick horses and dogs. She had a celluloid doll about 3 inches long which became an Indian princess in the buff. Because celluloid floats, her visiting Indian princess could swim through the lake while great majestic herons flew overhead. Vera had never seen a heron but Patty said they were majestic. Leaves became canoes, twigs afloat on the leaves became other Indian maidens. She built an island in the middle of her lake by piling up mud and stuck twigs and grass in her island to make a forest. She came to her wonderful virginal world almost every day. But when fall set in and the weather turned cold, her lake dried up and so did her canoes. She and her celluloid doll deserted the village and went home to hole up through the winter like little bears in hibernation. Everything was a fairy tale of some sort to the child who spent her days alone.

The search for something to do ended in the fall of 1908 when Vera proudly took her new tablet and her new pencil and presented herself to the first grade teacher, Miss Sullivan. Miss Sullivan was her first real-life heroine. Miss Sullivan taught her to write by the Palmer method, all those neat tight curlicues. She learned from Miss Sullivan when election day appears in the calendar. Every morning, after the class saluted the flag, Miss Sullivan asked, "When is Election Day?" The children answered in unison, "The first Tuesday after the first Monday in November in even numbered years." The child Vera had no inkling then of how important election day would be in adult Vera's life. Miss Sullivan also directed Vera to the library when she discovered Vera's love and aptitude for reading.

In a town the size of Tonopah there wasn't much for a curious little girl to do but read, once she knew how. She could walk down the hills past the polluted ponds where the effluence from the mines poured out into excavated holes in the area below the town called The Sewer Garden. Or she could go spelunking down abandoned mine shafts, an activity her brothers constantly warned against. Or she could peer down glory holes, abandoned shafts sitting like cisterns all over the landscape. As a rule, glory holes had greenish water in the bottom collected from the scant rainfall or underground seepage. Sometimes the dead carcass of a drowned animal sent up a horrible stench. A child could shiver with fright at the thought of falling in, and now and then a child did. But how many times could such activities be interesting? So Vera read.

By the time she reached the sixth grade, Vera had read every book in the town library. That year the teacher assigned an essay describing a sunset. Sunsets on the High Desert are moments of spectacular glory. The skies are swathed in tier upon tier of wispy tulle clouds ranging in color from blushing

20

pinks to flamboyant oranges and all the shades in between. Vera gave the poet in her soul full rein while writing that essay, but, instead of the praise she expected, the teacher ordered Vera to see her after school.

"What is the color mauve?" she demanded, staring hard at Vera while pointing to the paper in front of her.

"Why it's a color that's between pink and purple on the color wheel," Vera stammered, surprised.

"And how do you know that?" the teacher continued.

"I read it in a book. I've read every book in the Tonopah library," she replied.

The teacher stared open-mouthed, searching Vera's face for some sign she was lying. Vera looked back steadily, her eyes never shifting from the teacher's stern gaze. Obviously the child was telling the truth. It was incredible to think that a 12-year-old had read every single book in the Tonopah library. There had to be books beyond her interest or ken. Vera stretched the truth a mite. Once the librarian had found her checking out a book on Russian opera.

Amused, Margery Brown, the librarian, asked, "Could you really be interested in that?"

"Well, I think I've read everything else here." Vera sighed. Mrs. Brown was nonplused. The child before her was still in elementary school.

Margery Brown began ordering books especially for Vera. Many years later their paths crossed again in Mill Valley, California. After attending Mills College in Oakland, Margery married Hugh Henry Brown, a young attorney from San Francisco who now represented the mine owners in Tonopah. The Browns were among the elite of the city. One year they made a grand tour of Italy and when they returned, Mrs. Brown brought back recordings of operas they'd heard at La Scala in Milan. Vera's piano teacher saw to it that Mrs. Brown included Vera among the children invited to her home to hear her records. Those records were the first orchestral music Vera ever heard. She learned to love classical music in those sessions, a love that propelled her into being a founding mother of the Marin Music Chest many years later.

Mrs. Brown was the epitome of all Vera yearned to be: educated, modulated and sophisticated, a figure to be reckoned with in a world Vera was hungry to enter. When they met again years later, at an AAUW meeting held in Vera's living room in Mill Valley, Vera was as educated, modulated and sophisticated as her childhood mentor. The cygnet had become a swan too.

During her first year in Tonopah, Vera acquired the nickname that close friends and family used for the rest of her life: Bobbie. The Smiths' first house was on the milk route of a young lad named Bob Van Paten. Every day Bob brought his barrels of milk in from the dairy just outside town. Vera had a passion for milk. When the Smiths arrived in Tonopah, the only milk available was condensed milk which Vera hated. When milk delivery began the next spring, Vera was elated. Every morning Bob jollied the kids he met as he made his rounds. Every morning he found Vera hanging on her gatepost fearful he might not come. It was Jimmy who called the family's attention to Vera's obsession with the milk boy.

"Hmm," he taunted, "you're out there every day waiting for Bob. You got a case on him?"

"I'm waiting for the milk!" Vera cried. "I'm not waiting for Bob."

Jimmy wouldn't let it be. "Bobbie!" he called out from the house when he saw her at the gate. "Oh, Bobbie!" he'd call to her as she left for school. "Where's Bobbie?" he'd ask when they came home in the afternoon. Vera pouted, cried, and got angry, which made it all the more fun for Jimmy. Gradually little Tina became Bobbie to one and all. By the time she was in high school the family was using the name so consistently her high school friends picked it up. When she went to college the name went with her. In college she met her future husband and he adopted her pet name. After that, any hope of shedding it was lost. The *Pacific Sun* in Mill Valley picked it up. "Vera Bobbie"

Steve McNamara, the editor, called her. She became more comfortable with "Bobbie" than she was with "Vera."

GRIM REALITIES

Vera was a child in a world where children were not sheltered from adversity. A mining town is a hazardous place to raise children. Littered around the adits (mouths) of mines were all manner of tools and equipment, either discarded or temporarily laid aside. It wasn't uncommon to find sticks of dynamite scattered about. Two kids, the Sheroda brothers, picked up a number of sticks one Sunday morning and went in search of a fuse that was also easily available. Vera and her mother were in the kitchen that Sunday morning when a terrifying blast from up the hill above their house shook dishes off the table. Elizabeth Ann lit out with Vera racing beside her. What they saw when they arrived left an indelible memory on the future creator of Parks and Recreation in Mill Valley and later, Marin County.

For weeks, after the explosion, the children of Tonopah received repeated lectures about staying out of the mines. However, no laws were passed to force mine owners or miners, to be more responsible for the public's safety. Safety codes had been demanded successively by the Knights of Labor, the American Federation of Labor, and the United Mine Workers for over 40 years, but to no avail. Theodore Roosevelt had forced Congress to pass laws requiring mining companies and other corporations to compensate victims of industrial irresponsibility but there was no enforcement of federal law in remote places like Tonopah. The lack of legal protection for miners and their families was perennial conversation fare at Mrs. Smith's Boarding House table. Vera heard it all. The people, her people, were pawns in the game of profits with nowhere to hide and no power to protect themselves. There ought to be a state law, somebody said, but how could they get a law when the owners controlled Carson City? Poor people didn't have a chance. Vera not only heard she remembered.

One chilly winter morning, when pale sunlight shone through the window and warmed her back, Vera was again in the kitchen peeling potatoes with her mother. Again, the air was filled with anguished cries and the sound of people running. Huge billows of smoke poured out of the Belmont Mine shaft.

Such thick smoke could only come from a monstrous fire in the bowels of the earth. By the time Vera and her mother arrived at the mine shaft, miners were coming to the surface as fast as the cage could bring them up. A mighty hush settled over the scene broken only by the sound of the roaring echo chamber below them. All day, the people of Tonopah waited helplessly at the adit, unwilling to leave. When the smoke began to subside late in the afternoon, men began bringing out bodies of the dead.

Nine-year-old Vera watched with her mother as one after another of their boarders was brought to the surface. Altogether, 17 men died, 15 of them so young they scarcely needed to shave. All but two had taken their meals at Vera's Mother's table. Vera had laid their plates, filled their cups, and carried their dishes away when the meal was over. One of the dead men even lived in their house. Shaken by this grim reminder that life under the earth was even more hazardous than was life above ground, Elizabeth Ann numbly led Vera home in silence. It could have been Jack or Charles or Gene in that inferno.

The whole town went into mourning. All the mines and all the business houses closed for a full week to honor the dead. On the last day of mourning, every fraternal order in town, and every miner's association, solemnly paraded down the full length of Main Street. The town band, consisting almost entirely of miners, led the way. Trailing their elders came the school children of Tonopah, each carrying a cardboard sign, a written tribute to one of the dead that child had known. Vera was one of those children, and she had known them all.

After that tragedy, Elizabeth Ann decided to close the boarding house. There were too few customers left to support her effort. One of her remaining boarders, an attorney named McIntosh, was the catalyst in her decision. On a hill overlooking Tonopah, McIntosh had built a large house for his new bride before he brought her from the East to live in rackety, dusty, uncultured Tonopah. The bridegroom had spared no expense in surrounding his future wife with lovely things in the vain hope that such surroundings would make living in a rough mining town more palatable. But Mrs. McIntosh could not, or would not accept the boredom of life in Tonopah and moved out soon after she moved in. Mr. McIntosh rattled around in that big house, alone and lonely.

What he needed was a housekeeper-cook, and a lot more noise to fill the silent rooms. He proposed that the Smith family come to live with him. They could have free run of the house. All he needed was his master bedroom and bath kept completely private. The children wouldn't bother him much for he was seldom at home except to eat and sleep. He expected a good breakfast every day, his laundry done so he didn't have to send it to Reno as Mrs. Brown and the others did, and the house kept as dust free as possible, in that dry dusty world. Occasionally he'd want dinner at night.

The Smiths moved in and Elizabeth Ann set to work to give attorney McIntosh the best service she had to give. Vera resented the special attention her mother showered on him. He got the best of the berries, the best cuts of meat, the best of everything served at table. Her mother constantly reminded her of how well they were living because of Mr. McIntosh, and how nice they should be to him. Vera felt set aside and second class. From her viewpoint the family was getting short shrift, especially the youngest child in the family.

Below the ceiling of the dining room a plate rail circled the entire room and held a lovely collection of bone china plates. Elizabeth Ann lived in constant fear of something in the house being broken but the plates seemed safe in their out-of-reach location. One day, Vera stormed off in self-righteous indignation because she wanted her mother to do something for her but was brushed aside because of Mr. McIntosh's needs. The bedroom Vera shared with her mother opened off the dining room. To make sure her mother knew how angry she was, Vera marched into the bedroom and slammed the door behind her. The walls shook under the impact. Then came the terrible, thundering clatter of crashing china, a clatter that echoed through the whole house.

Vera stood transfixed with horror over the enormity of what she'd done. All those lovely plates broken! She heard her mother's shriek from the next room and braced herself. Then, after the first cry there was absolute silence, silence that lasted so long Vera was in a state of panic. She looked at the door knob but didn't have the courage to touch it. She couldn't bring herself to face the destruction she'd willfully created. Then she heard the swish of a broom on the carpet in the next room and the clink of shards being dumped into a pail. The clinking of broken china hitting metal went on and on and beat on her ears. Every one of those plates must have come down.

She heard her mother lift the pail and walk away, and after an eternity, she heard footsteps crossing the dining room. Vera braced herself. No one had ever laid a hand on her in her whole life but surely she would get it over this. Instead, Elizabeth Ann opened the door, came in, and sat down on the edge of the bed in front of Vera. Taking the child's chin in her hand she forced Vera to meet her eyes. Quietly, in a voice Vera never forgot, she said, "You see, Tina, every little cause has a consequence. Now we will have to pay for the wreckage and the cost will be very great. It will take us months to pay for it."

Vera was too unnerved to answer, but she never forgot the lesson. "Every little cause has a consequence." From that day, controlling her temper was one of her main goals in life. As an adult, Vera rarely spoke carelessly, almost never responded to anger with anger, and infrequently let resentment trip her up. In the heat of political battle she could diminish an adversary with caustic rhetoric but outbursts of temper were rare, and therefore memorable.

The loss of the plates was not the culminating crisis that led to the Smiths moving out, but the family remained in McIntosh's home only a few more months. Jimmy's dogs ate Mr. McIntosh's rabbits. The lawn suffered from too many feet on fragile grass in that arid place. The anticipation of what would happen next grew to be too much for the good Mr. McIntosh. He and Elizabeth Ann agreed that, as soon as she could find other quarters she and her children would move on. The forced change of residence happened at a propitious moment in the life of the Smith family. Mae, now a widow, was coming home with her child. There was no room for additional Smiths where they were.

Mae's odyssey had begun within months of Elizabeth Ann's and the younger children's arrival from Cedar City. Mae married Ross Peeler and soon after, the Peelers moved to Portland, Oregon. Two years later, Genevieve Lucille Peeler was born January 12, 1910. Word came within months of the baby's birth that Ross had tuberculosis. Ross and Mae moved to Colorado on doctor's orders. Breathing was easier there. Colorado was becoming the haven, as well as last resting place, for the victims of the nation's number one killer. The Peelers were in Colorado for three long years. When Ross died, he was buried in a graveyard for tubercular patients where he could not contaminate the dead in other cemeteries. Mae returned to Tonopah where the whole family could help care for her baby. She brought all her worldly possessions with her, plus her new found religion, Christian Science. Mae's previous resistance to any form of organized religion had evaporated in the face of Ross' illness. In hopes that Science practitioners could save Ross where medical science had failed, she wrapped herself around the teachings of Mary Baker Eddy.

As soon as she was safe again in the bosom of the family she urged them all to read Mary Baker Eddy's *Science and Health with Key to the Scriptures* and become practicing Christian Scientists. The women of the family succumbed to her evangelism but the men hooted at Mary Baker Eddy's ideas that there is no death. The idea that the soul's dwelling place is eternally the same, for Jack, Charles,Gene and Jimmy, was laughable. It was as foolish an idea as the Mormon belief that the living could be wed to the dead, thereby converting those on the "other side" to the true faith. The Smith women trooped off to the Christian Science Reading Room sans Smith males. Fourteen-year old Vera, taking all her cues and standards from her mother and Miss Patty, Vera's sister and Mae's best friend, threw herself into the new discipline.

Every Saturday, when the study topic for the week arrived by mail from the Mother Church in Boston, Vera hustled off to the town's newspaper office with the topic for the next day's discussion. Newspapers were bulletin boards in those days. They featured lodge notices, a lost and found column, sermon topics, notices of auctions, and advertisements. One topic Vera always remembered was, "Is the universe, including man, evolved by atomic force?" Vera knew about the mystery of atoms long before most people had heard of them. The debates that the questions engendered on Sunday morning fascinated her. Her ten-year commitment to the premises of Mary Baker Eddy comprised her only flirtation with "church stuff," but while she believed, she learned a lot.

With Elizabeth Ann available as a baby-sitter during the day, and Vera assigned the task after school, Mae went back to work. She took a job in the post office at the general delivery window. There she met everybody, including Elmer Berg. Elmer was handsome, smart, a real go-getter. Every Sunday he came around to see Mae, but he could never see her alone. Little Gen, Vera and Jimmy were always underfoot. Elmer solved the problem by arriving with dimes in his pocket to treat the kids to an afternoon at the movies. The children saw every show that came to town. The movies were Vera's peep-hole at the wider world beyond Tonopah. Later, in Reno she further immersed herself in the fantasy world of Hollywood as cashier at a movie house.

Once a month, Patty, who was teaching in nearby township schools, brought her pay envelop home to her mother. All the unmarried kids dumped the larger portion of their earnings into her lap. No one in the family was idle, even ten-year-old Vera had an income. Most enterprising of all the girls was Zet. Not bothering to finish high school, after a series of jobs— waitress, soda jerk, grocery clerk—Zet went to work as housekeeper for Tonopah's most important citizen, Senator Vail Pittman. Zetta studied the fine manners of Mrs. Pittman's guests. She had a lot to learn and she was in the right place to learn it. What she learned she passed on to Vera who listened avidly to stories of powerful people, and how they ruled the world. Being a senator was the pinnacle of success so far as Vera could see, but no woman could aspire to that. Being a senator's wife would have to do if only she could meet one someday.

By the time he was 14, Jimmy was big enough to be a Western Union delivery boy. It wasn't long before he knew the town inside out as he found his way up and down the hills carrying those familiar yellow slips in his hat band like the seasoned boys did. The Redlight district was wide open. Jimmy loved taking telegrams into the dance halls, the gambling parlors, the brothels—especially the brothels. The women pampered him, flirted gaily with "the kid" and gave him big tips. Elizabeth Ann was indignant. Sure he'd wind up in bed with one of "those hussies" some night she made him quit. Jimmy was furious. Instead of being a man with money in his pocket, he was just a kid again.

Jimmy's older siblings decided he was getting too big for his britches. He never walked, he swaggered. He needed to be brought down a peg or two by being thrown out of the house of women and into the world of men. It was a relief to everybody, including Jimmy, when Jack finally took him out of Tonopah and into partnership. In that partnership, Jimmy found what he was looking for. He stopped being Jimmy and became Jay. He and Jack remained partners until Jack died in 1938. Together they found and developed the "Chiquita," the gold mine that ultimately made them wealthy.

Vera joined the ranks of the employed by becoming a baby-sitter, a "professional" baby-sitter, she insisted. Gene was her agent. People who wanted her services contacted him. He took responsibility for seeing to it that she sat only in safe houses, that her employer walked her home or drove her back in his carriage, that she was paid in cash. She got 25 cents an hour at a time when miners' wages were $2.50 to $3.00 a day. After the children were down for the night, Vera read. Long hours of reading at night became a life-long habit. Vera hoarded her earnings. Elizabeth Ann had tacked a rug down on the floor of the room they shared and in the spaces between the tacks Vera tucked her savings. That rug was her bank.

She was 10 in 1912 when she began baby-sitting, and she continued baby-sitting until she started high school in 1916. With her earnings, Vera paid for her piano lessons, and after they moved to Reno she bought herself a steel guitar. When a carnival came to town with a troop of Islanders who played before the main tent to entice people inside, Vera was mesmerized by the sounds of Hawaiian music. For a dime you could see bare-bosomed brown maidens lasciviously gyrate their hips to the liquid, languorous, shimmering sounds of the steel guitar. Vera never saw the maidens, but she listened spellbound to the music. She made up her mind to have her own steel guitar someday, and she did.

In the spring of 1916 Vera finished elementary school. She'd been an excellent student. She'd studied hard, and though she'd baby-sat many nights while her schoolmates played under the arc lights at the school yard, she was a member in good standing of the "Amalgamated Order of Fun Makers," a formless club the kids organized that year. High school lay ahead and Vera was more than ready to expand her educational horizons. She read the newspapers every day. There was so much intriguing news and she wanted the background. For instance, everyone was talking about the Federal Highway Act just passed by Congress and signed by President Wilson. On a dollar-for-dollar matching basis, the U.S. Government was going to fund a series of federal highways that would stretch across state after state, from coast to coast. This series of connected highways was to be collectively called "The Lincoln Highway."

Also, the papers were full of news from the western front in Europe where war had been going on for almost two years. There were articles naming places, strangely wonderful in sound, located in areas few Americans had ever heard of. In that presidential election year, Americans voted their delight that President Woodrow Wilson had "kept us out of war." Later, in high school, all the issues discussed around the Smith table, as well as the geography of the world, would be grist for her mental mill in history and government classes. As she waited to enter Tonopah High, the summer seemed interminable.

To Vera's delight, when school opened her history teacher was female, young, recently graduated from the University. Her government teacher, older and more approachable, also female, was always in her classroom after school and would spend time answering the questions Vera hadn't the courage to ask in history class. Mentally, she and her government teacher roamed the wider world outside Tonopah, even outside Nevada. Vera never forgot either of those two teachers. It was a shattering blow when the following spring, as the United States entered the "Great War," Patty made the decision that the reduced Smith family was going to move to Reno where there was a University.

Two of the bread winners, Charles and Gene, were drafted and went off to boot camp. The Smith household was down to five females and a child who, with her mother, was practically out the door toward life with Elmer. There was no way to know when or if Gene and Charles would come back from their very different wars. Gene went to Siberia by way of Angel Island off the coast of Marin County, and Charles went to France. A university town offered more for the remaining quartet of women than Tonopah could.

THE TWIG IS BENT

Compared to the population of any other town between Kansas City and San Francisco, Reno's population was sophisticated and intellectually cosmopolitan. In addition to the stimulating permanent population centered on the university, men and women from all over the United States spent six weeks in residence in Reno to obtain a quick divorce with no questions asked. Nevada was the only state in the Union that did not make it difficult, if not shameful, to get a divorce. These floating members of Reno society needed diversion. Reno sported a lively night life of theaters and dance halls to brighten the visitors' wait, an environment filled with exciting new experiences for Zetta and Vera.

To earn her keep, Zet continued doing housework. Vera, determined to carry her own weight, became cashier and usher at the Majestic Movie Theater. She did everything at the Majestic but sweep up and run the movie projector. Never mind that the job didn't pay much; she saw every film that came to town. Needing to earn more money than the theater paid, Vera took a second job which left her inadequate time to study. She became a bill collector for the plumber who lived across the alley from their rented house. Creditors and businesses did not "bill" customers in the modern sense then. Instead, they sent someone around to pick up the payment. Vera trudged the streets of Reno with her collection receipts in hand, good training for a future politician. She learned to be persistent while being patient, to insist while being gracious, when not to respond to customer anger and when to push for resolution. One of her greatest assets, as a candidate for public office, was her ability to approach people who were strangers and leave them as friends.

Settled in Reno, Vera rented a steel guitar. By the time she graduated from high school she was providing background music during the lunch hour in a downtown hotel dining room. Idle ladies and well-heeled businessmen, not politicians and drummers (traveling salesmen), made up the luncheon clientele in Reno. With her earnings, Vera bought a steel guitar of her own and by the time she moved to Mill Valley she was proficient enough to perform for social events and women's club meetings all over southern Marin County.

After the outbreak of World War I, the town crawled with soldiers. War found the United States almost naked militarily. To produce an officer corps as quickly as possible, the government added war command classes to university ROTC curricula across America. When the Civil War broke out in 1861, most West Point graduates went South when the southern states withdrew from the union to become the Confederate States of America. The North was hamstrung for the first two years of the Civil War because of a lack of trained officers. Piggybacked onto the Morrill Act, passed in 1862 to establish Agricultural and Mechanical Arts colleges using public lands for funding, was the Reserve Officer Training Corps Act. Any state accepting the federal lands had to include ROTC in their "land grant" college curricula. In states where no university already existed, or where one had just recently opened, Morrill Act public lands could be turned over to those institutions, with the proviso that ROTC be part of their course offerings in perpetuity.

These new ROTC men also needed a place to play. Women's Clubs sprang into action sponsoring dances for the men in service. Assured of respectable chaperones, the young women of Reno were eager to dance since the government had so amply provided a stag line. The high-octane level of energy in Reno made the town most definitely Zetta's kind of city. Gene and Charles taught Vera and Zetta how to dance back in Tonopah, and dance they did, superbly. On Sunday nights at home, with no men around, Zetta would pull Vera away from her homework to teach her new steps she'd learned at the Women's Clubs dances. Small, light on their feet, the two sisters danced to the tinny music of an old gramophone and had a wonderful time. Zetta's exuberant personality, trim ankles, and flashing brown eyes attracted men like honey does bees. She always had a date for the dances. Sometimes she wrangled a date for Vera too and dragged her along as her private "chaperone." Later in life, after A.A. Milne's book, *Winnie the Pooh*, came out, the family started calling Zetta "Pooh Bear," a fitting endearment.

What more respectable place could there be where young women could go alone, or in groups, to dance with strangers than the University of Nevada gymnasium? Because of the sophistication of some of the older men in uniform, dances in the gymnasium became too cabaretish for the university trustees. Other dances, similar in format and regulations to USO dances held during World War II, were held by the women's clubs in a second location, a ballroom downtown. The atmosphere downtown was more adult so fewer coeds attended.

For Zetta those dances became the staff of life. Fred Starbuck wandered into the downtown ballroom one night and was bowled over at the sight of Zet. Abundant dark hair, the biggest sparkling brown eyes he'd ever seen, a smile that lighted up her well-ordered face, light and quick of step, she exuded sex appeal. Fred was older and from New York, attributes Zetta found enthralling. Fred had asked for this assignment so he could establish residence in Nevada at the expense of Uncle Sam. Only the humiliating charge of adultery was grounds for divorce in New York and being stationed in Reno was the best way for him and his wife to get a divorce. Before summer was out, Fred's divorce came through and Zetta and Fred, with Vera in tow as witness, went off to the courthouse and were married. The second daughter to be wed followed in the footsteps of the first and notified their mother after the fact.

That September, Fred went off to active duty leaving Zetta where she'd always been, at home with her mother. Mae and Elmer married soon afterward and, to relieve Zetta's boredom, whisked Vera and Zetta off to San Francisco with them for a honeymoon. Vera was enchanted. With Zetta abed with the flu, 15-year-old Vera walked everywhere alone and took it all in. The town more than lived up to its reputation as the most romantic city in America.

World War I was a short war for the United States. The U.S. declared war April 17, 1917 and signed the Armistice on November 11, 1918. The conflict was over. Fred came home and whisked Zetta off to Los Angeles where he could find work. Charles came home before Christmas and headed off to join Jack and Jay. Gene didn't get back for many months after that. The Smith Boys fought very different wars. Charles came back from France full of stories about "Gay Paree" and weekend leaves among the mademoiselles. Gene came back morose, bitter and silent.

At the invitation of the Russian government, to protect prisoners of war and refugees, the U.S. army went into Siberia. After the troops were well inside the country, the armed debate called the Russian Revolution broke out. The questions became: "Which government? Which refugees?" As the Red Army and the White Army see-sawed back and forth over the same territory, again and again, the American Expeditionary Force found itself facing first one hostile Russian army, then the other. Stranded far beyond U.S. Army lines of supply, the men nearly starved. Exiled for two long bitter years, in one of the most backward areas of the western world, Gene felt abandoned by his own government.

To add to his misery, Gene returned to Reno just as a typical postwar economic depression set in. He couldn't find work. Disillusioned, suffering post-war trauma, Gene holed up in the attic apartment of his mother's house, a haunted specter of his former self. Late in 1920, when the construction industry began to recover, Fred and Zetta moved back to Reno with their new baby, Betty Jean. They bought a house near the rest of the family. In the midst of all these relocations, Elizabeth Ann's widowed brother, Don Mathews, died leaving two little girls orphaned with no one to care for them unless Aunt Elizabeth opened her heart and home. When Thelma and 'Little Vera' Mathews came to live in the Smith household they took up what little time Elizabeth Ann might have found at last to devote to Vera.

Elizabeth Ann, Vera and Patty found themselves as cramped for space as they had been in the boarding houses of Tonopah. Jack, as usual, stepped in to solve the problem. He bought an old house at 214 Stewart St. for his mother, the first home she had owned since they left Dutch Flats. It was large enough for her to keep roomers again. "Ma Bell," the telephone company, had a large contingent of young men, temporarily training in Reno, who required lodging. After the first of them found his way to Elizabeth Ann's door, she sheltered and fed Ma Bell's boys for the rest of her days.

COLLEGE COED IN THE DAYS OF THE FLAPPER

Through all the family changes and confusion, Vera stayed her course. Having learned early to set her own goals, to turn inward for quiet and order, she was never diverted by events in the wider society or in her family-centered life. Conscientious application of time, combined with attending summer school every summer, allowed Vera to graduate from high school in 1919. By law, however, Vera, age l6, was too young to graduate. Faced with a year to idle away as she waited for her age to catch up with her achievement, Vera began taking elective courses at the University for which she would receive credit later.

Since she intended to pursue a degree in English she needed a good grasp of language and a good grounding in the intricacies of cogent argument. Ergo, she needed a high grade point average in English. Other girls her age went to high school proms and parties and spent most of their time thinking about boys. Vera thought about about the grand design of human affairs. She mulled over the results of the war in Europe, the physical future the Industrial Revolution was creating for mankind, and the political overhaul of society that the passage of the 19th Amendment would demand. She spent her "limbo" year as a classic "grind." However, life broadened out and became less profoundly intellectual when she entered college the following fall. At last, Vera was able to enjoy the playful side of being young that she had missed .

Nineteen-twenty was a watershed year for "Suffragists." Having won the right to vote after 50 years of prolonged struggle, they were nudged aside by a new form of feminism coming out of France and England called "The "New Woman." The American "Flapper" strutted onto the front pages of the newspapers of the world. U.S. women expanded their demands to include access to the employment marketplace and freedom to combine marriage with career. They wanted unchaperoned movement in society. F. Scott Fitzgerald, writing about the era, said that past generations formed a continuous line, the younger generation socially picking up where the last left off. By 1920, "an infinite and unbridgeable gap" between his generation and the one that preceded it. Vera eagerly embraced the heady new atmosphere.

Then as now, when students returned to campus, sororities jostled each other in a determined race to pledge one or two scholars to give their house an aura of academic excellence. Gamma Phi Beta decided Vera filled the bill. When she became a pledge Miss Patty crowed with delight. Patty felt the whole family had arrived. Vera's reaction was what it had been in Tonopah when she became a member of the "Amalgamated Order of Fun Lovers." She plunged into the social scene, delighted to be one of the inner circle. Though she was a day student who didn't live in the sorority house, Vera was so popular that she was elected president during her junior year.

Vera learned a lot from her madcap friends. Though library time was mesmerizing, skating on Lake Manzanita in the winter or swimming in Lake Tahoe in the summer were also stimulating. Many "favorite things" were not found in text books. Not frivolous enough to a be regarded a "flapper," nevertheless, Vera was seduced by the tone of the times, as enunciated by Dorothy Parker whom she loved to quote in later years. She also read everything she could find on the Algonquin illuminati whose quips were so quotable. Sorority fever and the New Feminism could have been her undoing. Vera was Vera, however. Parties and prattle might be fun, but nothing challenged and edified her like the classroom, particularly, classes in the social sciences and writing.

Vera enrolled in the first class in journalism ever offered at the University of Nevada. To learn the art of writing she went to work on the school newspaper. After two years of learning every step in the process of getting out a paper, she became co-editor. She dreamed of becoming a great writer, a second Edith Wharton perhaps, or, best of all, an Ida Tarbell. Her first project as a reporter took her to the hotel room of the wicked playwright, Maxwell Anderson. Anderson was in Reno getting a divorce. Vera, seeing a reference to his presence in Reno, called him and boldly asked for an interview.

Anderson was annoyed by the idea of spending an afternoon with an eager young coed. She probably had a very passing interest in his writing, or in him, just wanted to see her own name at the head of a column in the school paper. "How better to gain fame than by spending time with the infamous?" he twitted her. Within minutes of her arrival her eagerness won him over and he took her seriously enough to discuss his work in the abstract as well as the concrete. Triumphantly back at the University with her "column" clutched tightly to her bosom, Vera faced her journalism teacher with her coup. Not only was her success in getting in to interview the great man impressive, the teacher declared, but he lauded her ability to keep the interview on track. After that story appeared in print, Vera became very big on campus.

Beyond journalism she took classes in as many electives outside her field as possible. Vera already knew something critically important that the world of specialization glosses over: The broader the background the more specific the truly erudite can be. Political science intrigued her most of all. When she ran for class office the first time, she became keenly aware of how much she enjoyed the scuffles of the political process. Many young people threw themselves into discussions of Freud's startling new theories about the determining force of libido on human life. Vera was more interested in how legislation affected the U.S. She thought women would be liberated more effectively through exercising their right to vote than by indulging in discussions of uninhibited orgasms. While other young people learned to drive and took to the roads, Vera walked to the library. Many a night, when her friends were learning to smoke, to play the ukulele, to roll their stockings below their knees and make them stay up, Vera bent over a pile of books.

Every election, Vera ran for office and once she was elected vice-president of her class. She longed to participate in state and national general elections outside academia—to hand out campaign material, get signatures on petitions, attend political rallies, do something! The idea that one day she'd hold public office herself never occurred to her then. Neither did it occur to her that she'd have any options about a vocation. She assumed that when she graduated she'd teach just like Miss Patty. Writing would be a sideline.

To provide sufficient income to indulge in campus life outside the classroom, Vera continued the two jobs at the Majestic Theater through all four years of college. She gave up bill collecting though, she had no time left over for that. Reporting to the Majestic, night after night, loading herself down with classes, working on the newspaper, running for office, keeping afloat in the social swim, Vera met herself coming and going. "My candle burns at both ends..." she'd say when asked how she was. As long as she could, she continued that pattern of constant physical and mental motion for the rest of her life.

Being a sorority sister put new experiences in her path, foremost among them the college dances. When the war ended so did the city-wide soirees at the gym. College dances became college affairs again. Some Friday nights, when the gymnasium was taken over by sports, dances were held at the downtown ballroom at 2nd and Virginia Streets, the place where Zetta met Fred. On the corner outside that ballroom, one night in her junior year, Vera met a transfer student from the University of California, a slim, elegant young man who set out to "acquire her." They dated once a week on her one night off for over a year before Vera graduated. Sometime during that tepid courtship she said she'd marry him someday. For Vera, "someday" was a vague misty time in a distant future after she'd done many things. For her swain, Ray Schultz, "someday" was far more immediate than Vera imagined. Long before she was ready to honor that promise he held her to it.

In 1922, Zetta and Fred bought an established family resort named Camp Belle at the south end of Lake Tahoe. They renamed the place Starbucks Resort, and year after year for over three decades the entire Smith clan spent their Labor Day holiday in the big lodge that doubled as Fred and Zetta's summer home. The summer of 1922 Vera worked for Zetta as a chambermaid, making beds in the big lodge and cleaning cabins. Under stars so close overhead she could almost touch them, Vera played her guitar by the campfire to entertain the guests, or swam with Zet in the icy waters of the lake, invigorated and happy. That first summer at Tahoe whetted Vera's appetite for more freedom, more adventure, more of the world. She knew she had to work somewhere during June, July and August to accumulate money for the next school year but she could do it in places other than Reno or Tahoe.

Beth Hanchet, a member of the Amalgamated Funlovers from Tonopah school days, was living "Down on The coast" in Oakland with her mother. In Reno, "Down *to* the Coast" or "Down *on* the coast" meant going to or being in the Bay Area of Northern California. In the 1920s, Oakland was *the* city of choice in the East Bay. Oakland might not have "any there there," according to native daughter Gertrude Stein whose candle was burning in Paris, not New York, but there was enough going on in Berkeley, Piedmont and Oakland to merit a Hearst newspaper, which of course had a society page.

Beth's mother invited Vera to spend the summer of 1923 in Oakland so the girls could renew their friendship. Vera pleaded for permission to go. She promised her mother and "Miss Patty" that she'd find work to save money for her senior year's expenses. She already knew what kind of work she wanted to do if she could get it, but she didn't tell Miss Patty or her mother what she had in mind. She intended to try her hand at being a reporter on a big city newspaper. Hearst's *Oakland Post Enquirer,* one of the jewels in the Hearst Newspaper chain, was her target.

As soon as she unpacked her bag at the Hanchets, she went to the newspaper office to let them know she was in town. Full of her dream, sure of her ability to fulfill it, she walked in and astonished the editor by offering to work dirt cheap if he'd give her a try. Something about her energy, her enthusiasm, her perky self-confidence must have tickled his fancy for he decided to try her out.

Her test assignment was to submit a column that would demonstrate her nose for news, her ability to gain access to a source, or a celebrity, or officialdom, and her ability to carry on an in-depth interview. She had to find her own story, get all the facts, prepare the copy for publication and submit the end product. With Maxwell Anderson under her belt, Vera was undaunted. At a state-wide California teachers' convention in the Oakland Auditorium she found her quarry. The program featured a professor of national reputation. Vera succeeded in interviewing him, then culled the interview for the meat in it. The rest was easy. Vera could write. The *Post-Enquirer* published her piece and hired her. In spite of the pittance she received, (she'd made more money selling tickets at the movie house in Reno) she reveled in the job. She'd fallen into a pot of jam and wallowed in its sweetness.

When the glorious summer was over, she went back to the University of Nevada aglow from her success. In her first article for the school paper that fall she wrote glowingly about her summer as a cub reporter. As she told it, she'd been a working Journalist with a capital J, on a Hearst newspaper. The English Department faculty and students were agog over the fact that one of theirs had worked in the newsroom of a big city daily, if only for a summer. After that article appeared she was a "big woman on campus" again. She even received a letter of congratulations from the university president.

As her senior year wound down, Vera applied for teaching positions in nearby towns, avoiding the disappointment that her dreams of a career in journalism were slipping away. She lost herself in the flurry of parties, with commencement, rehearsals, and cramming for final exams. As long as she put off facing the future, it wasn't real. With less than a month to go, however, she began to have anxiety attacks.

The University of California at Berkeley had recruiters scouting the University of Nevada campus that spring hoping to lure University of Nevada graduates down to Berkeley to become teaching fellows in the English Department. The president of the University of Nevada, J. Walter Clark, put on a big dinner at a downtown hotel to entertain the recruiters. Vera knew Clark personally. Clark's wife was Jewish and the Clarks were keenly sensitive to the paranoia that swept the U.S. when the Russian Revolution broke out. The revolution was like kerosene poured on the smoldering passion in the United States for a law to halt the tide of immigration flowing into the country.

Resentment against the steadily increasing hordes of immigrants had been intensifying for over 20 years. In the peak year of 1907, over a million newcomers arrived. The "huddled masses yearning to be free" were responding to the invitation. By the outbreak of World War 1, one in eight Americans was foreign born or the child of foreign born parents. When the war ended, the tide of immigrants came in again. A smoldering anti-Semitism, even greater than the anti-immigration resentment, had been building since the Jews of eastern Europe fled the pogroms of the 1880s and 1890s and poured into New York City. By the time Vera was in college the number of eastern orthodox Jews on the lower East Side had reached close to 200,000. They spoke a strange language, huddled together in their own neighborhoods, had the most exotic foreign culture of any of the immigrant groups, and refused to intermarry. More important, most of the leaders of the Russian Revolution were Jewish, weren't they? Truth or fiction, Jews were tagged as radicals who led labor strikes. Little wonder there was such a violent reaction to their presence. Vera wrote editorials defending the immigrants. In particular, under the aegis of the 1918 Alien Act, she protested the deportation of Russian Jews without giving them their day in court first.

Her defense of the Jews endeared her to the Clarks. Additionally, she had dated the Clarks' older son a couple of times and a younger Clark boy, a bright eight-year-old, was in one of Patty's classes. When Clark arranged the dinner party, he seated Vera between himself and the head recruiter from Berkeley. She felt like a butterfly on the point of a pin. J. Walter began enumerating her accomplishments to the University of California man, stressing the fact that she was an honor student. The recruiter could assess her personality for himself. Midway through the meal he smiled down at her and said, "Well, Miss Smith, I think we'll just sign you up." Vera could hardly get her breath. Graduate school! No small town high school classroom after all? Graduate school meant college teaching. Overwhelmed, she was speechless.

That night, after the lights went out in the hotel ballroom, Vera sailed home like a kite on the wind. Her mother was asleep and Vera didn't wake her. Disappointed that she couldn't share her great news about how her whole future had opened up over chicken tetrazzini and fruit cocktail, she went to bed to toss and turn for hours, too excited to sleep. She allowed herself to spin wonderful fantasies about life on the campus in Berkeley. In the midst of her daydreaming she suddenly confronted the enormity of what this change in her life would mean to Miss Patty. It was not just her future that was being redirected, but her sister's as well. Patty had intended to take a sabbatical and go back to school herself to finally get a Bachelor of Arts degree. If she, Vera, went to Berkeley instead of getting a job she would still need help from home. The Fellowship paid only $60 a month. Her elation evaporated under a siege of guilt.

Unable to face Patty with the news, Vera kept the knowledge of her sudden freefall into a lovely future to herself for days. J. Walter Clark kept urging her to sign with the English department of the University of California. He kept telling her what a rare opportunity had come her way. "Think of your future, girl," he said. At last she shut her ears to her conscience, took the fatal step and filled out the application. After supper that night, she blurted it all out: what it would cost, how much help she'd still need, what it would mean to them both. Midway through her recital she began to cry. "I'm sorry I signed those papers. I won't take it, Patty. It's your turn."

Patty laughed until tears rolled down her cheeks. "Not take it! It's what we all hoped for, isn't it? A graduate degree, a real start? You're not robbing me of anything. You're giving me something. I'll get my degree without any sacrifice from you, you hear?" Vera went limp with relief. Her future was hers to make. Patty had set her free.

DOWN TO THE COAST

When Vera stepped off the train from Reno in the fall of 1924, her first objective was to find a cheap place to live. As a matter of pride she wanted to keep her monthly expenses within the $60 stipend. Scouring the want ads she found an apartment some distance from the University where the rent wouldn't eat her alive. For a week, she walked back and forth in order to save carfare. At the end of that week her feet were so blistered she could hardly put on shoes. The long walk was too difficult and ate up too much time. There was a limit to how much of her life she could dedicate to scrimping. Thoroughly frustrated, she searched again for a cheap, close-in apartment, or a room with cooking privileges.

She was beginning to believe she'd never find an affordable place when the proverbial Smith-family luck kicked in. Besides teaching four classes of Subject A English she was taking four classes of her own. Every night she faced long hours of work on lesson planning, paper grading, or homework for her Master's. One of her Subject A English students, Jack Thornberg, a young married man with a wife, a small child, and endless ambition, solved her problem.

Jack was a man of many talents, a whiz at budgeting time, and blessed with boundless energy. A building contractor, he built a small house for himself near the campus. The first essay he wrote for Vera's class was about the life of a married man with a wife, a child, and a business to run, while being a full-time student. Vera read his essay and was indignant. The assignment had been to write about something real in his life. An alleged wife, a storybook child, and a successful construction business were not the baggage of a student in the 1920s. She wrote a scathing note on his paper and ordered him to do it over. Jack stormed into her office and quickly disabused her of any notion that he was full of moonbeams. Amazed at the scope of his life and his ability to juggle so many roles, she retracted every word she'd written, regraded the essay carefully, and wrote a heartfelt apology in the margin. They became fast friends.

After that interview Jack added a room to his house and urged her to come to live with his little family. "You can help Frances with the baby to pay your rent," he said. Vera jumped at the offer. No rent to pay would keep her off Patty's dole and provide a little pocket money. Furthermore, she missed being part of a family. Eagerly she moved into the Thornburg's addition. An expert on child care after all her experiences with her niece Gen, her cousins Vera and Thelma, and all the hours of baby-sitting she'd done in Tonopah, Vera's expertise made her invaluable to the new mother struggling with the endless hours of work a baby demanded.

To earn extra income, the teaching fellows in the English Department at the University of California graded Subject A English essays sent to the University from colleges all over the state. Regardless of which college the applicant hoped to attend, public or private, applicants for college entrance wrote Subject A essays of 500 words. In reality the essays were matriculation exams written in standard "blue books." Blue book essays arrived all year long and required hours and hours of time to correct and rank. When the flow of blue books was heavy, Vera spent many nights pouring over the piles stacked on her desk, sometimes falling behind in her own studies. She gave over every weekend to grading blue books, ad nauseam, on a piecework pay basis.

One beautiful October Saturday, Vera went out into the Berkeley Hills above Jack's house and sat down at the foot of a glorious clump of brilliant red and orange foliage. With a lap full of work, she leaned back against the giant eucalyptus cloaked in its gorgeous drapery and scribbled away for hours. All afternoon, as the sun filtered through the branches overhead, she was aware of a tickling at the back of her neck that she tried to brush away from time to time, but it persisted. As the shadows grew long and her back began to ache from sitting hunched over her lap, she stiffly rose and went home to take a hot bath before going out on a date. A hot bath was absolutely the worst thing she could have done, but how was a girl from the desert to know? The next morning she frantically called Frances Thornberg into her bedroom.

"I don't know what's the matter with me," she moaned, "I can't open my eyes."

Jack's wife took one look at her and shuddered. "Oh you poor thing!" she cried, "You've got as bad a case of poison oak as I've ever seen!"

Vera fell back onto the bed and began to cry. She couldn't afford the time to be ill. Jack went to the pharmacy to buy everything Frances had ever heard touted for reducing the pain and itching. After two agonizing days of applying every compound the pharmacist could recommend, Vera was still a horrible mess. From her scalp to the bottoms of her feet, she was covered with a fine red rash. In the creases of the bends in her elbows and behind her knees her skin was a solid, puffy mass of livid red dots. Nothing gave her relief and the rash continued to spread. Vera went to the Infirmary at the University.

For a week she lay between rubber sheets, fearing to move once she found a comfortable position, thrashing about if she didn't. On the seventh day of isolation and misery she persuaded the nurse to help her to a phone so she could call Mae in Reno. Pouring out her tale of woe she pleaded piteously, "Will you come and get me? I think if I could come home, I might get better sooner." When there was no metaphysical cure, the poison oak episode ended Vera's belief in Christian Science. Mae kept the faith but Vera became an avowed agnostic.

After three weeks at home Vera returned to California. Her afternoon in the arms of the lovely poison oak had cost her five weeks of absence from classes. Worse, she had to hunt for another place to live; the doctors said she couldn't go back to the contaminated room at Jack's. Where to go? The mother of Bart Yarborough, one of the main characters on the beloved Sunday night radio serial, "One Man's Family," lived in Berkeley in a beautiful big square house near the campus. Mrs. Yarborough had come to Berkeley to make a home for her younger son who was a student at the University. She had brought two servants with her who did all her work. A stranger in town, time hung heavy on Mrs. Yarborough's hands.

Unhappy, and at loose ends, when she and Vera met at an affair on campus Mrs. Yarborough poured out her tale of newcomer-loneliness. Vera suggested that the restless lady audit her class, and there she'd meet people. Mrs. Yarborough eagerly enrolled and Vera had a number of tutorial sessions with her to remedy the lady's Texas speech habits. Those sessions gave Vera an idea. Mrs. Yarborough had rooms to let and maid service went with them. Vera suggested they trade tutoring for shelter? Mrs. Yarborough was delighted. But Vera's idyll at Mrs. Yarborough's was disappointingly brief, as were all her living arrangements that year. Soon after Vera moved in, the Yarborough menage had to close out the house because of a series of calamities that befell Mr. Yarborough down in Texas. The servants were let go, the big house was sold, Mrs. Yarborough went home, and Vera was out on the streets again.

When school was out in the spring of 1925, Vera eagerly escaped to Tahoe for the summer. Weekly, a constant shipment of blue books followed her. Blue books or no blue books, it was good to be back in the family circle, to eat her fill at Zetta's bounteous board, and not worry about the rent. When her vacation ended, she left Tahoe more reluctantly than she had sped away the previous fall. Her second school year slipped by with greater speed than her first. In the spring of 1926, with a master's degree in English almost in her grasp and her Fellowship running out, Vera began looking about for a school opening. Her interest in teaching was no greater than it had ever been, but she had to have a job.

Just as she was resigning herself to the classroom permanently, fate stepped in and shunted her into a divine direction. Out of the blue, Marie Onions, the club editor at the *Post-Enquirer*, came by to tell Vera that she was going to resign and go to Europe to live for a year. There would be an opening on the paper immediately and if Vera acted quickly, Marie said, maybe, just maybe, the job could be hers. Vera was thunderstruck. She had dropped by the Enquirer now and then to say hello and smell the ink, but she'd written nothing since she came to Berkeley. Could it be that she didn't have to teach after all? Crossing her fingers and holding her breath she hurried off to talk to the Editor. What if he didn't remember her?

He remembered, and without a moment's hesitation hired her to fill Marie Onion's capable loafers. When Vera left that interview she had to pinch herself to keep from shouting for joy right there on the street. She'd found Nirvana! She'd died and gone to heaven in that big, sweet pot of jam after all. Forget that she'd earn less than the schools would pay. She could make up the shortage by continuing to grade blue books.

The *Post-Enquirer* discontinued the society page in the dog days of July and August. Once the June weddings were over and the women's clubs took their summer hiatus, the club editor was furloughed. No sense of guilt overshadowed Vera's joy as she packed up a summer's supply of blue books and went home to face Patty. This time she was relieving Patty of responsibility for all time. If Patty was disappointed that she wasn't going to teach, so be it. The aborted Master's degree might be a sore subject. She hadn't taken her orals. She hadn't written a thesis. She wasn't going for a master's degree after all. That might disappoint Patty but she didn't care. This job gave her the world on a string and she was going to curl that string around her finger no matter what.

The sun sparkled on the lake that summer; there was no cloud in the sky. Vera was happy and life couldn't be better—except. A barrage of letters flowed unceasingly from Berkeley. When she took her Fellowship at Berkeley, Ray Schultz returned to "Cal" where he'd been a student before going to Nevada. After Vera's first year on campus he graduated in 1925 and went to work for an Insurance Company in San Francisco. Living in Berkeley and commuting by way of the ferry made such long days for Ray that for the past two years Vera and Ray had gone on with their a once-a-week dating pattern. It was an old habit they were too busy to change. It had been a comfortable relationship for Vera. It gave her something to do on Saturday night, and left her time free the rest of the week. Abruptly all that changed. Now that her Fellowship had come to an end, and he was making good money, Ray wanted her to consumate the "someday" promise she'd made back in Reno three years before. He wanted to get married now. Never a social animal, he had few friends and he was tired of living in rented rooms and lonely apartments.

When Vera had made that non-threatening promise three years earlier, she was living at home facing the future of a schoolteacher in some small town. She hadn't been given the option of big-time journalism, nor tasted the independence she now enjoyed. She hadn't sampled freedom. Now she was on her way with a job in a field she adored. Marvelous opportunities were coming her way. Marriage was not on her agenda. She wasn't ready to put on an apron. If she married, her promising career would be over before she even went to work. Why hurry? When she let her suitor know, in letter after letter, that marriage had no charm for her at this time and maybe he ought to look for someone else, Ray was impervious to her arguments. Knowing his prey, he insisted on holding her to her pledge. She had said she would marry him and he'd been patient while she did that Fellowship thing but it was over and he wanted her to marry him now. He didn't want to look elsewhere. Vera was caught between honoring her word and fulfilling her dreams. What was she to do? Hearst papers had a policy of not hiring married women, and women who did marry after they were on the payroll were expected to resign. How could she in good conscience take the job if she was to marry now?

The "New Woman" in her would not give up the right to a career. Honor or no honor, promise or no promise, she wasn't going to miss this rare opportunity to work for the Hearst organization, not before she'd even seen her name at the head of a regular feature. One of her reasons for going home that summer had been to avoid the issue as long as she could. There was no escape. Daily, the mails brought strident letters in which Ray harped on the fact that she had given her word. Despite her wild yearnings to be free, she felt trapped.

Vera's basic instinct was always to make everyone feel good, even if she had to set aside her own needs and desires to do it. So, with a troubled conscience she succumbed to his demand that she fulfill her promise on the condition that Ray join her in a conspiracy that would allow her to go on being "Miss Smith" to the newspaper world, and be Mrs. Schultz secretly.

She'd marry him now, as he wished, instead of later as she preferred, and in doing so, would twice compromise herself. She would lie to the editor, deny being married, and deny Ray the little housefrau he preferred to a career woman. Having laid out her terms, she hoped he'd refuse and bow out, but he didn't. Looking back at the end of a long fruitful life filled with an extraordinary list of achievements, Vera regretted the unfinished business of that Masters Degree, but when asked if she regretted the marriage, she ducked the question.

The future career-woman-wife set off from Nevada in late summer to start an unnerving, complex, new life in California. No one in Reno or Tahoe knew of the full agenda that lay ahead of her. On the 21st day of August 1926, Ray was waiting on the platform in Oakland as she stepped down from the train. He led her out of the station to the new little car he'd bought, put her bag in the back, and drove straight to San Jose for the wedding he'd arranged on his own without consultation. He'd found a minister by spotting a sign on a lawn advertising weddings for anyone who had a license. The cleric and his wife were waiting in their parlor when the bride and groom arrived. The minister's wife would be Matron of Honor. The housekeeper came out of the kitchen to be a second witness, and, noting the little gray satin dress Vera wore, said, "That's a pretty dress. Married in gray, rue the day." On that cheery note the bare bones wedding proceeded.

The wife and housekeeper "stood up" with them in the parlor, sans friends, sans family, sans anything old, borrowed or blue. The minister's children went out and tied tin cans to Ray's car so they'd make a racket like clattering horses in good old Nebraska farmer fashion when they left. Ray had grown up a dirt farmer's son from the Midwest and some his hard scrabble mentality never washed off. Vera Lucille Klingensmith (it was the first time she used the Klingen half of her surname) and Ray Schultz were married that day and, for better or for worse, headed into a 64-year alliance. They had told no one in either family they were going to take this fateful step so Elizabeth Ann got another of those telegrams from a daughter who married first and announced later. Before going to bed that night Ray sat down and wrote his mother a long letter while Vera stood in their hotel room in Santa Cruz looking out over the moonlit Pacific Ocean.

When the newly married Schultzes returned from a honeymoon in Southern California, Vera moved into the house Ray had rented while she was still in Nevada. Triumphant over her capitulation, Ray had acted alone as was his wont. He'd rented a little mouse-ridden, shabby cottage, located behind the Chesapeake apartments on Durant Avenue in Berkeley. At Montgomery Ward's he bought a skeletal array of furniture to fill the tiny rooms. If sparse was desirable, Ray had chosen both house and furnishings well. Vera hated it. That cottage was the worst place she'd ever lived except for a cockroach-infested apartment she'd occupied for one week the year before.

The next day Vera took matters into her own hands as her mother had done upon their arrival in Tonopah. She began looking for a better setting for the new Mrs. Schultz, who was about to become a great journalist. Ray got his first taste of what happened when his penuriousness pushed her too far. Jack Thornburg had built a rental house up on Cragmont Avenue. Cragmont was a healthy distance from the *Post-Enquirer* or the ferry landing, but that house was heaven compared to this collapsing cottage. Boxing her husband in at a party where he couldn't object, she announced to Ray et al that they were going to be the Thornburgs' new tenants.

As much as she loved the little house on Cragmont with its beautiful view of the Bay she had to admit defeat during the winter of 1926-1927. That year was one of those drenchers California periodically endures. Having a bit of a walk to the street car line, she arrived at work every day as wet as a rat terrier. No coiffure could survive the weather long enough for her to put in a decent appearance at the paper. The couple went down to University Avenue and rented a little cottage behind the new Casa de Manana Apartments just half a block off the car line. It was a neighborhood of poorly built small workmen's cottages at least 30 years old. Their's was one of the smallest, but it was clean and the rent allowed for a little savings.

On September 1, Vera Smith reported to the *Post-Enquirer* trembling with excitement. On her initial trip to the water cooler, she met Al Santoro, the sports writer for the paper. Al took one look at sparkling Vera, and was immediately smitten. Her easy banter, her high energy, her quick mind appealed to him. Whenever possible he found a way to casually drop by her desk for a quip, or a chance remark. Awake at last to the effect she'd had on the sports department, Vera slithered out of accepting his offhand invitations to go for a drink after work or to take in a movie and did it so skillfully he wasn't sure he was being direct enough. Al decided to take the frontal approach and trap her in her den.

One Saturday night as she was fixing dinner and Ray was puttering around the house, the doorbell rang and there on the stoop stood Al, a bottle of wine in one hand and a loaf of bread tucked under the other arm. Vera was thunderstruck. Open-mouthed for a breathless moment she contemplated slamming the door in his face. Then the hilarity of the situation struck her and she burst out laughing as she stepped aside to admit him.

"Come in, Al," she chuckled, "I've got to let you in on a little secret. I don't live here alone, I'm married. This is my husband," nodding toward Ray, "and we're about ready to eat."

Al stared down into her laughing face for what seemed an eternity to the waiting Schultzes, then threw back his head and howled. Relieved, Vera took his loaf of bread and his bottle of wine from him and put them on the table. "We'll just add these to the meal and you'll have dinner with us." she stated in a tone that brooked no objection

Throwing his coat over the back of a chair Al entered into the spirit of the ambush gone awry and pitched in to help get another place set and the food on the table. They had a wonderful time. He told war stories about life on the paper. He and Vera bantered back and forth about colleagues and their foibles. Ray described life on the ferry crossing to San Francisco. When it came time for Al to leave Vera said to him,

"Al, you know the paper's policy about married women. If Mr. Hearst finds out I'm married, I'm dead. Please, keep my secret?" As she spoke, she reached out and placed her hand over his.

He looked down at her hand and grinned, "Lady, you'd make quite a politician. Don't worry, I'll never tell."

He never did. A couple of months later, though, he had one delicious moment of sweet revenge during a hilarious episode that involved Vera's in-laws. Mr. and Mrs. Schultz had come to meet the bride and spend the holidays but newspapers know no holidays: 365 days a year there is an edition. Every December the paper threw a Christmas party for the *Post-Enquirer's* employees, their parents and their children. It was always scheduled for Christmas Eve afternoon at the Oakland Auditorium. For days, Vera's "Children's Column" had been filled with previews of what would happen at that party. Her coverage was intended to whip up readership for her Children's Page, and circulation for the paper.

Vera had complimentary tickets for her in-laws. Ray had to work until noon so he gave his new Ford to his parents to drive to the auditorium. When the show began, Vera stood in the wings of the stage making copious notes. She'd have to rush back to the office and pound out a story in time for the evening edition. Before the last child had taken her/his sack of candy from the Santa Claus hired for the occasion, Vera hurried her in-laws to the parking lot before she took off on the double for the newspaper.

Outside, Mr. and Mrs. Schultz buttoned up against a cold wind blowing in off the Bay and walked to where they'd left the car. It was gone! Someone had stolen their son's precious automobile. They were aghast. After the shock came angry indignation. The police had better find it fast. But there was no policeman around to help them. Stranded in a strange city, growing colder by the minute, the senior Schultzes forlornly trudged across downtown Oakland to the *Post-Enquirer* to find Vera. Fortunately for Vera, by the time her in-laws arrived, the building was practically deserted. The receptionist and most of the staff had gone home early on Christmas Eve. Only she and Al Santoro were at work in the huge silent room.

When Ray's parents came in looking lost and frazzled. Vera didn't see them. Al, looking up, saw the anxious couple looking bedraggled and bewildered standing beside the empty receptionist's desk and went over to see if he could help.

"We'd like to speak to Mrs. Schultz." Ray's father said. "She's our daughter-in-law."

"Oh," said Al innocently, "we don't have anyone by that name working here."

"But, she's right over there," protested Mr. Schultz, pointing to Vera bent over her work.

"Sorry sir," said Al choking back laughter, "you're mistaken. That's our Club Editor, Miss Smith. If that's who you think you'd like to talk to, I'll call her over and let her straighten this out."

Eyes dancing he walked over to Vera's desk and leaning down whispered in mock amazement. "There's a couple here asking for a Mrs. Schultz. What should I tell them?"

Vera stared at him stupefied for a moment, then following his pointing finger saw the forlorn senior Schultzes on the other side of the reception counter.

"My in-laws," she groaned.

"No no," Al laughed, walking away, "Mrs. Schultz's in-laws."

Glaring at his retreating back, she bounced out of her chair and hurried over. Ray's parents began talking at once, pouring out their tale of woe, eager to tell every detail of the calamity. As the story kept spilling out, Vera lost patience.

"I'll get you a cab," she said "and I'll call the police and I'll call Ray. I'll take care of everything. You just go on home and don't worry about a thing. Everything is going to be all right. I have to finish this column before I can get away but Ray will take care of everything. Come on, I'll find you a cab." Urgently she pushed them out the door.

Safely on the sidewalk outside, she hailed a cab cruising along the nearly empty streets of Christmas Eve. When she returned shivering Al was busily typing copy, whistling Christmas carols as he worked. He looked up, gave her a wink, then buried his face in his coat sleeve. Vera was not amused. She put through a call to Ray, quickly told him what had happened, then hung up without giving him a chance to let fly in her direction. Let him take it out on his parents or the proverbial cat. She had a column to finish. Fortunately, the police found the car the next day, but Christmas Eve was ruined. For Vera the whole episode became a joke she loved to tell in later years, but Ray never laughed at the story.

Vera passionately loved being part of the newspaper world. She'd gladly have paid membership dues to a Union if it had been required. She took over the children's page which Elsie Robinson had started earlier and became "Aunt Elsie," as well as continuing as club editor. In those days, newspapers across the country encouraged young readers, wooed them, and tried to build a readership for the future. Every Saturday, one whole page was filled with children's activities: contests, letters to Aunt Elsie, essays from school children, reports from camp by little readers who wanted to see their names in print, Boy Scout and Girl Scout news, puzzles to be worked, and advance information about cultural offerings for children in the Bay Area.

As Aunt Elsie, Vera kept in touch with the public schools of Oakland. She became a regular at Parent and Teacher Association meetings around the city. The club editor's beat included the scheduled events of every women's club in the triad of towns—Oakland, Berkeley and Piedmont. The clubs ranged from the League of Women Voters, to the Federation of Women's Clubs, to the Daughters of the Golden West, to the PTA. When the NEA held its convention in Oakland she covered that, too.

The League of Women Voters was Vera's favorite. Vitally interested in their programs, she used her typewriter to push their agenda. She covered all their meetings, advocated all their projects, and unabashedly urged women to get involved. The 19th Amendment had made women eligible to vote in the 1920 national election but women had not voted in the numbers the League, or Vera, had expected. Prophetic of the future, women demanded the right to vote and then neglected to exercise their empowering franchise. History would repeat the scenario 50 years later. The 26th amendment, allowing 18-year-olds to vote, was as stridently demanded, and as carelessly ignored, as the 19th. Through the Oakland and Berkeley LWV chapters, Vera got an education in California politics she would put to good use in Marin County later on.

One of Vera's most pleasurable assignments was to review all the movies that came to Oakland and Berkeley. Theaters "comped" the Schultzes, hoping for good reviews. Vera and Ray saw every film that came to town. One of the first critiques she wrote for the *Post-Enquirer* was about "The Red Mill," starring Marion Davies. Having no idea that Marion Davies was Mr. Hearst's "Other Woman," she reviewed that movie as she saw it, and roundly panned it.

When she turned in her copy, word swept from department to department, from pressmen to editors. The rookie reporter had written her way into immortality. There were whoops of laughter in the newsroom, in the lavatories, in the front offices, even at the newsstands when the paper hit the streets. People whistled and cheered, the place was in an uproar. They put her picture on the newsroom bulletin board. Vera was the darling of the paper. After that gaffe, everyone connected with the Post-Enquirer knew Vera Smith.

Only one incident marred her second year on the paper. After a year abroad, Marie Onions returned and came back to work. She transferred to the news department, and the club editor's job was Vera's. Marie was Vera's only confidante and Marie was irate about Ray's inflexibility. As the man in the family, Ray controlled both their salaries as if he'd earned them both. His possessiveness about their car was especially galling to Marie. It was his car, not their's. Vera, the "New Woman," was too intimidated to insist she be allowed to learn to drive. One Saturday, under the spur of Marie's feminism, Vera and Marie stole the car from its parking space behind the apartment and drove up to the Rose Garden for a picnic. Marie drove up the winding streets to the park but insisted Vera try her hand coming back. Unluckily, the car was scratched in a minor brush with a parked delivery truck.

Marie and Vera decided that since the scratch was almost indiscernible, what Ray didn't know wouldn't hurt anybody. They didn't mention the picnic or their joyride. Ray's eagle eye saw the scratch the next day. In a rage he demanded to know what Vera knew about the "damage to my car." Honest Vera owned up about hers and Marie's defiant escapade. Ray erupted in a tirade that left Vera exhausted. She didn't ask again to learn to drive for 22 years. No matter how inconvenient it was for her to take the streetcar, even after they moved to hilly Mill Valley, Vera either hoofed it or hitched a ride. She didn't even feel free enough to take a taxi.

If anyone had suggested to Vera that she would ever voluntarily leave the engrossing world of newsprint she would have objected strenuously. Yet in the Spring of 1928, in spite of her fascination with journalism, a spur of the moment impulse changed the locus and focus of her life forever. One beautiful sunlit Saturday in May, when the fog hung off the coast too lazy to roll in, the Schultzes attended a weekend house party across the Bay in Mill Valley. Mill Valley was blanketed that spring with a breathtaking sea of blue forget-me-nots and wild iris, the most glorious display of nature's flower garden Vera had ever seen. The Schultzes went for a walk along the village streets to feel the lightness of the air, to bask in the sunlight filtering through the canopy of trees overhead, smell the fragrance of the season, and drink in the wonder of a perfectly lyrical spring. They passed little summer cottages belonging to San Franciscans who crossed the Bay on the ferry as soon as school was out and stayed until Labor Day. They admired the larger, though less numerous, substantial homes of the permanent population. As they drank in the ambiance of one of the dearest little towns she had ever seen, Vera had an inspiration.

"Why don't we move over here just for the summer?" she enthused. "If I can get leave from the paper, what difference would it make to you whether you commuted to San Francisco from here, or from Berkeley? You could catch the ferry here just as easily as you can from over there and I could write. I've got several stories in my head, and this would be an ideal place to compose."

Ray couldn't think of an answer so he kept walking while she talked. For Ray, silence was a good retreat. If you let Vera talk long enough, she might talk herself out of whatever it was she wanted, or give up. This time she didn't do either. Scratch the surface of any journalist and you'll find an embryonic novelist hatching plots and itching to "do a book." Vera's itch and the lure of the bowery town were upon her. As Ray kept walking, she kept talking. Finally, Ray caved in. On Monday, Vera approached the editor and proposed a leave of absence for three months.

"Sure," he said, "happens all the time. I don't see any problem. Take two or three months and write your stories. Everybody has to get that book out of their craw sooner or later. Better now than have it building up frustration."

Vera was thrilled. In her mind's eye she saw herself seated behind tables signing books in bookstores, posing for photographers, an invited guest at readers' clubs, banked by the committees that made book awards. Besides a fertile imagination, and the ability to put coherent thought into arresting metaphors, writing required discipline, just plain discipline. One sat in a chair hour after hour and pounded away at a typewriter applying persistence and self-control. She had talent, she had determination, and she'd learned long ago that the investment of time was the essential ingredient for doing anything well. She could write a book in a summer in an inspirational setting like Mill Valley.

LOOK OUT MILL VALLEY, HERE SHE COMES!

Vera set out in a flurry of activity to finish the spring season before taking off for the far side of the Bay. Nights, she hurried home from the newspaper to pack their stuff for storage during their absence. To find an author's hideaway where they could live for the summer was the only obstacle they faced. Early the following Saturday morning, they drove to Mill Valley to choose a secluded retreat. To their surprise they had no choice. They couldn't find any place in Mill Valley, furnished or unfurnished. They didn't even run across a big old house cut up into apartments where one could find a studio, or a bedroom with cooking privileges. With only two weeks to go before they were scheduled to move, they walked up and down the streets for hours looking for "For Rent" signs. Finally, after climbing two long flights of wooden stairs against the hillside from Miller Avenue. below, they trudged up Heuters Lane where they found a cramped little cold water flat not suitable for a long-term abode. They grabbed it.

Putting down a deposit, they drove back to Berkeley to wind up their affairs and store their furniture. They had the telephone disconnected on Monday to save the utility bill. Everything went into storage except that which they'd need for two months in a cubbyhole. They loaded into the car cooking utensils, bedding, their clothes and Vera's typewriter. Mid-morning, moving day, they drove up to the house on Heuters Lane eager to get settled. Happily, they crossed the little patch of lawn and rang the bell. A distraught woman answered, all chagrin and full of apology. Three days after she'd let the apartment to them, her daughter had unexpectedly been released from the tuberculosis sanitarium in Napa and needed a place to live. She had no choice. She had to give her daughter the flat she'd promised to the Schultzes. The Schultzes had stopped their phone service to save money and she'd been unable to notify them of this unhappy turn of events. She wrung her hands in apology.

Vera and Ray were speechless. Turning dumbly away they left the embarrassed woman standing in her open door. Numb with shock, they stumbled back across the crab-grass lawn. Now, they literally had no place to hang their hats or lay their heads. Deflated, dazed, they climbed disconsolately back into the car and grimly set off to look again for "For Rent" or "Guest Cottage" signs tacked to trees at the fronts of lots or sitting in windows. Signs for any kind of rental space were as non-existent as they had been two weeks before. Worse, there was no hotel in Mill Valley in 1928, no roadside inn. Where to spend the night? Too spent to look further, they camped on a vacant lot at 190 Ethel Avenue. Ethel Avenus was a narrow little street cut out of the side of the hill above Miller Avenue, the main artery into town.

"We could make our bed on this lot to sleep tonight," Vera said resignedly, "then go down to a Realtors in the morning and hope they can find us a place to live."

They cobbled some brush into a mounded pile, then spread bedding from the car over it. After trudging up and down the hills of Mill Valley, they were so tired they could have slept on the bare ground. As they crawled in between the blankets they discovered to Vera's horror that they were sharing their make-shift bed with a mole busily rooting around in the earth beneath them. Vera bolted upright. She couldn't sleep on top of something alive. Most of the night she sat leaning against a tree, gazing at the stars overhead which shone fitfully through the quivering leaves above moved by a light breeze that stirred the branches. The longer she listened to the night sounds around her, the more she absorbed the complete isolation of this spot so near the center of the town's activity. This lot was a superb combination of complete alignment with nature and convenient proximity to urban life.

Woodsy, quiet, substandard in size, 190 Ethel Avenue was an ideal lot on which to build a hideaway amid the overgrowth of trees and shrubs. Down slope from 190, the land was too steep for houses to be built across the street from them, unless they were perched on stilts. Only the trees would be their neighbors. The lot had one obvious drawback. A big culvert ran along the base of the property that would prevent them from ever having access to a garage if they built here. Furthermore, the street was so narrow there was no off-street parking on either side. Residents who could, drove onto their lots; the rest left their cars down on Miller Avenue and walked up the wooden stairs that hugged the hillside. At a curve a hundred feet or so down the block, there was a spot where the cut in the hill widened out and on that one tiny level bit of ground stood a small empty, rickety barn obviously built to hold one horse and a buggy. If 190 Ethel Avenue became theirs, they'd have to rent that barn to shelter their car.

When morning came, Vera sat on the edge of the pallet impatient for her husband to open his eyes. Unable to wait any longer she gently shook him. "Ray," she said triumphantly, "I've got the solution. Let's buy this lot and build a house. We could easily put up a little cottage this summer. Did you ever see such a glorious spot in your whole life?"

Rubbing his eyes, Ray grunted and looked around. It was a far cry from Nebraska or Berkeley. Build a cottage? It was the first time he'd thought about being a homeowner and the idea felt good. Gritty-eyed and disheveled, they loaded up the car and drove downtown to the Swiss Chalet building that was the railroad station to clean up in the restrooms before going to a nearby bakery for breakfast. In the bakery they inquired about the woman whose name was on the For Sale sign posted on the Ethel Avenue lot. She lived just a few steps away. Excitedly, they phoned from the bakery to ask if they could come to talk to her about the property she had for sale. Surprised that this couple had squatted on her lot the night before, she agreed to see them immediately.

When they were face to face with the owner, she said she wouldn't take less than $250 for her property. Vera couldn't believe it. $250? Such a charming lot for that price? Not bothering to think things over for once, Ray wrote out a check immediately. On a sunny Sunday morning in June of 1928, Vera and Ray Schultz unwittingly chose to sink their roots permanently in Mill Valley. With the bill of sale in hand, they went back to Berkeley to find Nick Klein-Shoorel, a one-eyed Dutch contractor whose work they'd seen and admired. Fortunately, he was at home. Without wasting time in idle chatter, interrupting each other in their eagerness, the Schultzes spilled out a long litany of the frazzling events of the past few weeks. Ray whipped out the bill of sale and asked,

"Would you come over to Mill Valley for two weeks and build us a summer cabin?"

"Two weeks?" Nick scratched his head. "Is the lot improved?"

"No," they admitted a bit fearfully "at least we don't think so."

Bemused, Nick pondered awhile. "I'll have to go over and have a look at it," he finally said.

"Well, come on," urged Ray, "Let's go right now."

They went that afternoon. They found there were no improvements of any kind on the lot—no water, no power line, no sewer line, no septic tank. Nick paced around the woodsy lot assessing the best siting for a house and a septic tank.

"I'll make a bargain with you," he said finally. "If you two will help, if Ray will take a vacation and pitch in, if he'll dig the rock out of that embankment to use in building the fireplace, I think we can do it in two months. I know we cant' do it in two weeks."

A house in two months was too much to hope for but the inexperienced Schultzes let themselves believe and took the gamble. The three of them rented a house up on Hueter's Lane they'd not seen before and Nick came to Mill Valley for the duration.

That night they sat down and drew a plan which every night thereafter they changed. Instead of building a one-room cottage with a grill in one corner and a fireplace in another they built a five-room house with a full kitchen. Instead of two months, it was just under a year before the Schultzes moved in to the unfinished shell. The town of Mill Valley brought the utilities to the site immediately but it took much longer than two months, and a change of contractors, to finish it.

Vera threw herself into being carpenter's assistant and was soon pounding nails like a veteran. When Nick had to get back to his own life, they sent out an S.O.S. for Fred and Zetta. Fred had become a contractor in Reno after he and Zet returned from Los Angeles. If a Smith was in trouble the family rallied. The Starbucks came when called and Fred set to work. It wasn't long until Fred and Zetta, like the Schultzes, were trapped by the insidious pull of Mill Valley. The fall and winter the Starbucks planned to stay to help Vera and Ray stretched into a permanent change of residence, for the Starbucks as well as the Schultzes. The influx of people coming into Mill Valley in the 1920s, and the dearth of houses available to accommodate them provided Fred with a gold mine of his own. He worked on Hollybush House, so named after a large holly bush on the property, until the house was far enough along for the Schultzes to move in. They could finish the rest of their house themselves.

With the Starbucks settled in Marin County, the two couples decided to take a vacation in the late summer of 1930. Ray wanted to go to Detroit to buy a new car and the Starbucks wanted to visit some friends in Chicago. Fred and Zetta were in no hurry. Going east as far as Chicago in the Starbuck's big Packard, stopping early and starting late each day, the four of them had a wonderful time. The tempo changed once they parted in Chicago. The Schultzes, much to Vera's disgust, set the metronome at higher speeds and headed off for Detroit post haste on the Greyhound bus.

Vera and Ray wasted no time sight-seeing in Michigan. After they bought a new Chrysler in the motor city, they rolled down the windows, and headed west. That was the last trip they took that was not done totally on the cheap. Years later, when they went east again to buy another car, they took the Greyhound bus nonstop from Marin County to Detroit to save overnight hotel bills. It was a cheap, horrible trip. Every bone in Vera's body ached by the time they arrived. After that, Vera refused to take any long trips unless she traveled on official business with some agency paying the bill. If she was going to leave Marin County, she was going to go head high in comfort, and enjoy herself, or she would stay at home.

On May 2, 1929, Vera went to her nearest neighbor's, a Mrs. Brown, the school nurse at Old Mill Elementary, to have a cup of tea. As they sat looking out the kitchen window, talking about this and that, they saw a column of smoke rising on the mountain. Conversation stopped abruptly as they watched mesmerized. In a fraction of a second, the column grew into a veritable funnel cloud. Frantically, Mrs. Brown began throwing things into boxes making ready to run. Fire on the mountain in a high wind, who knew what would happen?

What happened was stupefying. The fire grew in sound and fury and raced down the mountain like a freight train without brakes. Some townspeople followed Mrs. Brown's lead and fled while others were immobilized by fear and watched in terror. Nothing was being done to obstruct the fire's careening course down the mountain. The Mill Valley Fire Department refused to go. The fire was not in their district. It was not their problem. By the time the fire was in their district and should have been their problem it was beyond control and beyond containing. Flames were shooting hundreds of feet into the air, leaping from treetop to treetop.

Compounding the horror was a rude awakening to the fact that Mill Valley hydrants varied in size. The fire department's hoses fit some hydrants and not others. Furthermore, the water pressure was so low it was impossible to shoot a stream of water high enough to reach the flaming treetops. Mill Valley faced a calamity. A horse and buggy town council had not taken responsibility for its fire equipment. There was no policy on uniform equipment, no inspection, no mains large enough to provide adequate water pressure. Whether it was compatible with what was purchased in the next district or not, for his district, each councilman bought fire-fighting equipment he thought was the best bargain. The result was monumental tragedy.

The Mount Tamalpais railroad should have been harnessed as a workhorse to carry water up to the fire before it reached Mill Valley, but the train sat idle in downtown Mill Valley. Ironically, one of the train's passengers had started the conflagration in the first place by lightly tossing away a burning cigarette shortly after boarding the open cars. Racing ahead of the fire the train hurtled down curve after curve at full speed then slammed to a halt in the car yards behind the station. Immediately the crew "abandoned ship," and fled to try to salvage their own belongings. Firefighters didn't know how to get the steam up in the train's boiler and, even if they had succeeded, none of them knew how to drive it.

Vera hurried down to the railway station not knowing what else to do and stood watching helplessly. She had no available car in which to flee and there was no other means of escape. In the brief moment of hesitation during which she stood on Ethel Avenue, fixated by the fire, the commuter train had pulled out of the station below headed for Sausalito. As it careened down Miller Avenue people clung to whatever projection of the cars they could grasp. At Sausalito, everyone, including the motorman, headed for the ferry to San Francisco. The trolley didn't return. All hopes of escape blocked, Vera watched numbly as the fire picked up speed until it was an avalanche spilling down the mountain in great waves, voraciously consuming trees and houses in its path.

As Vera listened to the roar of the flames and watched the onrushing inferno, fire equipment from surrounding towns began to pour in. Even units of the San Francisco fire department were brought over by car ferry as soon as the catastrophe was sighted from across the Bay. It was all for naught. Without water pressure all the fire equipment in the whole Bay Area was useless. Luckily, Nature at last took a hand and a shift in the wind stopped the fire's advance. The crowd went limp with relief. The fire had come all the way down to Lovell Avenue behind Old Mill School, a few blocks from where Vera stood. Altogether 110 houses had gone up in smoke.

Lost in the drama going on in front of her, Vera hadn't noticed an old buddy from the *Oakland-Enquirer* among the crowd of onlookers. She and K. B. Reynolds, a photographer and colleague, had worked together on many stories. K.B. had also moved to Mill Valley. Now, as the fire subsided, people coming out of shock began to turn to fellow onlookers to share the euphoria that took over. It was then that K.B. spied Vera and hurried over.

"Vera!" he cried. "What a day, eh! What a story! My God, I wish I'd had my camera! Say, if you don't get back to the newspaper, you're going to lose your job. Homer says he's covered for you long enough."

Vera stared at K. B. in disbelief. She hadn't thought of the newspaper in months. Her pot of jam had dried up without her noticing. "K.B.," she said shamefacedly, "will you please do me a favor? Will you tell Homer I'm not coming back. I'm in the middle of building a house over here and I've taken another job. My roots in Marin get deeper and deeper all the time."

"You don't mean it?" K.B. was incredulous. "You're really going to give up the paper? For good? We thought it was just taking you longer to write that book than you thought it would."

With a hollow pit in her stomach Vera turned back to stare unseeingly at the dying flames. Was she really turning her back on the world she'd wanted for so long and in which she'd been lucky enough to find a place for herself? Had she let an impulse send her irrevocably down another road? It took some minutes for the momentary panic to pass and for her to realize that she had indeed turned a corner. The newspaper job in Oakland was no longer relevant. This community, this place, this little town of Mill Valley was her world. It was where she belonged.

Once rooted in her new community, nested in her new house, Vera looked over the cultural landscape of "life in Marin" and found it wanting. Intellectual ferment was a basic necessity for her, like bread and water. The only intellectual focus in town was the library that had opened under the proddings and financial support of Mrs. William Kent in 1926. The Kents were still regarded as the patrones of Southern Marin as late as 1929. As much as she appreciated the library, Vera felt a community like Mill Valley should offer women like herself more outlets than a library card. A chapter of the American Association of University Women in Marin would be just the thing, she decided. There were plenty of bright young university women around to make up a substantial membership. The young women she knew were vegetating under diapers, dirty dishes and PTA meetings. Vera went to see her new friend, Iris Engels. Iris Engels was a fount of energy and a do-gooder of the first water.

"What interest would you have, Iris, in seeing an AAUW branch organized in Mill Valley?" Vera asked.

"AAUW? I never thought of it!" Iris cried. "Of course we should have a chapter!" Iris's enthusiasm for any new stimulating venture was as infectious as was Vera's. "But," she added,"the person we need to talk to if we want to get this off the ground is Flora Drake."

Flora Drake lived next door to the Engles and was a few years older than Iris, and a lot older than Vera. A mover and shaker, Flora was involved in every event held in Marin County. When they told her what they wanted to do, Flora's response was to get out a calendar and set a date for their first meeting. This was something they should have done long ago, they said. With three such dynamic women behind the idea, things were bound to happen fast. They secured permission to hold meetings in the auditorium at the high school. They wrote to the national AAUW organization for guidelines. Vera composed an article for the Mill Valley newspaper announcing the first meeting, outlining the purpose of the organization. Optimistically, they drew up the draft of a constitution to present to the very first meeting. Why waste time?

Janet Gavin and her husband Bill had become new close friends of Vera's. Janet was elected President. As soon as the constitution was adopted, Vera, who became program chairman, sat down with Janet to create a series of thought-provoking programs that stretched the minds of the membership. No matter what organization Vera belonged to, "program" was forever her bailiwick. She could always internalize the unique "raison d'etre" for any organization's existence and design programs to further its purpose. Women came from as far away as Novato to attend the AAUW meetings, and more and more of the meetings were held in San Rafael, the central city in Marin. Soon it became clear that a cleavage was developing between women from North County and those from South County. North County women wanted less high-minded programs, and more social events.

In December 1941, when World War II began, the organization split into two branches. Instituted to save tires, - rubber was in shorter supply than gasoline - gas rationing prevented trips of greater distance than five miles from home. After the war, the surge of "inmigration,"--a demographer's word for incoming persons who take up residence in a new place within the same country--brought more and more college and university women into the county. There were too many applicants for membership in the two chapters to think of returning to one organization. In December of 1949, a charter was granted by the national organization of AAUW to the Mill Valley chapter. Later another charter established a separate new branch in Novato.

Vera found other ways to further expand the cultural menu in Marin. Three musical organizations were already in existence. The Tuesday Musicals, a Ladies Club that Adeline Kent had been instrumental in founding, a group that was very private, very precious, very prestigious with a membership limited to the number of ladies who could gather in one parlor. There was also the Marin Symphony, formed in 1925 by Clinton Lewis, head of the music department of the College of Marin, to give talented music students an opportunity to play with members of the San Francisco Symphony. Third, there was the Marin Choral Group, organized in 1927 and made up of lovers of song who could read music. These latter two groups, largely amateurs, gave concerts for their families, friends, and the larger community a few times a year.

Vera had loved classical music ever since Mrs. Brown played her wonderful recordings from La Scala for a room of little children back in Tonopah. Since 1926 Vera had bought season tickets to the San Francisco Symphony. Once she was resident in Marin, that meant an hour across the bay by ferry, followed by a long trip by street car to the Opera House. She became acquainted with many members of the orchestra on the ferries coming home from the concerts. The long trip brought everyone home so late that many people in Marin wouldn't bother to attend the concerts. That caused Vera to ponder. Why, she asked, should Marinites have to set aside so many hours of travel time for a two-hour concert? Why not have professionals performing in Marin itself?

Mrs. Powers Symington, known as Maude Fay in operatic circles in Europe and the United States, had asked the same question. Quoted in the local paper as saying that Marin County was "a cultural desert," the opera star asked why Marin didn't do as so many communities in Europe did? In Europe, a group of townspeople would set up an event, sell tickets to it, and with the proceeds bring major artists to their community. When Vera read the article she immediately asked herself, "Why not indeed?"

Never hesitant about jumping into a void, she immediately contacted Mrs. Symington and invited her for coffee. Within 10 minutes the two women were wrestling with what course of action to take. Neither wanted to do something on a piecemeal basis, one event at a time. They wanted a rooted organization that would carry on a twelve month program, year after year. Together they set out to sell Southern Marin on their brainchild, The Marin Music Chest. The Music Chest would schedule an outdoor summer concert series to be held in an open grove on the grounds of Dominican College. In the winter they would move indoors to the auditorium. Summer, open-air programs, however, meant building some kind of seating which would cost money.

Vera brought "Maude Fay" to the Outdoor Art Club to make a plea for support and Maude generated enthusiasm for the project. One means of selling The Marin Music Chest and raising the funds for collapsible bleachers that could be stored away when not in use, was to recruit women who would be willing to go door to door selling 25-cent memberships in the new organization. Vera set out at once with her membership slips in hand, her little sales pitch memorized. Though it was 1932, the year the Ross Valley Players organized and began their performances in a sylvan grove on the Kent Estate, the Depression was nearing its nadir. Depression did not keep memberships from going like hot cakes. Before the summer season began they were solvent and programmed. Not settling for second stringers, they went after stars, big stars, musicians with at least statewide stature. One of the biggest fish they ever landed was Nelson Eddy. Few people know today that Vera Schultz was one of the founding mothers of the enduring Marin Music Chest, but she was.

Almost concurrently with co-founding AAUW, and the Marin Music Chest, Vera got involved in the Outdoor Art Club. Painting classes and painters' groups abounded in Marin by the turn of the century. Garden clubs sprang up in places like Ross as early as 1902. All the gardeners and the artists co-joined into the Outdoor Art Club, the most inclusive of all the clubs in clubby Marin. As a child, Vera's special task was to help her mother in the garden. In Tonopah, Elizabeth Ann had raised vegetables. In Reno, before they moved to Stewart Street, she raised what seemed to Vera like acres of flowers. Vera had weeded and thinned and mulched under the manicurist eye of the chief gardener, her mother, and learned to love gardening.

When Vera let it be known that she'd like to be a member, the ladies of the club were delighted to not only bestow membership on her but to put her to work as Vice-President and, of course, Program Chairman. Movers and shakers rarely hide their lights under a bushel and no one moved more quickly than Vera. Once she had an idea, transforming that idea into action became a relentless goad. For the Outdoor Art Club she came up with the idea of "Art In Action." Rather than focus on the gardens of individuals, or on the landscaping of the town itself, why not spend a year looking at the ways Art could be brought into community life, especially the ART involved in landscaping?

Not far from her house lived a struggling young sculptor named Richard O'Hanlon and his wife, Ann Rice, a painter of great talent. The two young artists were hard-pressed to make ends meet. Ann painted in the house while Dick sculpted in the yard as neither of them had a proper studio in which to work. One day, as she was walking by, Vera saw Dick busily chiseling away on "a piece of considerable dimensions," a lovely doe with her little fawn. He called the piece, "Forest Madonna." It was enchanting, one of the most beautiful pieces Vera had ever seen. As she gazed at the graceful figures, she had an idea.

"Would you be interested in putting on a demonstration of your sculpting techniques for the Outdoor Art Club?" she asked. "You'd get lots of exposure and you might get some commissions as well as pupils."

Dick O'Hanlon thoughtfully studied his creation, then turned to Vera and said, "Why not? I think that might be fun."

The program was a smashing success. Women stood around the artist and asked questions long after the demonstration was over. Dick O'Hanlon's reputation was made in one afternoon. He became one of Mill Valley's instant celebrities. His wife, benefiting from his exposure, began to attract favorable attention to her work, boosting her standing in the art community as well. Once established, she became a leading innovator in the art world of the Bay Area. With the rewards of wider recognition, they bought a piece of ground in Mill Valley where they built an art center with studios where other artists could work. Yet today, that center is in operation and is a Mecca for artists. Later they both taught at the University of California. The "Art In Action" programs were the most popular programs the Outdoor Art Club ever had, possibly the most important as well. They shifted the focus of programming from finished product to artistic process.

A second purpose of the club was to interest members in civic affairs. Vera was indignant that Mill Valley had no Parks and Recreation Department. The town had enough taxpayers to pay for some of the refinements available in a full-fledged city. Children in Mill Valley were in danger of falling into their own "glory holes," glory holes that came from nothing to do. Vera had had to make her own entertainment on Mount Brougher. She wanted more for the children of Mill Valley than had been available in Tonopah. Under her urging, the Outdoor Art Club petitioned the Mill Valley City Council to create a Commission of Parks and Recreation to study the recreational needs of the community.

Once the idea was on the table, it didn't take a major campaign to sell it. The Mill Valley City Council established the requested commission, and the Outdoor Art Club recommended Vera for membership, a position she held for eight years. Under her spur, the commission hired a park director, and through his efforts, a summer program for children was immediately inaugurated. With recreation assured, what was needed was a park in which to carry out the program. Vera began pushing for the acquisition of a piece of land, or the takeover of an already existing facility, where Mill Valleyites and their kids could play.

In 1934, the Roosevelt Administration introduced various programs to relieve the debilitating tedium of the lives of poor people and give them hope. April 26 of that year, the county formed the Marin Recreation Council to receive a portion of the California Emergency Relief Agency funds earmarked for recreation. Those funds could be used to buy up land forfeited because of non-payment of taxes. Marin County bought the old Duffey Airfield but could not get enough money from the state to develop it. January 1937, three years after Mill Valley established the Recreation Commission, the Mill Valley Golf and Country Club came on the market. Organized before the turn of the century, the old club could be purchased for $25,000.

The Recreation Commission believed that if Mill Valleyians would sit still for a bond issue the town could buy the Golf and Country Club for a civic center. They urged the City Council to place a bond measure on the ballot. The people of Mill Valley passionately hated bonds but this was a once-in-a-century opportunity. No other such property existed within the city limits. Passion or prejudice, antipathy toward bonds prevailed for three years. The voters turned down a bond initiative to fund the purchase of the country club in 1937 and again in 1938. Finally, in 1939, the voters held their collective nose, swallowed the bond pill, and forthwith acquired the property. It was 42 acres of fairways and tennis courts, an amphitheater, the grand old clubhouse, a swimming pool, several outdoor patios around both the clubhouse and the pool plus ample parking space. The city had bought the Park and Recreation Commission a marvelous playground for a mere $25,000. All one needed was a bicycle or a car to get there.

Only one other recreational need remained: neighborhood playgrounds. Kids too young to ride bicycles in the streets needed places close to home where they could congregate and play. The country club did not meet the daily needs of toddlers and small fry. Miniature parks with playground equipment too large for the average backyard in Mill Valley did not exist. During summer vacation and on weekends, school grounds were alive with the activities of older children. Little ones got shoved aside or knocked around. With Iris Engels' husband George on the City Council, Vera had almost an open channel through which her ideas reached the council's docket. One of Vera's ideas was that the city should establish public playgrounds by setting aside vacant lots that fell into its lap because of unpaid delinquent taxes. Most of the lots were in residential neighborhoods so Mill Valley could have dozens of little neighborhood parks where the children could play and still be within hailing distance of their mothers. The council bought her idea, and Mill Valley children today are still playing on a multitude of small neighborhood playgrounds, thanks to Vera's foresight at a time when so much real estate was undeveloped within the town limits.

Much of Vera's effectiveness as a community activist came from her effectiveness as mentor to the Superintendent of the Public Schools. Ostensibly she was his assistant. In reality she was his CEO. In 1929, an academic-administrative assistant to the Superintendent of Schools of the Mill Valley district was to be hired. When the job was formulated and described, it was labeled "Secretary to the Superintendent." The scope of the job in a rapidly expanding school district went far beyond dictation and typing. Hollybush House was nearing completion, Vera now had time and energy left over to do something more mentally challenging than pounding nails or wielding a paint brush. She applied for the position of Secretary to the Superintendent and got it. She was overqualified for the job as outlined but she would enlarge it. Her intention was to overhaul the school system once she was on the payroll.

The Mill Valley School District and the Sausalito School District, located in adjacent towns, were each too small to provide all the services their respective communities needed. To meet the challenge of expansion costs stemming from the broadening of curriculum, they put the office of Superintendent of the Mill Valley District and the office of the Superintendent of the Sausalito District into the hands of the same elected official. On Monday, Tuesday and Wednesday, the superintendent, Roy Huffman, and his secretary-lieutenant, Vera Schultz, were ensconced in Mill Valley at the Old Mill School. On Thursday and Friday, they shifted their seat of operations to an office in Sausalito.

Each district had a distinctly different school population with distinctly specific needs. Mill Valley was a haven for artists and intellectuals. Sausalito was a port town for the fishing industry and the agriculture market town of southern Marin. The ethnic mix of Sausalito was not replicated in Mill Valley. Mill Valley was lily-white Anglo-Saxon. Sausalito had a few Chinese, a few Blacks, many Portuguese and a handful of Mexican-Americans mixed in with the white population that ran the town. A curriculum to teach the basics to the children of farmers and fisher folk was too restricted for children who came from homes filled with books. To meet the needs of both districts was like wearing alternating think caps. Vera plunged neck deep into understanding both student populations, and soon was highly regarded in both districts for her comprehension of their difference.

For Sausalito it was necessary to have small classes because of the difficulty of teaching children whose parents spoke a different language. In Mill Valley there was a need to enrich the educational experience by expanding the range of learning experiences. Always the teacher-journalist, or journalist-teacher, Vera started a newspaper in the Mill Valley District called *The Old Mill Wheel*. The kids were enthusiastic about putting out a paper. They wrote and edited copy, they interviewed and editorialized, they drew cartoons to illustrate their stories, and they learned about layout. Today, copies of that paper are on file in the Mill Valley Public Library. In addition to direct contact with the kids, Vera loved the dynamics of relating to the teaching staff.

From time to time Vera dropped in on PTA meetings to learn what issues were current causes of concern to parents. At one meeting, mothers were railing against the City Council over water for the wading pool in Old Mill Park. The town had built the pool as a memorial to its World War I Veterans, but the water to fill it had never been turned on. It stood dry as a bone, year after year. Vera, sitting in the back of the school auditorium, listening to the heated discussion, couldn't remain silent. She rose and urged the women to take their gripe to the City Council. A PTA meeting was not an effective place to voice their discontent, she said. The women responded with hoots of derision.

"That council doesn't listen to women. We can't get anything out of them."

"But they're your representatives," she protested.

A woman quietly sitting off to one side challenged her. "You go down to City Hall and ask the council to put water in the wading pool. Tell them you represent the PTA and you'll find out how representative they are."

"But," Vera protested, "they'd take it more kindly if one of the PTA members herself came to ask them." She paused, then made a decision. "No," she said, "I'll be glad to do that."

Vera thought she'd taken on an easy task when she went to the council. Logically and clearly she laid out all the arguments for filling the pool, ending with the observation that as it stood, empty and full of leaves and dirt, it was an eyesore. Sympathetically they heard her out and at the end of her little speech thanked her for coming. They assured her the problem would be corrected.

"You see," she told herself as she exited the Council chambers, "all they needed was to have the matter brought to their attention. They'll do it." But they didn't. A month, then two months went by and no water. The whole summer went by without anyone paying any attention at all to the pool. Puzzled, Vera went over that evening again and again in her mind. She'd been so sure they meant what they said. Usually, she wasn't easily duped; they hadn't been feigning interest. Yet, if those men believed her and believed they'd take care of it then why was the pool still empty?

Mulling over the dichotomy between what was said and what was done, she came to the conclusion that power turned over to a collection of citizens not personally responsible for what does or does not happen, is a poor way to run a government. Any one of those councilmen could have taken it upon himself to see to it that water was provided for the pool by contacting the gardener, then keeping a check on that worthy. Council members seemed to think that attendance at the meetings was the only requirement of the job. The more she thought about it the more convinced she became that the government in Mill Valley needed overhauling. First the antiquated fire department, and now this.

Mill Valley was a primitive little town run in a primitive way. No one was trying to bring about the changes needed to keep up with the changing times. Who or what agency could force a government to overhaul itself, she wanted to know. She harkened back to the influence of the League of Women Voters on the cities of Berkeley and Oakland. That's what Mill Valley needed; the political clout of organized women. Until women became involved politically, they'd never be heard in this rustic cow county where wading pools were trivial. As she went about her daily school routine, Vera thought about the complexity of introducing women into the political arena. Aside from starting a League of Women Voters, which she intended to do, she was at a loss about what action to take to force modernization and promote efficiency.

Modernization and efficiency were also lacking in the superintendent's office. Schools are one of the first institutions to feel the impact of increasing population in all times and all places. It didn't take many newcomers long to become as unhappy with the Superintendent as they were with the City Council. His business-as-usual style ignored the changing composition of each of the student bodies. Sausalito kept growing more urban and sophisticated while the population of Mill Valley became more permanent. Year-rounders outnumbered summer folk at last. Indignant parents began to organize to oust the superintendent. To run against him, they focused on two candidates who advocated change: Edna Maguire, teacher and principal of Old Mill School, and a Building Contractor in Mill Valley named George Kendall.

Edna Maguire made it one of her principal goals to know all the parents of her pupils and they supported her. Sensing that the time had come when a woman could be elected as superintendent of schools, Edna mulled over the pros and cons of entering the race without telling anyone she was considering it. Vera, not knowing that Edna was contemplating a run for office, at a social function met George Kendall who had already filed as a candidate. The two naturally launched into an animated discussion of school issues. The longer they talked the more Vera became impressed with his knowledge about the art of teaching, and what was required of a school district to give creative teachers full rein. At that party, she pledged her support for his candidacy and offered to help with his campaign. By the time she learned of Edna's decision to run it was too late. She had given her word. There was no going back on it.

The superintendent's wife was a bosom friend of Edna Maguire. When Roy Huffman recognized his days were numbered, his wife urged her friend, Edna, to run for the office. When Mrs. Huffman learned that Vera had endorsed George Kendall, her wrath knew no bounds. Having hand-picked her husband's successor, she resented his lieutenant's support for the opposition. She organized a band of Edna's other supporters and led them to a meeting of the school board. They urged the board to pass a ruling mandating that only *un*married women could be employed in the district. Nationwide, in 1935, such a policy, in one variant or another, was already in place in most school districts. The Unmarried Women ruling was an easy sell and it sold. Though Kendall was elected, Vera was out of work. Out of work meant out of pocket money. Out of work meant ennui. Out of work felt like "out of order." As usual, Vera's hands were filled before they could become empty. Like other university-educated women in a day when only a fraction of the women of America went beyond high school, involvement in public affairs attracted Vera like a moth to flame.

A TOE IN THE WATER

It was a complicated chain of events that brought the federal government into Marin, first to establish Muir Woods, then to move rock dug out of Mt. Tamalpais to create reservoirs that would provide a water system for the little towns on the leeward side of the mountain. William Kent had mortgaged his half of Mount Tamalpais back in 1904 to buy a small valley of redwoods about to be drowned to provide a reservoir for the town of Ross. He and John Muir persuaded Theodore Roosevelt to take the valley into federal custody under the guise of a Federal Monument which Kent insisted be named Muir Woods. Reimbursed by the Federal Government for his purchase, Kent began pressuring the State of California to take over his mountain for a state park. In 1927, the year before Kent died, his beloved mountain was at last secured for all time from the avarice of developers. Once California took over his Mount Tamalpais property to create the Tamalpais State Park, the land he and Sidney Cushing had earlier given to The Mountain Play Association was turned over to the state park to own and protect in perpetuity. CCC boys came in in 1934 to build the seating in the Mountain Play Theater out of the aforementioned stone, quarried first for the dam and then for the theater.

William Kent was a member of the "Progressive millionaires" coterie of northern California—fellow conspirators: Rudolph Spreckels, John Randolph Haynes, and James D. Phelan. Progressives, inside and outside of Congress, they had supported the Newlands Act of 1902. That act established a series of reservoirs in the foothills of the Sierras as catch basins for snow melt, to provide the Central Valley with water for irrigation. Now they tried to put the government in Sacramento into the power distribution business. They argued that the taxpayers had paid for the dams that generated the power, therefore, the taxpayers were entitled to electrical power at the lowest possible rate. Pacific Gas & Electric, a recent amalgamation of over 400 little power companies, fought tooth and nail against the well-heeled do-gooders, out-spending them four to one. With the help of Southern California Edison Company, PG&E prevailed. William Kent was always one of Vera's heroes. Much of her work in Conservation was inspired by the laird of Kentfield.

The 1930s was a decade of social experimentation on a colossal scale all across the nation. Experimentation in ideas and programs, derived from the old Progressive Party platform, became the philosophy of the Democratic Party after Franklin D. Roosevelt went to the White House. Not even Republican Marin County escaped the reform fever. Because of the dearth of pockets of poverty, Marin was relatively immune to the catastrophic economic depression gripping the rest of the country. Still, Marin youth faced as bleak a future as did young people nationwide. The job market was saturated and business wasn't expanding. Who was to speak for the young people? In 1935 Eleanor Roosevelt proposed an idea to Harry Hopkins, product of the inherited Settlement House movement of the previous generation, that he instantly embraced. Hopkins hesitated to approach the President. It could be one project too many to lay before FDR, or Congress, or both. Hopkins feared a political boomerang.

Eleanor shared Hopkins' apprehension, but she was not intimidated. It was reported that she went to Franklin's bedroom, just as he was drifting off to sleep, and made a pitch for the creation of a National Youth Administration. Established the following year, the new agency was put into the hands of young Lyndon B. Johnson from Texas. NYA was designed to keep high school and college students in school and off the streets of the cities. Marin had no cities and did not have a major problem with drop-out rates.

As for legislation to assist migrant-based agriculture, a major problem in Southern California and the Central Valley, agriculture in Marin was not large-scale enough to face a major migrant problem. Migrant-based agriculture was the special province of Helen Gahagan Douglas who became politically active after she made a singing tour through Europe in 1937. Suddenly awakened while in Salzburg, Austria, to the fact that Americans were somnolently uninformed about the Nazi assault on all those who espoused opposing political views, Gahagan Douglas came home to alert all who would listen. America didn't want to hear. Douglas joined the

Democratic Party hoping to make herself heard, but even there she found more ostriches than watch dogs. As things turned out, Helen Gahagan Douglas catapulted into national prominence through her work as a member of the John Steinbeck Committee to Aid Migratory Workers.

Living in Southern California where migrant workers picked oranges for starvation wages and lived in hovels no self-respecting dog-lover would assign to a pet, Douglas was appalled at the conditions John Steinbeck reported. She toured migrant camps, attended meetings of concerned citizens, and went to government hearings on the problems attendant with migrancy. In early 1939, she joined Steinbeck's committee and became its chairman. From that pulpit she worked hard to publicize the plight of the migrants, solicit money for the alleviation of some of their most deleterious conditions, and encourage the public to push for labor laws and social security programs designed specifically to put solid ground under migrants' feet. Brought to the attention of Eleanor and Franklin Roosevelt by Aubrey Williams, then head of the National Youth Administration, the Douglasses were invited for a weekend in the White House. A close friendship developed and Eleanor stayed with the Douglasses when she was in Southern California.

Studying sex roles out in New Guinea in the 1930s, Margaret Mead wrote: "If those temperamental attitudes which we have traditionally regarded as feminine, such as passivity, responsiveness and willingness to cherish children, can so easily be set up as the masculine pattern in one tribe (the Tchambuli Lake district in New Guineas) and in another be outlawed for the majority of women as well as for the majority of men, we no longer have any basis for regarding such aspects of behavior as sex-linked." Mead was far from the political upheaval going on in America, but the Depression was revealing the fallacy of proscribed sex roles here in the United States where women were forced to assume the traditionally masculine role of breadwinner and head of household. With their husbands out of work, women were learning that marriage was not a safe harbor. When the nation found itself in economic straits, wives were as vulnerable as unmarried women.

Carolyn Bird, in her penetrating tome on the impact of the Depression on the life of the nation, *The Invisible Scar*, published in 1966, wrote: "As long as *women's work* is whatever needs to get done at the moment in a society that values people in terms of what they *do,* preferably for money, women can never afford the luxury of a settled character." Bird saw that life in the United States during periods of economic dislocation was as precarious for one sex as for the other and that American society's differentiation of roles in the 1930s was archaic and unworkable.

None of the women mentioned above allowed themselves to be bound by a national consensus on women's roles in society. Neither did Vera. The 1930s was the decade of her baptism in activism and politics. When, in 1935, her job with the Mill Valley-Sausalito school districts was over, Vera was poised to move on to even meatier roles in Mill Valley affairs. The wading pool issue had come along at the right time to propel Vera into the wide range of problems in Marin that were going unattended. Though not yet politically ambitious for public office herself, she was cutting her teeth on civic problem solving that would lead her into the political fray.

THE LEAGUE OF WOMEN VOTERS

Under the leadership of Fern Andrews, a handful of women began meeting in the Outdoor Art Club library once a month in the early 1930s to study current affairs. When Vera began involving herself in the political arena in 1935, she told Fern that her current affairs program was too amorphous, her focus too scattered. If all she and her fellow students only studied current affairs, their study could be a screen for inaction. They needed to tighten their parameters and deepen their commitment, to move from inaction to involvement. She wanted the study group to become the nucleus of a Marin League of Women Voters (LWV).

Inspired by Vera's vision of what they could accomplish through the League, Fern and Iris Engels wasted no time in converting their loose association into a tightly disciplined LWV. The Marin League of Women Voters was chartered in 1936. The women of Marin enthusiastically welcomed this new organization that gave them orchestra seats in the theater of politics. LWV members began reading journals and newspapers and treatises and political platforms. They went to the meetings of the Board of Supervisors to listen and they found themselves excited by politics, an area of public life from which they had previously been rigorously and routinely excluded.

Early in the decade the League of Women Voters of the United States made a scholarly study of town government to help all the little towns in the United States better understand themselves. The national organization urged Leagues nationwide to form study groups to educate women about the lack of democracy that prevailed in their own communities. Iris Engles and Vera were determined to push their membership into an intensive study of Mill Valley government. To kick off the proposed study of their backward, one-horse government, Dick Richards, chairman of the State Council of Mayors, was invited to be the keynote speaker. The meetings were thrown open to the public.

Each month, a member of the Mill Valley City Council, or the Planning Commission, was invited to appear before the League to explain her/his duties and how the job she/he filled, fit into the town's chain of command. One by one, every elected official and every employee of the town, right down to the gardeners and bookkeepers, came to make their presentations. Anyone who seemed reluctant to appear, was nudged by Iris Engels' husband, George, who was a member of the City Council. The presentations and discussions spread out over most of the summer. Even at the height of vacation days, interest in the series grew instead of tapering off.

That study, ultimately, led to a LWV delegation proposing to the City Council that a city manager type of government be adopted. The council dithered and diddled and did nothing. To educate more of the citizenry about what their town government did or did not do, Iris and Vera worked long hours putting together a study guide for public distribution. The notes taken during all the summer meetings, in addition to excerpts from the national study, were combined into a 28-page pamphlet called "Your City and Its Government." It was well-written, readable, and, they thought, very salable. They had it printed, bound, and then set out to sell it. To their dismay not even their own membership bought their little 25-cent book. They had to give it away. Now what to do? Vera proposed they advocate the election of a Board of Freeholders.

Men in the county became so intrigued with the "Know Your Town" study and the idea of a Board of Freeholders that they formed an organization called The Mill Valley Forum. The new organization was coed, had more clout than the League, and was more determined to reform the town's laissez-faire government. The Forum met once a month to study Mill Valley's needs and formulate programs for improvements. They discussed the same topics in open forum that men had previously discussed in barber shops and on street corners. They brought in speakers. They put together discussion groups, had debates. Don Fowler, a popular internist who carried weight in Mill Valley, and his wife Carol, who had been part of the League study, were eager to promote the new organization. When they asked Vera to be president she didn't hesitate. The Mill Valley Forum was so successful that when that group threw its weight behind the idea of a Board of Freeholders, the City Council was forced to call for an election.

Under the constitution of the State of California, a Board of Freeholders is a body of 15 homeowners that operates like a Grand Jury. Freeholders are authorized by an elected city or county government to study a specific issue and nothing more. A Board of Freeholders can exist for only one year. At the end of that year, a report must be made by the Freeholders to the level of government that it was mandated to study, i.e., county, city, or unincorporated area. In this case the mandate was to scrutinize the city government of Mill Valley and make recommendations to the City Council for its deliberation and action. The League and the Forum were certain that if a Board of Freeholders scrutinized the crude engine of government to which Mill Valley was currently attached, they'd recommend the city manager plan of town government the League advocated.

Forty-five non-partisan candidates filed for the 15 seats which by state law constitutes a Board of Freeholders. Each candidate put her/his own name on the ballot. Vera was one of the 15 elected. Another woman elected along with Vera was Nettie Evans, a future political activist who worked with Vera on many projects after Vera became a county supervisor. Once established, at the expense of the State of California the Freeholders brought in experts to educate them about many issues. "Everything is made easy for you in a democracy," Vera said, referring to the functioning of that board. "No department of the government being studied could refuse to open its books or to submit its regulations to their scrutiny."

Week after week the Freeholders pored over the duties and achievements of the Mill Valley Council. The majority of the Board voted to recommend that, before their proposal for a City Manager type of government was presented as a ballot measure, the City Council would have open meetings to educate the populace concerning what a city manager does. If this type of Government was established, the Freeholders stipulated, it should be permanent, never altered nor voted out of existence. At first the City Council obstinately refused to hold public hearings or recommend changes and stoutly maintained that maintained that they would not put a measure on the ballot even if ordered to do so by the Freeholders. In the end, the Freeholders prevailed and the issue did appear on the November ballot. A city manager system was handily voted into existence.

Immediately after the adoption of the new government framework, and as recruitment for the right man for the new office began, it became clear that the council itself did not understand the concept of a city manager. Mayor Sloan, thinking "mayor" meant boss, thought they were hiring an errand boy for him, an assistant who would carry out his orders. When Sloan learned that the other council members thought they were hiring a city manager-engineer to take care of the streets, he was further incensed. They already had an engineer—him. He could be city manager, i.e., engineer, and Mayor, and not cost the taxpayers the expense of bringing in an outsider who would expect a big salary. The confusion might have become laughable if the city had not been suddenly confronted with a problem that overshadowed the debate, and all other issues facing the county as well.

A county-wide political crisis, brewing for some time, was brought to a head by the State of California. The state demanded that Marin do something about its Poor Farm. The state had made such demands before, but they were always ignored. Merle Tharp had earlier urged the League of Women Voters to study the situation concerning the county's care of the elderly poor out in Lucas Valley. The League had demurred, had not advanced the poor farm to the top of its agenda. The isolated, dilapidated, rambling old building in which the discarded and neglected old folk were housed was also home to the county hospital. The only other hospital in Marin was a little institution called The Cottage Hospital which was much too limited an operation to be mistaken for a fully-operative medical facility.

Marin County lagged ominously behind much of the rest of the nation in its oversight of the health needs of its population. Not even the affluent could receive the medical attention they needed in their own communities. Rich and poor had to go to San Francisco for x-rays and hospitalization. Conditions out in

Lucas Valley were deplorable, and no agency had the authority to order changes except the Board of Supervisors. The Board of Supervisors more passionately hated to spend money than did the Mill Valley Council. To hold the state at bay, the League at last formed a study group to find a solution. Vera was appointed a member of that committee too.

Outside Mill Valley, throughout the rest of the county, the League had been regarded as little more than a sewing circle of women who neglected their homes as they nosed around in public affairs they could not understand. That opinion of the League was about to change. Iris Engels and Vera Schultz set out on a fact-finding mission that took them to every county within driving distance of Marin County that had a health department. In Santa Cruz County they found a model health department overseeing a modern county hospital. One wing of that hospital was given over to the care of the elderly. The doctor who had established the hospital, and who was a member of the health department's executive committee, took Iris and Vera through his elderly wards. He asked them to use their noses to see if they could pick up the scent of incontinence, a telltale feature of charity wards and "old age" Institutions. The place was not only visually spotless but the air was fresh and clean.

When the two women reported what Santa Cruz had in operation, the League decided to begin a detailed, thorough study of the Lucas Valley facilities. Their report was impressive. The "ladies" had studied everything from the foundations of the building to the ridge poles and all the activities conducted in between. Every item that needed repair, from tattered sheets and skimpy clothing down to the dangerously faulty wiring system that could result in a fire at any time, was noted and written down. The report was excruciatingly thorough, and very sobering. They presented their findings to the Board of Supervisors accompanied by a request that the county establish a health department, an agency that was notably lacking in Marin. A Health Department would have the right to condemn, quarantine, force compliance, set standards and open up or close down programs as needed—including a county hospital—for the public's health and safety. All costs were itemized to the best of the committee's ability, without the expense of hiring an accountant, to do a professional analysis for them.

That report made the Board of Supervisors blanch. What the League proposed was an ongoing, permanently expensive county health department. Expensive was not a relative term, like benefit versus cost. Expensive was the outlay of one red cent that absolutely did not have to be spent. The Board shut its eyes to that report and to a potential intervention by the state, already a reality in several other counties across the state. The Board of Supervisors risked having the state legislature mandate a health department more expensive than the one they devised for themselves. In the midst of the stalemate unexpected events beyond anyone's ability to foresee erupted. An epidemic of communicable children's diseases—measles, mumps and chickenpox—hit the county simultaneously and the schools were forced to close.

Children needing hospitalization had to be taken to San Francisco by ferry, forcing parents to spend hours commuting back and forth to be with their children. The costs that accrued to the county were high, both monetarily and in voter dissatisfaction. Citizens of all walks of life, and from all parts of the county, joined the League's advocacy and badgered the Board of Supervisors to establish a permanent Board of Health and to build a county hospital. Besieged but not bowed, the Board kept mum about the fact that there was federal money, as well as state funds, available for public health facilities. They were matching funds and the county would have to cough up its share.

When the League became cognizant that such funds existed, the citizens' cries of outrage could be heard all the way across the Golden Gate. Even the San Francisco papers took note of what was going on in Marin. Not to be thwarted by five pig-headed men, the League turned to the doctors. The doctors seemed more amused than amazed that a group of women thought they knew enough about medicine to make proposals concerning the regulation of health care and the proper organizational structure for such regulation. The LWV retaliated by threatening the local medical association with a publicity campaign that would hold them up to ridicule throughout the whole Bay Area. At first, the AMA got its back up and indignantly refused to meet with the ladies privately or publicly. They said they would not show up on call like a pack of dogs.

The doctors of Marin said they didn't want a bunch of meddling bureaucrats telling them anything about medicine, much less passing rules they'd have to abide by. The League was prepared for exactly that reaction. Many of the doctors' wives were members of the League and they had listened to their husbands sound off about politicians who knew nothing about medicine but presumed to set medical agendas. Those same wives now brought home word that if their spouses boycotted the public forum, a publicity campaign would start immediately. If that happened they, the wives, would be humiliated in front of their friends. Browbeaten, the doctors reluctantly attended the meeting, almost en masse. To their credit they listened. The League had done its usual thorough job of organizing materials, charts, and analyses, for their presentation.

What surprised the doctors most was that the League's proposal did not impact in any way on their freedom to practice medicine without government supervision. What the League was proposing was something the doctors decided they themselves should have advocated in the first place. They joined forces with the League so that the Board of Supervisors now faced pressure from two well-organized groups, one lay and one professional. Both groups were determined to extricate medical facilities in Marin from the grasp of folk-remedy policy-makers who circled their wagons against modernizing and updating at the public's expense. Against such formidable adversaries the Board wilted. A department of health was established that would be run by the county but which would be under the eagle eye of the medical profession. The doctors would be in charge, *not* the politicians. The League had carried the day.

For Vera, those two League victories in major areas of public welfare and good government were a siren call for deeper entry into the thickets of politics. The embryonic "good government kook," so named by George Jones some years later, was infected by a need to reshape the government of the county in accordance with textbook principles of governance.

Many social problems needed attention and not all of them could be cured through political action. Three years into the most crushing Depression the world had ever known, Iris Engels came to Vera one day and said, "Bobbie, I've got to do something about those people down around China Camp and in Sausalito. Some of them are starving. I have an idea and I want your help. I want to start a store. Not a store where people go to buy, but a store where women can come in and ask for things off the shelves—food and shoes and clothes for their kids—and not pay for them. Let them have the dignity of choosing what they want if we have it. Don't you think that's a good idea?"

Puzzled by the notion of a store where no money exchanged hands, Vera looked at her friend in bewilderment. "Where are the food and dry goods to come from, Iris? How do they get on the shelves?"

"Why," said Iris, "from all of us, of course. Volunteers put it on the shelves. Every time any of our suppliers goes to the grocery store to feed her own family she shops for another family too. Every time we buy our kids something new, we take something from their closets to the store. Five days a week, the store is open for women to bring in the goods and one day a week it's open for women to come and carry the goods out. Accepting help doesn't smack so much of charity this way."

"Oh Iris," Vera said over the lump in her throat, "what a marvelous idea!"

It was a marvelous idea, a tangible thing to do, a truly workable, lovely idea! The year was 1932 and America was staggering under disaster. Every day heart-wrenching pictures of gaunt women and emaciated children appeared in the newspapers, pictures that aroused either a sense of hopelessness or an urgency to do something to stem the tide. Iris had come to the right person with her "notion." Within weeks, their store was in operation and it functioned throughout the rest of the Depression years continuing into the first years of World War II. During the war, the purpose of the store changed to help military families stranded far from home. It was a one-of-a-kind program for alleviating want which only needed organization and energy. Vera and Iris had both.

Somehow, in the midst of all the confusion of Vera's hectic first decade in Marin, the Schultzes found time for a speculative venture in real estate. The nation might be suffering through a depression that put a lid on home building, but Marin County was not in dire straits. Anticipating the opening of the Golden Gate Bridge, a building boom was underway. The promised easy commute to the city made Marin County a magnet for "inmigrants." Once the bridge was opened, people would be able to drive to work in San Francisco in a quarter of the time it took to go by ferry. Trucks could deliver goods directly from warehouses across the Bay to Marinites' front doors. Marin would become a full-blown suburb of San Francisco. Speculation fever gripped Southern Marin. Many future suburbanites were already scouring the county for available properties and vacant lots.

Some years earlier the Schultzes bought four steeply sloping lots abutting their Ethel Avenue property. Those four lots were standard 50-foot frontage lots. The Schultzes paid $250 each for them, then proceeded to replat them into three lots of 66 plus feet width. Ray and Vera believed, along with the intellectuals and artists who made up the most influential elements of Mill Valley circles, that Mill Valley's greatest asset was its wonderful naturalness. Great swaths of trees should not be cleared to build new homes. People loved the virgin feel of Mill Valley's wooded hills. The town was full of houses hidden in shady bowers. Lots over 66 feet wide allowed for larger houses without despoiling woodsy neighborhoods.

The busy Schultzes bought the lots, replatted them, then set them aside awaiting the influx of prospective buyers in the mid 30s. Hollybush House was free and clear; they had a healthy nest egg. Under the spur of Iris Engles, who insisted that the time was ripe to build for the coming market, Vera and her husband were energized to start developing their lots. Brother-in-law, Fred Starbucks, who had just returned from

Schultzes. Under the spur of Iris Engles, who insisted that the time was ripe to build for the coming market, Vera and her husband were energized to start developing their lots. Fred said "No!" but Ray was relentless. Giving in at last, Fred costed out plans for a Swiss chalet, the currently popular house design Vera loved. Knowing the "let's change the plans a bit" pattern of the Schultzes, Fred found a young house designer to sit down with Ray and Vera to draw up final blueprints for the house before he started to build. Fred wanted no surprises, no brainstorms once the construction was underway. Work began in the winter of 1936 and continued through the spring and summer of 1937.

The Golden Gate Bridge opened on a cold foggy day in May, 1937. No vehicular traffic was allowed on the span opening day. Hordes of people, bundled against the wind, walked back and forth, high above the surging channel below. They gloried in the majestic structure, and in the adventure of being pedestrians on the roadway. The opening of the bridge meant the opening of floodgates to Marin. A whole new epoch was about to begin. Instant demand for housing drove real estate prices sky high in southern Marin. Every weekend, eager buyers combed Mill Valley and Sausalito searching for houses for sale. By September, 1937, all that was left to do to the new house to ready it for the soaring market was to sand the hardwood floors.

Vera and Ray planted a "For Sale" sign in the yard, not bothering to put an ad in the paper. They didn't need to. Browsers traipsed through the house, threading their way among paint cans Many admired 219 Molino Avenue, but few could buy unless the Schultzes carried paper. The Schultzes would rather not. They needed the cash to develop two more lots. One day, as Vera pushed the big electric sander back and forth, a young couple short of cash who yearned to own a house of their own in Mill Valley, presented her with a proposition. They didn't have the money for the Molino house but they had enough money to buy Hollybush house. If Ray and Vera sold them the Ethel Avenue property and moved into 219 themselves, the Emmets could move to Mill Valley immediately. The Schultzes would then have the necessary money to begin work on 215 Molino. The idea had not occurred to Vera or Ray, but once the Emmets made their offer it was too good to pass up. In October the Schultzes moved one street up the mountain.

Vera was still within walking distance of downtown Mill Valley and the street car line that ran down Miller Avenue to the ferry landing. The house was light and airy and had an attached garage for Ray's car. The den-office-playroom downstairs faced out onto the lower slope. With its own outside entrance, the room made a great place for committees to spread out around a long table. Best of all, the width of the street out front was enough for two directional driving and off-street parking. More furniture. new drapes, all the yet unpurchased items a new house needs, remained on Vera's shopping list when, without warning, New Year's Day, 1938, Ray sold the house out from under her. Before the Schultzes were out of bed, an elated young couple rang their bell. Ray left Vera drowsing under the covers as he went to the door. On the stoop stood a couple he'd never seen before.

"We've come to buy your house!" the man announced triumphantly. "We were here when you were working on it and we wanted it then; but we had to scrounge up the money first. Now we're ready. We want to buy our first home, on the first day, of a New Year, to bring us luck."

Clear-eyed and freshly dressed, they gazed steadily into his bewildered face. Disconcerted by being awakened on a holiday by two young enthusiasts who wanted to buy a house that wasn't for sale, Ray almost shut the door on them. The scent of quick profit, however, stayed his hand. Inviting them in, he excused himself long enough to dress and clear his head. Rushing back to the bedroom he scrambled into his pants as his mind raced. How much could he ask for the house and not blow the deal? Hurrying back to the living room, expecting to bargain, he set a price on the high side. They met it without argument.

"How soon do you want it?" he gulped. "I've got to have time to build us another place to live."

"We need it by April 1."

The 1st of April was three months away. Fred was knee deep in work. If he refused to juggle his schedule then what would they do? Still, a deal like this was too good to let slip away. Ray scribbled out a simple contract that stipulated the price and date of occupancy and the three of them signed. Scurrying back to the bedroom, Ray summarily re-awakened Vera to present her with pen and paper.

Vera stared up at him in astonishment, "You've sold the house?" Now thoroughly awake she started to read the document but Ray shook the edge of the paper in irritation.

"There's no time for that. They're waiting in the other room. Just sign it, you can read it later." She signed, and he flew back to get his hands on the check.

Of course there was no house ready in three months. They had no building plans, there were no utility connections to the lot next door, the site had not been graded. Fred went through the ceiling. Told he was expected to build the Schultzes a house in three months, he stormed and ranted. Just because Ray had rashly, impulsively, sold his house, he wasn't going to disappoint people he'd already promised. In three months, what could he accomplish, even if he paid overtime for weekend work? He'd have to build something higgeldy piggeldy and he wouldn't do it. He'd never built a cheap house and he wasn't going to start now.

Fred might rave, but the fact remained that the Schultzes had sold their house! They would be out on the street after April 1. Furious, Fred juggled things around as best he could and set to work with a will. Never again would he build them a house he fumed. Try as he might, he couldn't pull off a miracle. Not only was the new house not ready in three months, 215 Molino Avenue was not ready for occupancy for nearly two years. The Schultzes crowded in with the Starbucks on Throckmorton Avenue. There they remained until their third house in a decade was finished. Vera, at loose ends and under Zetta's feet, looked for ways to stay out of the house and to keep busy. Happily, the League of Women Voters and the Board of Freeholders gave her plenty of reason to be out and about frequently. Now that Ray owned his own agency, he was out almost every night selling insurance. With Vera out at night meetings of the Board of Freeholders, the Starbucks at least had their evening hours to themselves several nights a week. If the Schultzes had not been able to make themselves scarce, the Smith family serenity might not have prevailed.

As the decade of the '30s ended and the decade of the '40s began, the United States was in the throes of an unprecedented presidential election. Franklin Roosevelt broke with tradition and ran for a third term. According to Joseph Lash, who knew Eleanor Roosevelt as few other people did, "For herself, (Eleanor) she had a real horror of four more years in the White House with its lack of privacy, innumerable ceremonial occasions, things that had to be done in which she was not interested, and the people who would have to be entertained who meant little to her. She preferred to retire to Hyde Park...and be a useful citizen doing productive and helpful work...."

Eleanor Roosevelt was an enthusiastic booster, member, and officer of the League of Women Voters before her role in national politics removed her from the circle of nonpartisan women. Vera, whose admiration for Eleanor Roosevelt knew no bounds, had no interest in retiring from the political arena. In 1940, she eagerly entered a two-year odyssey as one of the two LWV of California resident advocates in Sacramento. League advocates spent five days a week in the state capitol following the legislature through its labors as long as it was in session. Vera, still enamored with the romance of the political process, was about to have her illusions shattered and be bruised by this rude exposure to reality. Resident advocates are chosen at a state-wide convention of the League to watchdog the Legislature and track every piece of legislation as it wends its way through the Assembly and/or the Senate. Advocates divide the Assembly and Senate committees between them and together cover all the action, buttonholing every lawmaker to inform her/him about the League's position of the bill in question.

Advocates must be able to pay their own living expenses in Sacramento. In 1940, that meant the women either had inherited wealth or they had husbands with deep pockets. Vera's husband could hardly claim poverty. Reluctantly he allowed they could afford it. Afford it or not, Ray Schultz hated it when Vera took on the big boys in Sacramento in public debate. He was always of two minds about her public life. On one hand he was secretly proud of her accomplishments. On the other, he complained, he carped, he fumed about the embarrassment he felt when men reproached him for something she'd said. If only she'd soft-pedal her opposition to the way politics worked. Her passion for reforming everything spilled over on him and on his business. His business was where the money came from to pay for her political activities. Why couldn't she be persuaded that his business was enough reason to keep still?

Vera's fellow advocate, Fern Andrews, was also from Mill Valley. Fern and Vera were old campaign buddies who had been through the "Know Your Town" series together as well as Vera's run for the Board of Freeholders. During sessions of the Legislature they drove to Sacramento every Monday morning and back every Friday night with likable Dick McCollister. McCollister had just been elected assemblyman from the Sixth District which covers Sonoma and Marin Counties. Vera came to know one of her future opponents well, and she was disgusted with the way he failed to do his job.

Whenever a new bill was introduced into legislative chambers, Vera and Fern took their rosters and set out in search of every assemblyman and every senator to remind him of the League's stance on the issue. If legislators weren't able to duck the interview, they listened politely, then brushed the ladies aside. The Ladies were a nuisance. The bank lobby, the insurance lobby, the transportation lobby, the publishers lobby—those advocates were powerful and legislators listened when they spoke. The League got short shrift.

Lobbyists, other than the aforementioned, who wanted favors went through Arthur H. "Artie" Samish. Samish was the lobbyist for a coalition of liquor, oil, bus, trucking, mining, billboards, theatrical, racetrack interests, etc. He began in 1924 by representing the Motor Carrier's Association, but after the repeal of the l8th amendment in 1933, he organized the state's brewers, distillers and tavern keepers into a pro-saloon league. By 1935, the Brewers Association was paying five cents on the barrel into Samish's political fund, a fund for which he was not accountable. As a result California had the lowest liquor taxes in the United States. Between 1935 and 1938, Samish forced oil severance taxes in California down to the point where similar taxes in Louisiana and Texas were 100% higher. The only lobby powerful enough to avoid the out-stretched palm of Samish, was the banking lobby.

With his huge campaign contributions, Samish held the state legislature in thralldom. A 1949 Collier's Magazine expose called Samish the "secret boss of California." The ponderous Samish—his weight was estimated to be above 300 pounds—operated through minions. Samish sat in his office blocks away in the Senator Hotel and controlled the legislative process by telephone. No political boss in the United States wielded such political power without having to resort to physical enforcement. Samish's lieutenants sat in the balcony and gave hand signals to the legislators below. Vera and Fern watched them do it and they saw how the legislators furtively looked up for instructions before marking their ballots. Word filtered back to Artie that "that Shultz woman" had guts, that she'd take on anybody.

Samish ruled the state for over 20 years before the Kefauver Senate Committee on racketeering set out to crush him in the 1950s. Samish ultimately went to prison but before he did, in 1950, he blocked Vera's path to a seat in the Assembly. When Thomas Keating, sheriff of Marin County, ran for the state Senate he urged the Democratic women of Marin to organize and become politically active. The "Democratic Women's Organization" was outside the Central Committee of the statewide Democratic Party. 'The good old boys' in the party had never given more than lip service to the 19th Amendment. The women had to go it alone. Elected primarily by the women, Keating secured floor passes for Vera and Fern so they could sit with the legislators on the floor of the Senate rather than in the balcony with the other lobbyists. Vera and Fern saw everything from their intimate proximity to the proceedings.

By the time her term as advocate expired, Vera was convinced that, regardless of the odds, women had to run for office, win elections where they could, and use governmental power to clean things up. Power was the prize in the political game, not the public weal. In the wrong hands, political power is one of the greatest evils of mankind, she declaimed repeatedly. Women had no access to the inner circle of elected legislators in Sacramento and that had to change. Vera was beginning to contemplate personally breaking the iron grip men had on the legislative process at all levels of government.

In the summer of 1941, home from the lobby wars after the legislature had folded its tents for another year, Vera did some serious thinking. The democracy she passionately believed in was compromised and defeated by the avarice of the very people to whom it had been entrusted. Women were shut out of the halls of power by societal prejudices. Where could humanity look for hope if women didn't enter the lists? On the national scene there were a handful of women in positions of power, usually as wives of powerful men. The number swelled slightly at the state level, but in Marin no woman held elective office.

MOTHERHOOD

All summer she wrestled with the twin issues of collective morality and personal responsibility. Her family had always stood for the virtues she believed in. Morality was almost the first consideration of every Smith. In their rollicking debates about what constituted good citizenship—how far did individual responsibility go, what was the role of government in everyday life—she and her siblings had developed an abiding faith in the democratic process. By now her family had dwindled to two offspring: Gen and Betty Jean -- neither of whom showed any inclination toward involvement in public affairs. Vera decided it was time for her to have a baby, to raise a feminist of her own. Her biological clock was ticking. If she was to have children, children who would make their own contribution to the future, it had to be now. In the past, Ray had put her off about a child. "Wait until we're really settled," he'd say. Or, "Wait until we have a little more money laid by."

One morning she practically ordered Ray to sit down with her in the backyard.

"We need to talk," she said. "I'm not going back to Sacramento. I'm so disillusioned with what's going on up there I'm heartsick. We've been married for 15 years, Ray, 15 years. I want a baby. It's time."

Ray sat silently rubbing his thumbs together while she waited. Finally he rose and said, "Well, if that's what you want, I guess it's all right." So Vera got pregnant and began incubating. In good health, pregnancy did not confine her.

With her usual self-confidence in her ability to do whatever needed to be done, Vera took on the presidency of the League of Women Voters. This would be her temporary swan song. She pledged to herself, to Ray, to Mae and Patty, to anyone who cared one way or the other, that once the baby was born she'd take three years off from all committee work. All of her energy would go into the task of nurturing and educating the new little democratic Smith-Schultz. She'd give the League as much time as she could before the baby arrived, then someone would have to take over and finish her term.

She breezed through the first six months of her pregnancy at the same pell mell pace she usually went through life. Then came the third trimester and she began to tire. Being a prospective mother at age 40 was proving more difficult than she had expected. Her feet swelled. It was hard to breathe while she talked. It became difficult to conduct meetings. Vera announced she was handing over the gavel. Nobody wanted it. Reluctantly, Dorothy Owens finally succumbed to her pleading, but just as Dorothy was finishing Vera's term, she discovered *she* was pregnant. It became a joke in the League that the presidency was a sure way to become house bound with a baby.

Home from the hospital with her baby in June of 1942, for the first time Vera faced the reality of mindless chores that swallow the days of any new mother. She discovered how totally a baby was a forever thing, not a sometime thing as it had been for when she was a baby-sitter. No wonder God made girls physically ready to be mothers at such tender ages. She felt strangled, strait-jacketed by her voluntary pledge to stay at home with the child for three years to give it a good start in life. When she'd dreamed of a child, she'd really dreamed about the woman that child would become. The baby was adorable, and Vera poured herself into adoring, but devotion to adoration wasn't fulfilling enough. Ennui had her by the throat. To be out of the current, lolling along in middle age living the life of a young mother who had not yet grappled with the world, filled her with angst. She felt her life so maddeningly unproductive she almost developed ulcers. There were days when she lay doubled up on the floor with stomach pains. She reminded herself again and again, "You asked for this."

Nineteen Forty-Two, '43 and '44 were terrible years to be out of circulation. The advent of World War II sent every able-bodied adult and most "bobby soxers," male or female, into the war effort. Fear of invasion brought blackouts to both coasts. Americans found themselves regulated as they had never been before. In the Bay Area, after sundown the two new bridges across the Bay were closed to all but emergency traffic. Civilian planes were not allowed to fly over the area at any time. Cars had to drive at night using only hooded parking lights. In the months following Pearl Harbor hysteria gripped the West Coast as people fearfully anticipated a Japanese invasion. Shipyards sprang up around the Bay. Rationing affected all goods that used imported raw materials needed by the armed forces or war production plants—everything from sugar to steel.

Confined at home, all Vera could do was use the telephone. She poured herself into the work of Traveler's Aid and the Red Cross, serving as Home Service Chairman for both organizations. She spent every moment she could spare from child care on the telephone finding housing for service men and/or their families, and for the new shipyards' incoming workers. Travelers' Aid served couples stranded in the Bay Area as they waited for the men to ship out to the Pacific Theater. These young couples needed a place to get in out of the fog. San Francisco was packed. Hotels had five-day limits on occupancy. If a serviceman couldn't find another billet for his wife when the five days were up, she had no choice but to go home. People all over the city were letting out rooms, making apartments out of attics, anything. In Marin County, carriage houses became homes, guest houses were sometimes shared by two or more young couples from Akron or Memphis or Sioux City. Even filling stations, closed down by gas rationing, were converted into dwellings.

Vera and the president of Traveler's Aid put their heads together to try to combine their various functions into an organization that would last into the post-war era. They formed what they called Family Services and began to badger the county to take over. Vera believed Family Services was an organization worthy of ongoing funding beyond war's end. Taxpayers should pay for it, and free the volunteers from fund raising so they could get on with what they should be doing— serving people. Because war knows no class, and patriotism was running at high tide, the county adopted their program and it continues to this day.

At night, after the baby was finally asleep, Vera would gorge on printed matter until she couldn't keep her eyes open. During the day, as soon as she finished making formula, washing bottles and diapers, mixing pabulum, Vera would put her little girl in the stroller and head off to some meeting that was within walking distance of the house. Or she would take her weekly contributions to the food store established during the Depression to help the poor. She'd wedge her sack of contributions in between the baby's seat and the handle frame of the stroller and away she'd go. The store was now serving the families of servicemen at Hamilton Field.

News from the war zones was confusing. Casablanca, Guadalcanal, the Solomons, Sitka, Chungking? Where were these places? U.S. citizens needed geography lessons. Women's International Relations Clubs sprang up all over the country. Under the spur of Elizabeth Kent, widow of World War I Congressman, William Kent, and daughter-in-law of Adeline Kent, an International Relations Club was organized and most of the members of the LWV hastened to join. Elizabeth Kent ranked among Vera's echelon of heroines, almost as high as Carrie Chapman Catt. One of her favorite stories about Mrs. Kent was when Elizabeth carried placards and picketed the White House in Washington, D.C. to attract the attention of the press. The suffragists were demanding the passage of the 19th amendment and Mrs. Kent, a woman of dignity and wit, felt the arrest of a Congressman's wife for demonstrating would symbolize the second class citizenship that demeaned women of all classes. Civil disobedience by their own wives might shame legislators into voting to make women enfranchised citizens of the United States.

Mrs. Kent was also instrumental in getting Mills College to offer two-week summer institutes on International Relations during the war. Mae, Patty and Vera left the baby with "Little Vera" Mathews, the orphaned cousin who had come to live with them when Vera was in high school, and the three sisters traveled back and forth from Marin to Oakland to attend the sessions. At Mills College, Vera was thrown daily into the company of the esteemed "Queen of Kentfield," mother of Democrat Roger Kent. Later, after Vera found herself in the mainstream of Democratic politics, Vera and Roger campaigned separately and together in 1950 when Roger ran for the U.S. Congress and Vera ran for the state assembly.

Among the speakers and consultants at Mills College was Congressman Jerry Voorhis from Southern California, another public figure whom Vera much admired. In a position for the first time to rub shoulders intimately with political reformers of such caliber, Vera loved the contact. All the passion she'd felt for the political process during her college days and as a member of the Board of Freeholders flared anew. Her distaste for politics in Sacramento was chalked up to local corruption. The larger dream was still alive. Pent-up energies from being house bound, plus the stimulus of exposure to people who had made a difference nationally at last unleashed her latent desire to hold office herself. She was aware that other women were stirring up political tempests in other parts of the country, even in conservative California.

Helen Gahagan Douglas was elected to Congress from the 14th Congressional District in Los Angeles in 1944. Douglas was elected primarily by men and in spite of the hostility of housewives who felt threatened by a woman in the Congress. She was the target for "Jew-baiting" epithets thrown at her because her husband's father was a Jew. She was also accused of Communist ties because she was backed by the CIO. In spite of all that, with backing from her friend Eleanor Roosevelt, Helen Gahagan Douglas persisted and won. She was an object lesson for Vera who followed the Douglas's campaign with avid interest. Her victory poured kerosene on the flame of Vera's ambition. She was practically pawing the ground when her three years' commitment to motherhood ended in June of 1945.

OUT OF THE CAGE AND BACK IN THE FRAY

September I, 1945, Japan signed the articles of surrender prepared by the victorious allies and U.S. troopships poured out of foreign ports headed for home. Vera was poised to set in motion some of the ideas that had percolated in her fertile mind during the nation's preoccupation with war. Before she could find a cause to embrace which could propel her into office, Elizabeth Ann Mathews Smith died on November 10th, 1945. Cremation was not legal in Nevada so they brought her body down to Sacramento to the only crematorium they could find. All seven of her surviving offspring gathered on the front verandah of the Hotel Senator across the street from the funeral home where the "ashes to ashes, dust to dust" process was underway. There would be no memorial service; the Smiths left this world without "feathers or fuss."

Her mother's death delayed her, but by Christmas, Vera was looking about Mill Valley for an opening into public life. Government in Mill Valley had skidded off the new track during the war. With many of the inmigrants off to war, the old guard on the City Council had continued to run the town as imperiously as ever. Vera was approached by her buddies of her "Know Your Town" days to take a hand. She'd been the catalyst to get a city manager in the first place, and now she had to do something. The office had become a "gofer" arm of the Mayor's domain. They urged her to run for the City Council, hoping to elect the first woman council member in the history of Mill Valley.

The city manager plan was not working because Bob Baumberger, the current manager Sloan thought they'd hired to be his assistant, was too timid to dis-abuse Sloan about where power was supposed to lie. He let Sloan emasculate the office. Everything Vera thought they'd accomplished was being rendered ineffectual by Baumberger's timidity. Baumberger was not even protesting Charlie Sloan's abandonment of the Southern Marin Sanitation District by Mill Valley.

The sanitation district, born in 1944 while Vera was in reclusion, was designed to take sewage from all of the various towns and districts of Southern Marin, and pipe it out through the Tennessee Valley to the ocean. It would provide sewage service to 16 separate incorporated and unincorporated areas at minimal cost. Mayor Sloan opposed the unified district because of pressure from contractors and sewage plant suppliers who stood to make small fortunes out of a multiplicity of sewage districts. His opposition to the "Jenks Plan," drawn up by an engineer hired to assess the situation, was sold to the voters as a matter of town pride: Mill Valley should have its own plant under its own control. Voters, who didn't understand the ecological issues, voted Sloan's way. The result was a proliferation of sanitation district facilities, spread out along the Bay, that counted on ocean tides to flush away their effluence. The costs to be borne in the future were discounted or denied. Just the same, Mill Valley proudly had its own.

When the election to dismantle the Southern Marin Sanitation District was held, Vera was in Tahoe holding Zetta's hand. Fred had found a playmate and Zetta's marriage was over. Confident that the voters of Mill Valley would not buy a chauvinistic argument about something so basic or mundane as garbage, Vera had not waited to vote. She had hurried to Zetta. Patty called Vera in Tahoe to tell her the unbelievable results of the election. Practically frothing at the mouth, Vera came down from the lake and went straight to the newspaper. She took out a full page ad in the *Mill Valley Record* denouncing Sloan and the subversion of a sane sanitation solution. Her righteous indignation embarrassed Ray. His wife was taking on the men again. Sloan resigned and Vera's itch to get back into politics had found a "raison d'être."

An attack by Margaret Mead on a new book then on the best sellers list provided Vera with ammunition. Margaret Mead had women like Vera in mind when she attacked Ferdinand Lundberg and Marynia Farnham's bestseller, *MODERN WOMAN: The Lost Sex.* Mead argued that women suffered less from Freud's penis envy, as Lundberg and Farnham claimed, than they did from envy of the special powers men were allowed to exercise at the exclusion of women. Women wanted some of the prerogatives men enjoyed because of those powers. Mead's thesis substantiated Vera's assumption that women had to run for office, had to challenge the stranglehold men had on the political process. However, Margaret Mead's assumptions about, and Vera's impatience with, male autocracy were not shared by the majority of women at the end of World War II. Popular propaganda was pushing women out of the workplace and back into the home to have babies. The war was over, the men were coming back, women should confine themselves to home and hearth and let the men have back their jobs. They'd valiantly reached beyond themselves to serve the war effort, but they were free now to return to the nest.

To be elected to the City Council, to seek the necessary power to bring about change, Vera needed to persuade more than 4,000 voters that a woman could be trusted with public office and should be allowed to take her place in the world of politics. Mill Valleyians generally shared an ingrown opposition to change, any kind of change. A woman on the council would be a tidal change. A healthy debate followed. Many were convinced that society was not ready for women politicians, others thought it was definitely time for women to challenge the prevailing entrenched male-political-preserve-mentality. Who better to be the standard bearer in such an effort than Vera? All agreed that boldness and audacity had to be hidden in velvet gloves by any woman seeking office, and all agreed that Vera had the diplomacy and tact necessary to allay fears of aggressive feminism.

Margo Dick offered to take over publicity and she and Vera spent hour upon hour in Vera's basement writing ads for the *Mill Valley Record*. The LWV's mimeograph machine, housed in Vera's basement, was rented by her campaign committee, and cranked out all sorts of campaign missiles. Vera drafted a statement about the subversion of prior reforms by the mayor, foremost among them the office of city manager. More personally disappointed than she, in the way things had gone, Bob Baumberger carried around copies of the statement to hand to everyone he met.

The announcement of Vera's candidacy brought Elizabeth (Libby) Rudel Smith Gatov, the future Treasurer of the United States, into Vera's path. Libby was not a political animal at the time of   their meeting; her interest lay in political figures, people of power. She was a reporter on The *Independent Journal* when they met. She made an appointment to interview Vera for a feature story about "The Woman who Dared." Ostensibly, Libby came to interview Vera, but, before the meeting was over, Vera had interviewed Libby and given her a push onto the path of political involvement. Libby became deeply immersed in local Democratic politics, and both she and Vera were subjects of a major study, *California Women in Politics*, done by the Bancroft Library at the University of California in Berkeley.

Previously apolitical, Libby now led a drive to establish a Mill Valley Chapter of the Marin County Women's Democratic Club. Being a Democrat in Marin in those days meant being a political nobody. Libby changed that. Vera attended every one of the meetings Libby called, adding her vigor to the new partisan energy Libby was whipping up. All the stalwarts got involved. Carol Fowler had fund raisers for the Club in her home while the others handed out informational materials and talked Vera up in their social circles. Before Vera's campaign ended, Libby was chin deep in the currents of Democratic party policy making with no way to shore except to get busy and swim.

A campaign for the City Council in Mill Valley, a non-partisan office, was usually a pedestrian kind of electioneering. Vera made few speeches. Instead she tramped the streets of Mill Valley. She rang doorbells, she shook hands, and when people were surprised to find a woman candidate on their doorstep asking for their vote in the next election, she addressed that issue, usually to their satisfaction. She addressed the Chamber of Commerce and she was the luncheon or dinner speaker for a small number of clubs and organizations. What carried the day was her technique of hoofing it around to talk to people, one on one. Five candidates ran and Vera got 86 percent of the vote. Eighty-six percent of the ballots cast went to the one female candidate. Another California woman, Helen Gahagan Douglas, ran in the 14th Congressional District, but she was unable to campaign in person because Truman had appointed her to the United Nations General Assembly. Nevertheless, she won reelection with twice the margin of votes she'd received in 1944.

Vera's success at the polls brought problems at home. There wasn't enough time for everything. Daily, she face the question of how to oversee a household, take on the problems of the town, and be well-groomed every day. After having read half the night, Vera had no time for beauty parlors or for "dressing her hair" every morning. Anything that slowed her down had to be eliminated. The solution was wigs. As for hats, there are few pictures from the 1940s, '50s and '60s of Vera without a hat. She loved them. All through high school, after she learned the milliner's trade, and later through college, she wore hats even to dances, and refused to take them off. Once on the council, with the help of the best milliner she could find in the Bay area, she acquired a large wardrobe of hats that she wore with presence and pleasure. A hat and gloves were the signature of the well-dressed woman in that those decades.

Traditionally, the mayor was the council member who received the highest number of votes in an election. That did not happen in 1946. Humiliated enough by the election of a woman to their sacred bench, the men would not have a female mayor in the bargain. In secret caucus, they changed the rules before she was sworn in, and again chose their old buddy, Charles Sloan. When Vera quietly took her seat without fanfare, nothing was said about the change in the rules. She let it pass. She felt she had more important things to tackle at that time than the gender issue.

One of Vera's most admirable qualities was that she never sought power for the sake of wielding power or to aggrandize herself; she wanted power because it was the most effective tool with which to make the changes she had in mind. Once she had power, however, in her haste to get things done, she sometimes used that power to mow down opposition to her ideas. Because she did her homework and was sure of her ground, she had little patience with other public servants who were unprepared, or whose service was to themselves and their cohorts, not to the public. Vera was at her best rallying the troops and leading them into battle against that person or plan she considered detrimental to the public good.

Once sworn in as Councilman (in 1946 all public office holders were "men"), Vera attacked the issue that garnered her the most support among the voters. She proposed that the council immediately begin to search for a more qualified civil servant to fill the office of city manager. No one more heartily endorsed the idea than the current manager, Bob Baumberger. Bob knew he'd been diddled by Sloan and had no stomach for further humiliation. In the face of her overwhelming endorsement by the people, other councilmen didn't dare refuse. Harrison Leppo, one of the inmigrants who had come across the bridge, also a new member of the council, was a bright man wedded to the same ideas of modern government as those Vera held. He joined her in insisting they go outside the county to look for a replacement.

At their own expense, the two of them went down to Pasadena to meet a young miracle worker named Ted Adsits. Vera and Harrison were so impressed they invited Adsits to appear before the whole council. Charles Sloan, alone, demurred. He threatened to resign if Adsits was hired. Adsits was hired and Sloan resigned. With Adsits in and Sloan out, Mill Valley became a model city almost overnight—problem-oriented, productive, attuned to the new breed of Mill Valleyites pouring into their little town in the late '40s and early '50s. Mill Valley never abandoned the city manager plan once it was instituted.

On the southern edge of Mill Valley lay 17 acres of marsh bordered by the town on the west and north, and by Richardson Bay to the east and south. The land was owned by the Biggio family whose scavenger company used it as a dumpsite. The Biggios' scavenger company serviced Mill Valley. Little by little, the marsh was drying up, becoming a solid mass of junk and garbage. Rats from the desiccating mass invaded the downtown. Citizens living near the dump wanted relief from the smell as well as from its ugliness. How to wrest control of the land from its owners? Vera came up with the idea of annexation. Annex the land and Mill Valley could resolve the situation their way. They could re-negotiate the town's garbage contract with the scavenger company and close down the operation. Mill Valleyians eagerly voted for annexation.

Once the land was annexed, Vera wanted to protect Richardson Bay from being ringed by apartment buildings. Buildings were already being drafted in a number of Mill Valley's architects' offices. She went to see Mary Summers, planning director and head of the County Planning Department. All plans for land development in Marin were supposed to reach the Board of Supervisors for approval. Both women knew that the interested developers planned to create an enclave of apartments featuring a private boat harbor for their renters on the shores of Richardson Bay. Vera wanted a review from Mary of all existing laws dealing with the preservation of land in Marin County. No one had ever asked the County Planning Commission about laws regarding land use before. Mary was impressed. There were no laws; decisions about land use lay entirely with land owners, in this case, the Biggio family.

Mary assured Vera that when the City of Mill Valley became the owner of the 17 acres, Mill Valley would decide the fate of the Bay. Vera was elated. Doing her usual thorough search for ways and means to sell an idea, Vera moved fast and came up with a scheme whereby once annexation was complete, the Mill Valley School District would be ceded six of the 17 acres for a middle school. Once those six acres were in the possession of the school district they would be safe from development. For the remaining 11 acres, the clever thing to do was to draw up a contract with the scavenger company allowing them to continue under the present contract until the dump site was saturated, but add a clause that would force them to cover the whole 11 acres with a deep layer of topsoil when they were through. Those "sanitary engineers" would then "gift" the land to Mill Valley specifically for use as parks and recreational areas. With no money to buy out the garbage men's contract, it was a brilliant solution. The remaining shoreline to the south and east of the Bay was in the county's domain and would have to rely on county protection from developers.

Very little research had been done at that time on the impact of waste sites on such things as underground water or nearby surface streams, lakes, bays, oceans, and so forth. Some long-range planning needed to be done for such a prime and delicate piece of real estate. In the short run Mill Valley could do nothing because of a lack of funds, but the city could put into place regulations and pass legislation that would keep the developers out until funds became available to develop the Bay front for recreational purposes. Some time after acquisition of the 11 acres, Mill Valley built a public safety building on one corner. That was all they had the money to do. The rest of the annexed bay front remained undeveloped, the natural habitat of virginal reeds and water weeds.

Today, the "gifted" land is called Bayfront Park and there is no recreation facility in town used more heavily. Mill Valley built bike paths, walking trails, softball diamonds, volley ball courts, and a horse shoe pit—all compatible uses. Kids, dogs, the elderly sunning on benches, young Mill Valley mothers pushing prams. The traffic in the park is terrific. Mill Valley has more developed and yet-to-be-developed park acreage than any comparably sized town in the county. The city fathers are building the community center that Vera envisioned so long ago, not on the corner of E. Blithedale and Camino Alto, but close. It took a crusading "good government kook" to break the hold the "good old boys," born and bred to rural county politics, had on Mill Valley, and to turn the town's face toward the future. Bayfront Park is one of Vera's more visible legacies.

In the last year of her life, old, blind, and isolated on her mountain, Vera still followed unfolding changes in Mill Valley. Still pondering "ways and means," Vera suggested that the school district cede back the remaining parcel of land that fell into their laps in 1947. Still undeveloped by the school district, the property should be transferred to a different public use. The school district did not cede; it sold. Vera's memory bank of data was amazing. She remembered complex legal issues in all their detail, a feat boggling to younger people who can't remember the fine print of negotiations that took place last year. Since her death in May 1995, it has been suggested that the name of the new community center being built on land she saved, should be The Vera L. Schultz Community Center.

Vera always said there are no dead issues, only delayed ones. People in Marin today are hearing some of the old proposals offered up as new idea about schools, about traffic, about building moratoriums. Perhaps they should review council proceedings from 1946 to 1950. Following acquisition of the waterfront acreage, the next thing Vera scrutinized was property assessments. Favoritism kept the little town of Mill Valley broke. Vera played sleuth checking the real values of properties and comparing them with the assessed value according to the county assessor's roles. What she found was stupefying. Properties next door to each other, homes or business buildings built by the same builder in the same year, had assessed values so at variance with each other they made no sense. In many cases, they had even been assessed on the same day. It had to be favoritism, the "good old boy" network in all its insider exclusivity. Friendly favors for favored friends.

Vera persuaded the Council to hire two tax factors to come in at the town's expense and reassess all property of every kind in Mill Valley. George Hall, the county assessor, was fit to be tied, but he had no authority to prevent a town from doing its own assessing. Using the values assigned by the tax factors, not those whimsically established by Hall, equitable property taxes were levied on all. An outcry came from outraged individuals who faced greatly increased tax bills. Incensed office holders, responding to the outrage, condemned the officials who had meddled with the status quo. On the other side, taxpayers previously up in arms over the inequity that had existed, rubbed their hands in glee. The Mill Valley council let the war of words blow where it would. They now had the money needed to catch up with the town's growth, particularly money for building more schools.

In the fall of 1948, midway through her term on the Mill Valley City Council, Harry S. Truman ran for the presidency for the first time. He had succeeded to the office when Franklin D. Roosevelt died in 1945. All pundits predicted, according to polls favored by the pundit, that Truman's candidacy was doomed. Thomas E. Dewey was about to move into 1600 Pennsylvania Avenue in 1949. Vera stumped for Truman all spring and summer. Now it was fall, and he was scheduled to make a campaign swing through California. Vera and Ray were not in Mill Valley during the week before Truman's visit to the Bay Area. They were not at home when the telegram arrived from Washington requesting Vera's presence on the platform in San Francisco for Truman's major speech in the Bay Area.

The Schultzes were at Knott's Berry Farm. Visitors to this tourist attraction can be arbitrarily handed a summons and locked up in an old western jail that has been brought in from some old ghost town. "In jail," the "outlaw" gets her/his picture taken peering out through the bars. Vera had been served a summons and was in the calaboose when suddenly the loud speaker blared, "Is there someone here by the name of Vera Schultz?"

"Yes" she called out in surprise.

"President Truman has a message for you," the voice came back.

Vera thought it was a joke. They all thought it was a joke. It wasn't. When she was "released on good behavior" and hurried out of the jail, she was handed a telegram. Truman was inviting her to sit with him on the speaker's platform at a sell-out event sponsored by his presidential campaign organizers. The telegram further requested that Vera accompany Mrs. Truman and her daughter Margaret to another event in Oakland the next day. Vera was dumbfounded, thrilled, and speechless. On the platform the following night it was wonderful to sit, bolt upright, ankles crossed, her face beaming, behind the current and next president of the United States. More satisfying were the two hours she spent alone with the Truman women the next evening. They talked about cabbages and sealing wax, and what Mrs. Truman liked about life in the White House. Bess Truman was honest, intelligent and easy to know. They talked about what it meant to Margaret to spend hours on the campaign trail smiling and smiling and smiling. What they discussed was not as important to Vera as the level of candor with which Mrs. Truman entered into their conversation.

From Eleanor Roosevelt to Rosalynn Carter, every Democratic president's wife came to know Vera Schultz by name. All but one met the people of Marin with Vera by their side. Eleanor Roosevelt came to Marin County after the war to give an address at the College of Marin. Vera was part of the welcoming committee and stood in the receiving line with the First Lady. Only Jacqueline Kennedy did not come to Marin. Lady Bird

Johnson was her favorite of them all. Vera liked spunky women who could think for themselves. Lady Bird could and did speak her mind frequently. When she did Lyndon listened.

In 1950, Vera's term on the Mill Valley council was up. Her appetite for further participation in the political game had been whetted, not dissipated. Scanning the political landscape for another challenge she determined it was time to unseat her old carpool buddy, Richard McCollister, as the Sixth District Assemblyman. In her view McCollister played the role of small time politician to the hilt, drinking his way through every session of the Legislature. He missed more days than he appeared. His vote was as predictable as boss Samish's preferences. During a decade of incredible change, he'd introduced not one piece of legislation other than bills to allow gambling in California. The Sixth Assembly District covers Marin and Sonoma Counties. Marin was more heavily populated than Sonoma, but Sonoma covers four times the land area.

Running for the state assembly meant running as a party candidate. The new Democratic Party organization Libby Gatov had put together in Mill Valley was still so small and so quiet it had yet to make a political ripple. From the start, Vera was a closet member of that little party. The charter of the League of Women Voters prohibits partisan political activity by a board member. To run for the Legislature, she'd have to step aside and give up any further leadership role in LWV. Marin County shared with Orange County the distinction of being the most Republican county in the state. So commonplace was it for anyone coming into Marin to be a dyed-in-the-wool Republican that when Vera went to register as a voter for the first time, Will Falley, the town clerk, automatically enrolled her under the elephant's symbol. When she demurred, he didn't want to put her on the registration rolls at all.

Cross-filing allowed Republicans to cross over for the primary. For a Democrat to be the Democratic party nominee for Assembly was a major coup in 1950. Democrats always wound up with a Republican candidate running under the Democratic label. The November elections inevitably boiled down to a fight between two Republicans, or a no-contest shoo-in for the Republican running on the Republican ticket.

123

In 1950, the first woman candidate ever to run in the Democratic primary became the first Democrat in 16 years to survive the June primaries and get to the November ballot.

Roger Kent was the Democratic candidate for the U.S. House of Representatives that year and Libby Gatov, now a Democratic kingpin in the county, ran Roger Kent's campaign. Vera had her own organization and her campaign was in other hands, but the two committees coordinated speaking engagements when it was in the best interests of both candidates to do so. Vera and Roger appeared frequently on the same platform, but neither wished to be known as "Little Sir Echo" to the other.

At that juncture, Vera L. Schultz ignored the opposition and learned to drive. After almost a year of living on the middle ridge without her own transportation, she'd had enough dependency. She'd gotten by, hitching rides and taking taxis. Now she'd be campaigning all over the hills of both Marin and Sonoma Counties. Who would be willing to be her constant chauffeur? Friends were available to assist much of the time but there were many invitations to speak on short notice that left her scrambling to find a ride. Ray capitulated, bought her a car and handed her the keys. With nary a driving lesson, she held her breath and drove down the mountain. To her great delight, she didn't hit anything. The freedom wheels gave her was sheer bliss. She remained gloriously mobile until she could no longer pass the vision test to renew her driver's license. Ray, bought all her cars without her input. The cars were big, used, and had good maintenance ratings. As long as they were presentable and ran, Vera was happy. The old sense of being out of control of her life was gone.

Nineteen Fifty-Two was a lucky year for Democrats in Marin. They had two energetic candidates, both blessed with the requisite charisma to galvanize their party, and attract a wide following among the new voters who had come into the county since 1948. In her home county, Vera was well-known for her "Good Government" ardor. A new face in Sonoma County, however, she was seen as an upstart woman who wanted to sit with the seasoned boys in Sacramento where she could carp about policy like a fishwife. Vera had other handicaps. She was from artsy-craftsy, readers'-clubs Mill Valley, and also she was one of those damned "Save the Trees" people. Admittedly, they said, somebody should run against McCollister, but not a woman. In the long run, however, neither Sonoma nor Marin could come up with another candidate as savvy as Vera to wage a long and possibly futile campaign. Grudgingly, Democratic forces in the two counties united behind her candidacy.

Undaunted, Vera filed the necessary papers with the Secretary of State and set to work. Roger Kent owned the Keystone Building in Mill Valley and gave her headquarters space in his building, rent-free. Strategically it was a great location, right downtown. A former partner of McCollister's, who now hated his guts, put up the money for 5,000 campaign buttons. Vera covered the cost of mailers with money of her own. Campaign expenses were tight but Sada Stevens from the central committee knew where to find more money. The Brotherhood of Engineers, other labor unions, and a handful of organizations that usually contributed money to Democratic candidates came through. From many sources Democrats eked out funds for both races.

It was an acrimonious campaign. Vera accused McCollister of do-nothingism; he accused her of being Carrie Nation, wanting to wreck things. One night at a meeting in El Verano in Sonoma County, McCollister referred to Vera sneeringly as: "this woman who wants to wear the pants ..." Roger, seated in the audience, jumped to his feet and blasted McCollister for his ungentlemanly behavior. The hall was immediately in an uproar. People reacted with wild applause or outraged booing. In the newspapers, Roger was cast as "the knight riding to the rescue of the beleaguered lady." Beleaguered didn't sound like front runner. The newspapers weren't helping.

Finally, Vera received the endorsement of the Sonoma *Press-Democrat*. At that point, Artie Samish sent word from Sacramento that if Vera would promise to mind her p's & q's and not meddle in other people's business once in office, they'd help her out. Vera indignantly turned down the offer. Obviously, Samish retaliated by pouring money into McCollister's campaign. Smoke-writing in the sky began soon after, along with showers of leaflets denouncing Vera.

McCollister's local forces could not have afforded either. Someone, other than local constituents, was filling his coffers.

Campaigning, whether one wins or loses, produces interesting incidents that often provide the candidate with new friends and cherished memories. When Vera announced her candidacy, Earl Warren, then governor of California, was quoted as saying, "Who is this woman who thinks she can be an assemblyman?" In Petaluma one day when both were in town campaigning, he for reelection, she for a first term in the Assembly, she confronted him. "Governor Warren, this is that woman you were reported to oppose running for the state assembly."

Embarrassed, Warren effusively assured her he'd been falsely quoted. He'd never commented on her candidacy one way or another. That encounter was the beginning of a warm friendship between them. They were thrown together a number of times in Sacramento after she became a supervisor, and before Eisenhower placed Warren on the Supreme Court. He and Vera were together in New York at a conference on welfare. They were jointly interviewed by *Harper's Magazine,* for an article covering the age-old topic: "To what extent should the government take responsibility for the welfare of 'the least among us' of our country's citizens." After Warren was sworn in as Chief Justice, Vera was free to call on him at his office in the Supreme Court Building whenever she was in the capitol. Over the years she was often a guest at his home in Chevy Chase.

In every campaign there are other events that are simply puzzling. One episode left Vera completely mystified. Michael Wornum, a neighbor, threw a huge cocktail party as a fund raiser to support her run for the Legislature. Loudly, he espoused the need for a woman in Sacramento to act as yeast for reform. His cocktail party was the kind of social splash duly reported on the society page of the county papers. Everyone who was anyone was invited, and most of them came. Tray after tray of delicious food was served by uniformed waiters. Conversation in every corner was sparkling. Vera had a wonderful time.

The next day Wornum turned over the caterer's and florist's bills to her along with the gate receipts. When the bills were paid there was little left for campaign expenses. Like most grand social events thrown for charitable purposes, more feeling good than doing good resulted from that party. "Wouldn't more money have come in if they'd had hot dogs and beer and passed the hat?" Vera asked. Vera's campaign was forced to rely almost entirely on hoof and mouth efforts, walk and talk. She could afford only a few radio spot ads and interviews, not enough to counteract the extravagant campaign McCollister was able to wage.

That same year, Helen Gahagan Douglas ran for the United States Senate against fellow congressman, Richard Milhous Nixon. Nixon had defeated Jerry Voorhis for Voorhis's seat in the Congress in 1946 by tarring him with being "Communist Leaning." Now he used the same smear tactics on Helen Gahagan Douglas. Douglas came to Marin to campaign and Roger Kent, in charge of arrangements, seated Vera and other Democratic candidates whose names would appear on the November ballot with hers on the speaker's platform. Vera was thrilled. When she was introduced as the party's choice for the Assembly from the 10th District, Vera's allotted time to speak was only enough to tell a little joke that ended with "Me, too." Immediately, she was tarred with the same "red" brush Nixon used on Douglas. This was too much for the Republican Petaluma *Argus-Courier* which had crossed party lines to endorse Vera. If she had the slightest taint of association with "The Pink Lady," the sobriquet Nixon had cleverly made a public synonym for Helen Gahagan Douglas, the *Argus-Courier* wanted no part of her.

Vera might have lost the election anyway, but Samish money and the Communist charge were too great a combination to overcome. Both she and Helen Gahagan Douglas were knocked out of their respective rings by "McCarthyism," a term Herb Block coined that year when, in one of his cartoons in the *Washington Post* he labeled an overflowing barrel of tar: "McCarthyism." Within the six months of the 1950 elections, China had fallen to Mao, the Russians had exploded an atomic bomb, Alger Hiss had been convicted of being a spy, and Klaus Fuchs had defected to the U.S.S.R. The country was scared.

Richard Nixon used McCarthy's tar brush not only on Douglas but on Vera as well because of her appearance on the same platform with Douglas. Her first attempt to affect legislation at the state level in California ended in failure.

But in a larger sense, Vera had won, not lost. As a Democrat, she'd won the Democratic party primary; as a woman candidate, she'd cracked open the door for other women to enter the assembly later on. Helen Gahagan Douglas was trounced by "Tricky Dick" Nixon in the 1950 election. That defeat ended her career in politics. She would re-emerge as a political figure in 1973 in a cameo appearance when the Watergate scandal produced bumper stickers that read: "Don't blame me, I voted for Helen Gahagan Douglas." Once out of the House of Representatives in 1950, Douglas was never again part of the Washington, D.C. "Inside the Beltway" drama.

Vera, on the other hand, resolved to find a way to reenter the political fray in Marin, was biding her time. Her opportunity would not come for another two years, but in the interim she focused her attention on a non-political project of great import to the county. In doing so, she enhanced her growing reputation as someone to reckon with. Nothing had been done to alleviate the woeful lack of hospital beds in the county after the establishment of a health department in the '30s. Marin babies were still born in San Francisco. All serious operations were performed either in "the city," or in Oakland. Marin needed a modern hospital of her own.

Opposition to county indebtedness was as entrenched as ever. There was no point in trying to raise funds by putting a bond initiative on the ballot. A group of hospital advocates decided the way to get around this conservative roadblock was to create a hospital district, then levy bonds against it. They hoped that, labeled differently and funded euphemistically apart from any form of tax structure, it might fly. The District was established in 1950 and Vera and Roger, both trounced in their respective elections, joined forces to co-chair the bond drive that followed. With that duo leading the forces, Marin General Hospital opened its doors in 1952.

THE SEVEN CANDIDATE PRIMARY

One day in 1952, as Vera was crossing Throckmorton Avenue, she ran into Dick McCollister. As civilized people are wont to do, they stopped to exchange pleasantries. He surprised her by saying, "Why don't you run for the Board of Supervisors? There's going to be a vacancy so there won't be an incumbent to run against. Right now, after the campaign you've just been through, your name is well known. You might get it."

Startled Vera asked, "Why would you want me to do that?"

"To keep you busy so you won't run against me again," he said.

That chance meeting awakened Vera to new possibilities. The Board of Supervisors? She'd ignored county government until then; ignored the very arm of government where a single individual could have more influence than at any other level of power. There'd never been a woman supervisor in the state of California so far as she knew, certainly not in Marin County. Going after an Assembly seat she'd tried to fly too high too fast. Another woman, Carmel Booth, was also trying to crack open the door for women by running for Supervisor in the Second District. One of Booth's three opponents was no-nonsense, in-charge, incumbent named William Fusselman, the candy maker from San Anselmo. Bill Fusselman was a paid spokesman for the Marin Chamber of Commerce and a solid member of the "courthouse gang." Carmel didn't have a chance. But, as McCollister pointed out, there was no incumbent running in Vera's Third District.

Letting herself in the kitchen door that afternoon, Vera went straight to the study. Her hat still on her head, she sat down at her desk and pulled out a legal-sized yellow pad. She began listing every reason she could think of why she should *not* run for supervisor. Then she listed every reason why she should. The "not" column was short but the "should" column grew longer and longer. The more she mulled over the pros and cons, the more convinced she became that she should and could make a run for it. The trick would be to persuade voters who had rejected her so recently to reconsider her adequacy for office.

129

In the Assembly race, her campaign had been based on the issue of Dick McCollister himself. There was no rascal to throw out this time. She needed to give people a reason, or reasons, to vote for her. Thoughtfully she formulated eight objectives to make up her platform.

Most important was the need for a major overhaul of the structure of Marin County government. The old cronies, busy milking the county, were doing nothing about the problems of an exploding population. Such an overhaul would call for:

I. A county administrator, someone who could be held responsible for the way things were managed in San Rafael.

2. Centralization of county offices in a new building. County offices were housed in 13 different locations around San Rafael creating massive inefficiency.

3. Centralized purchasing. Every department head and every district in the county did its own contracting. How much less costly if the county handled all purchasing out of one office. Together all the little towns and school districts, as well as all the county agencies, issued a plethora of contracts with suppliers for identical items thereby increasing the costs for taxpayers.

4. A personnel commission to hire people on the basis of merit rather than nepotism and favors to friends.

5. Better roads. Pure "pork" determined where roads were built and how they were maintained. Healthy campaign contributions brought good roads to a contributor's part of the district; inadequate contributions assured that existing roads went to pot holes.

6. Badly needed flood control. In California the "Average Rainfall" does not refer to yearly rainfall but to the difference between wet years and dry years. In wet years flooding on a grand scale is routine. In dry years, when the land is not underwater, flooding falls into the category of the proverbial leaky roof.

7. Fair assessments. Property taxes were even more a matter of political pork than roads, and outside Mill Valley, inequity in assessments prevailed.

8. Planning. A toothless planning commission could recommend its collective head off but nothing ever changed.

As soon as Vera was clear about why she intended to run, she began to make phone calls, to send up trial balloons.

Publicity photo; 1952 campaign for
first term on the Board of Supervisors

County Clerk George Gnoss and Vera Schultz

To Vera Schultz
with Love and Admiration
On this the First day of January
In the Year Nineteen and Sixty-one
In the County of Marin
State of California

From Her Devoted Supporters

"To appreciate the noble
is a gain which can never
be torn from us" Goethe

The fabulous scroll of admirers' names presented
to Vera at the Meadow Club dinner

In her book-lined office at home

Vera
At the presentation by Frank Lloyd Wright
of his plans for the Civic Center.

March 25, 1958, San Rafael High School Auditorium
Wright presents his plans for the Marin County Civic Center

The Marin Civic Center
Administration Building
1962

Vera wrote to Lou Dandelet:
"Your beautiful photograph
of the roof and sky and
golden pylon under the
gorgeous dome of heaven
is giving me daily happiness.
It is the first thing I see
every morning and starts
my day in the best possible
way. I'm glad I own it."

Head Table at the Gala
Vera, Peter Behr, Betty Deedy, Bill Gavin, and Gary Giacomini

With Diane and Rollin Post at the Gala

Vera proudly holds statuette of herself created by
Betsy Debs and presented to her at the Gala

1981 - Vera at "First Lady of Marin" gala

Sally Behr, Jane Drexler, Independent Journal Editor Jack Craemer,
the Author, Mill Valley Record Editor Fred Drexler

At the twenty-fifth anniversary party for the Civic Center
Joan Brown, S.I. Hayakawa, Aaron Greene,
Wesley Peters, Bob Roumiguiere

William Gnoss and Vera Schultz
Surviving members of the Board of Supervisors
that brought Frank Lloyd Wright to Marin County

Addressing a public meeting of the Save Our Counties Libraries Committee

With Aaron Green at the booksigning of his new book,
"An Architecture for Democracy"

Margaret Myers, first Vera Schultz Fellow, and Vera

Aaron Green with Vera at 90th birthday party. Background:
Supervisor's chair in the Civic Center she never got to occupy

Independent Journal columnist Beth Ashley with Vera at 90th birthday party

Vera read every book in this building

Marin's favorite icons memorialized

The response was exhilarating, especially from the people she polled in Mill Valley. It looked like the entire town was ready to back her. What else did she need? She already knew the trials of the campaign trail. Physically fit and raring to go, she still vacillated. The Third District was bigger than Mill Valley. How would she play in West Marin? The cattlemen of West Marin marched to the drum beat of George Jones, the political czar of Marin County. Did she have a chance with stalwart conservatives? One big surprise came when she had a visit from Fred Drexler, editor of the *Mill Valley Record*. He'd heard she was sounding out some of the more influential people in town and he came to tell her he wanted her to run.

"You know I didn't support you before. You're a Democrat and I'm a Republican. But this is a non-partisan office and if you'll run for the Board of Supervisors the *Mill Valley Record* will endorse you."

That was the irresistible call to arms. If the local paper was behind her she'd have a good chance against the big pack of six male candidates already in the field. All six of those men were committed to upholding the generally held prejudice against women being in politics. The moment she filed her papers and announced her candidacy, opposition flared as she had expected it would. Her pledged support for Estes Kefauver as the presidential candidate of the Democratic Party was trumpeted from the County clerk's office. Non-partisanship went out the window. Republicans, so long in the saddle, mobilized all their familiar forces to wipe out this usurper of the male prerogative, this upstart female Democrat. Her candidacy threatened the Republican Establishment that had run Marin county since 1850 when the Constitution established Marin as one of the original 27 counties.

Fortunately, the new Republicans in Marin were an individualistic lot. They were not embroiled in the eternal squabble that went on within the small coterie of czars who played poker together at the Rod and Gun Club. They were not adherents of Chief honcho, George Jones. The "Courthouse Gang" had taken over Marin County more than three decades before and their boss Jones ran it like a fiefdom. He controlled "My County" as firmly as Samish controlled the state legislature. Years later in reviewing the battle over the Civic Center, Mike Mitchell, Marin County Auditor, said: "There was a sixth member of the Board who had as much power as, or more, than the other five — George Jones, The County Clerk."

Seven candidates made the balloting more like a popularity contest than a bona fide election. Traditionally, being on the Board of Supervisors was not a job for a reformer but for a loyal team player. All the male contenders were Jones' boys so any one of them was as useful to him as another. The unpredictable factor in this election was how much attention the new suburbanites would pay to this race for an office that had previously been a matter of routinely soothing troubled waters and running the county the same way year after year. The inmigrants were numerous enough to determine the outcome but would they vote? Would they vote for a "Good Government Kook," Jones' now-familiar sobriquet for Vera, in spite of the Kook being a woman?

Roger Kent again gave Vera office space in the Keystone Building. Again she could practically coast down the mountain from home to walk the streets of Mill Valley rubbing shoulders with the populace. Sada Stephens, staunch Democrat and colleague of Vera's in the League of Women Voters and an activist in Vera's first campaign, was preoccupied with campaigning for Adlai Stevenson, Democratic candidate for president that year, so Libby Gatov masterminded Vera's race. Again, Margo Dick did the publicity and organized volunteers who manned the office and passed out handbills. Men who knew the political ropes in Marin pitched in by going into liquor establishments, whether public bars or private clubs, to campaign for her. That was where the pay dirt lay. The good old boys had always done business in such settings. As the days wore on, more men, new Marinites determined to unseat the old Courthouse Gang and modernize the county, went to work for Vera. They too canvassed the drinking establishments.

If the members of the old guard could have agreed among themselves and only one of the six made the race, it would have been a shoo-in for Jones. Of the 9,810 votes cast, 4,235 went to Vera. She had come within 500 votes of winning in the primary. It was a stunning upset. The five men who were now out of the race threw their weight to the runner-up, Steven Balzan, dairyman from West Marin, friend of George Jones, member of the Rod and Gun Club. Balzan knew almost nothing about government. He had no political agenda of his own and he'd done nothing in politics before. Balzan had entered the campaign as front man for George Jones and William Fusselman. They pulled the strings, he was the puppet, and if he was elected, the cracker barrel days were assuredly going to continue unmolested by reformers.

With the run-off election months away, Vera turned her attention to the National convention of the Democratic party to be held in Chicago the last week in July. That year, Dwight D. Eisenhower, America's beloved godfather, was running as the Republican candidate for the presidency. The Democratic candidate, whoever he might be, would have an uphill fight. Before the primary, Vera was invited to become a member of the Democratic National Committee. National committee person is the brass ring of party politics, short of a seat in Congress or the presidency. Vera yearned to hold that seat. Earlier, at the State Convention, she'd been elected to the California delegation to the national convention. Could she juggle all three activities at the same time? Could she successfully be a national committee member, a delegate to the National Convention in Chicago in July, and a candidate for the Board of Supervisors, all three at one time?

The Chairperson of the Democratic Party of Berkeley also wanted the vacant seat on the national committee. She upbraided Vera for even considering the post. "You can't run an election campaign, go to the National Convention, and have any time left over for the job of committeewoman. A committeewoman has to be in Washington from now until the election and three times a year in non-presidential election years" she said. Alarmed at the prospects, Ray added his voice to the upbraiding coming from Berkeley. Being a national committeewoman cost a lot of money. All her expenses in Washington would have to come out of their bank account. She shouldn't even think of it. Agonizing over the long-range impact of passing up the national stage for the local arena, she kept her husband on tenterhooks for weeks. After much soul

133

searching she let the national party office go, hoping that the chance would come again. It never did.

Going to the convention as a California delegate was exciting. The *Ladies Home Journal* did a feature article on one woman delegate to the Democratic convention and an identical article on one woman delegate to the Republican convention. The magazine chose Vera as the Democrat delegate for their article and laid out a plan whereby a bevy of reporters would try to get inside her head and stay there throughout the week. Every day, the lead interviewer would meet her after every session to debrief her on what had happened and how she felt about it. Every night, she would have dinner with the whole team of reporters who would interrogate her again. Then, after the evening session, before she could go to bed at night, she would be debriefed again. The article was published one month before her election to the Board of Supervisors. That article stressed her "to-the-death" belief in the Democratic party. After that, it was a wonder her candidacy for the non-partisan office of supervisor had any chance of success at all.

California's Democratic state party rules bound the delegation to vote as a block. Estes Kefauver had won their allegiance when, the year before, he headed a Senate committee digging into the issue of illegal lobbying practices. The Kefauver Committee had put Artie Samish on trial and convicted him. Samish was in prison and California Democrats were committed Kefauver supporters. So sold on Kefauver were they that when Stevenson won the nomination, Californians had to be brainwashed into joining the national Democratic excitement of being "Madly for Adlai." Vera went to Chicago personally committed to Kefauver, bound not just by party rules but by inner conviction.

Seated in the California Section on the floor of the convention hall, Vera, who had always been contemptuous of the hoopla of Convention demonstrations, had her worst expectations amply fulfilled. "You'd think we'd come two thousand miles to see a circus" the *Ladies Home Journal* reported her saying. "Do they really think this sort of thing helps elect a President of the United States?"

Yet, when Estes Kefauver's name was put in nomination, and his delegates took to the aisles to snake their way around the hall while the band played Kefauver's fight song, Vera fell in line to dance as enthusiastically as any of them. She had fun cheering and waving a banner which read, "The Women of America want Kefauver." It was a great lesson in mob psychology and a terrible let down when, after all their adolescent cavorting, Kefauver lost the nomination. Vera was crushed by the manipulation of the movers and shakers of the party who pushed a reluctant Adlai Stevenson onto the national stage, steamrollering Kefauver and his supporters. Delegates, carefully chosen, had come thinking the choice of the nominee was in their hands. Instead, they found they were superfluous. Democracy in party politics proved to be as elusive in national convention as it was in boss-controlled cities like Chicago. Machine politics prevailed everywhere.

It took weeks for her wounds to heal and for her to open up to Stevenson's charm. Ultimately, she took Stevenson's measure for herself and found him worthy. She became as ardent a campaigner for his election to the presidency as she was for her own election to the Board of Supervisors. As soon as the gavel sounded ending the convention, the Schultzes headed west to the home front. Vera needed to plunge into her own free-for-all. All the national attention being focused on her through the *Ladies' Home Journal* article about her being a woman delegate to the Democratic national convention, was bound to affect her non-partisan race for supervisor. Non-partisanship, corrupted by the very partisan national election and her open advocacy of the Democratic candidate, might seem incongruous to third district voters, to put it mildly.

Aware of her mounting reputation as a "comer," back in Marin her supporters were eager for her return. While she was at the convention, the *Mill Valley Record* wired that they wanted an interview as soon as she got home. Advance publicity about *The Ladies Home Journal's* article giving her national exposure was making her run for the Board of Supervisors much more significant. The hometown press wanted to trumpet her role in Marin. On the other hand, the business-oriented *Independent Journal* of San Rafael published in the second district, was not seduced by the national spotlight. It refused to endorse her even though it gave its blessing to Carmel Booth in her run against an incumbent who was a small San Rafael businessman. Most people county-wide read the *I.J.*, but Vera wasn't in a county-wide race. In the third district the *Mill Valley Record's* influence was a far more important channel to Vera's constituency.

The *Ladies Home Journal* article focusing attention on Marin County caused the Schultzes to be lionized by groups and individuals they had not known well before. Their social life picked up geometrically with every article that appeared about her in the papers. Their house was more and more frequently the location of huge cocktail parties which Vera hosted but hated. The vapid banalities that passed for conversation irritated her. Nevertheless, her wit and her charm scored success after success. She kept what Beth Ashley of the *Independent Journal* called her "1000 watt smile" sparkling and her amazingly retentive mind remembered names of new people for future encounters.

The two campaigns, waged simultaneously, required a prodigious amount of time and extemporaneous stump speaking. There were cocktail parties at Peacock Gap, at the Meadow Club, in private homes and public halls. Over great platters of hors d'oeuvres and glasses of bubbling champagne, she met the upper crust of Marin society. At chicken dinners in all the fraternal orders' clubhouses, church basements, and recreation centers, she rubbed shoulders with citizens lower on the social scale. Her mental acuity allowed her to shift subjects in all social strata as fast as each new person approached. Standing in high heels for endless hours tested her physical stamina. Luckily, Vera was blessed with amazing ruggedness. Had those parties not been so good for Ray's business, he would have balked at how much time he had to spend on her campaign. Instead, he threw himself into these affairs as far as his natural reticence allowed. Attending was good for his balance sheet.

While Vera was shaking hands like a centipede, and doing the luncheon circuit, her campaign managers, Margo Dick and Moishe David--another inmigrant of strong Democratic affiliations--put together one of the most energetic campaigns ever waged in Marin County. Door-to-door, street-by-street, volunteers carried Vera Schultz campaign literature to every house in town. A corps of dedicated volunteers eagerly talked about Vera's eight-plank platform for change and modernization. They drove up and down the narrow roads of Southern and Western Marin, ringing doorbells at the end of long lanes leading off the main roads. Or, at the tops of driveways in Sausalito and Mill Valley, too steep for anything but goats to climb.

New Marinites were easy to approach for they were eager to know more about the place they now called home, and about the issues Vera was confronting. They lauded the spunky little woman who had shown her mettle in the spring primary and was now bucking the entire phalanx of a hoary Establishment. Other enthusiasts included long-time Democrats whose party had never held a seat of any kind in county government but hoped that at last someone of their political persuasion would sit in the Supervisors' Chamber in San Rafael. Margo and Moishe kept their troops marching in cadence to the battle between the Illinois governor and the great war hero from Abilene.

Vera wore out several pairs of shoes tramping the hills, ringing doorbells, canvassing neighborhoods of the third district. She'd flash her sunny smile, hold out her hand and say, "My name is Vera Schultz and I'm running for the Board of Supervisors."*The Mill Valley Record* kept her name in the forefront of local news, almost daily, in spite of complaints from their Republican advertisers. As election day approached, she began to believe she was going to win.

THE ATTEMPTED BALLOT THEFT

Election day fell on the 4th of November. As soon as the polls opened, Vera cast her ballot, then started chauffeuring any and all who needed a ride to their polling places. She kept up a mad pace as long as the polls were open. When the polls closed, Vera went home exhausted but confident, to wait for election results on the radio. As the evening wore on, her lead was never enough to feel that sweep of exultation she itched to enjoy. At midnight, she had a wisp of a lead, 6,373 votes to Balzan's 6,211. By morning the margin had narrowed. By mid-morning her lead had dwindled to seven. The counting went on for days and on November 10 her lead had climbed back to 115. Still she could not celebrate. None of the absentee ballots had been counted and would not be until the 20th.

The absentee ballots were finally counted in the County Clerk's office on the 21st of November. She won by 170 ballots, 125 from the general election and 45 from the absentee ballots. The cork was out of the bottle and the celebration began. For days she wallowed in congratulations and basked in paeans of praise that arrived through notes, bouquets, editorials, and well-wishers who stopped her wherever she went to celebrate about her victory.

One week later, on the 28th of November, her soaring triumph plummeted into a slough of indignation. The Balzan organization filed with the Marin Superior Court for a recount. Recount? Vera was thunderstruck and her supporters were outraged. The county had never had a recount. On what grounds could there be fraud? The ballot boxes had been in the hands of Balzan's supporters ever since election day. After the initial shock, Vera lifted her chin, set her mouth in that determined line her opponents knew so well, and vowed she'd not be cheated out of her hard-earned victory without a fight.

Next morning, flanked by her attorney, Delger Trowbridge, and her old friend, Sam Gardiner, who had been a fellow delegate to the national convention in June, Vera marched into the courtroom in San Rafael to hear the reading of the petition for a recount of the ballots. The three of them had to stand silently by as Superior Court Judge Jordan L. Martinelli, father of Balzan's campaign manager, ordered the infamous recounting that would take place in the County Clerk's office where the ballots had been counted before. According to law, after the original count is complete, precinct envelopes containing election ballots are sealed with sealing wax before being sent to the County Clerk's office for safe-keeping.

The recount revealed tampering. No sealing wax had been affixed to any of the envelopes. They had been sealed with scotch tape across which nothing had been written. There was no way to know whether or not the envelopes had been reopened before the recount began. Sam Gardiner, who later became a superior court judge himself, Vera, and Del Trowbridge stationed themselves as close to the Clerk's desk as the Clerk allowed. There, one, or all of them, stood every day, all day, until it was done. On the second day of the recount, ballot envelopes from three precincts in Marin City amazingly held exactly 20 ballots per envelop more for Balzan than the original tally showed. According to the contents of those envelopes, Marin City had not cast as many ballots for president of the United States as it had for county supervisor. No other precinct showed such an overwhelming interest in the Supervisorial race.

Libby Gatov and Roger Kent's wife, Alice, immediately rounded up 28 other Democrats and headed for Marin City. On a rainy muddy night, when a fire on the hearth at home would have been much more appealing, they slogged through the wartime public housing going door-to-door. They canvassed those three precincts carrying affidavits Sam Gardiner had drawn up for the purpose. People, recorded in Jones' office as having voted for either one of the candidates for supervisor, were asked to state whether or not they had voted for supervisor at all. Many of them declared they had not and willingly signed the affidavit which said simply, "I voted for neither candidate for supervisor." Not all of the reputed voters could be reached and some were fearful. They were reluctant to become embroiled in a political battle among white folks which could have repercussions for them. They would not answer the question. But the group brought back enough signed affidavits to indicate chicanery. When the affidavits were handed to Jones, he laid them aside without comment.

Jones used a magnifying glass to scrutinize signatures while Vera's supporters watched from afar. He allowed no one close enough to track the tallying. On technicality after technicality, Vera's ballots were thrown out while not one challenge to a Balzan ballot was honored. If a corner was torn off, if there was a pin hole in the ballot, if an X had been drawn with a great flourish so that the Clerk could question which candidate's box it was supposed to fill, for any foolish little cause, Schultz ballots went into the discard basket. Finally, in the general election ballots, Vera was defeated. Only the absentee ballots remained to be recounted. Jones protested they'd been counted in his office the first time so there was no need to recount them, but Sam Gardiner stood his ground and insisted. Again, ballot after ballot for Vera Shultz was declared invalid and none for Balzan were discredited.

When the recounting of absentee ballots began, Vera had a margin of 45 votes; when it was finished the number had dwindled to 21. By those 21 votes, Vera Schultz squeaked into office. Pent-up tension among her supporters exploded in cries of joy but Vera was too limp with relief to rejoice. She should have taken the whole mess to court and charged Jones and his cohorts with election fraud, but she was out of funds. Years later, long after her tenure on the Board of Supervisors had ended, Vera said: "I recognize that I could never have been elected without support from both Democrats and Republicans, and it was forthcoming. I have always felt that the strength of, shall we say 'public work' in Marin County, our success as a county in making progress, has been due to the common ground that exists—about Marin County. We coalesce on these issues and we quite forget our political labels." In truth, the Supervisorial fight had not been about party, it had been about a woman's challenge to naked cracker-barrel, courthouse gang power.

The recount took so long Vera barely had time to collect her thoughts before the swearing-in ceremony of the first woman supervisor in Marin County was upon her. That morning, the Supervisors' Chamber was jammed with a jubilant standing-room-only crowd waiting to watch someone they would later call "First Lady of Marin" take the oath of office. Vera dressed carefully for the occasion, savoring her anticipated grand entrance into county government.

Vindictively, George Jones denied her her hour of adulation by waylaying her in the hall before she entered the chamber. He insisted on swearing her in then and there. She demurred. He persisted. She caved in. The meanest man in Marin County politics, by all accounts, cheated Vera and her supporters out of their moment of triumph. Why didn't she refuse? Why didn't she reward her friends and well-wishers by insisting that they be allowed their celebration? It was another of those instances when she "kept the peace," as she had done when the Mill Valley Council changed the rules to keep a woman from being Mayor. In both instances, there were bitterly disappointed women who thought she'd sold out.

Before the meeting, William Fusselman, also out in the hallway, was elected chairman of the Board. He made no mention of her when he opened the meeting. It was so demeaning, such a low-spirited snub, that some people indignantly walked out. Fred Bagshaw, whom she replaced, simply got up when Vera came in and gave her his seat at the long table behind which the supervisors sat. Vera, struggling to maintain her composure, quietly slipped into the proffered chair. At the time, Vera told herself she was saving her fire for more important targets, but in later years she rued her passivity. Ray was sick of campaign spending and of time away from his business. The idea of spending more money to sue powerful men because a woman had her feelings hurt was nonsense. So, Vera, for more domestic reasons than she was willing to admit, convinced herself that to insist on prescribed procedure was the wrong fight at the wrong time.

Once the meeting began, it took all of 10 minutes for conflict to flare and for it to become painfully obvious that her agenda was not the agenda of the four men on the Board. Further, it was obvious that the two agendas were on a collision course. The first frontal assault came over a spurious, trivial, and most unexpected issue. Jones, assuming an air of lethal innocence, called into question the right of the new supervisor from the third district to vote on any issue before the Board having to do with Insurance. Vera's husband was the Agent of Record for the county, a profitless responsibility he had carried for years. Agent of Record refers to that insurance agent, chosen by other agents belonging to the Association of Insurance Brokers, who places the county's insurance policies with various agencies in the county, but never his own. Agent of Record carries a certain aura of importance within the Insurance community, but nothing more. If Vera's right to vote on any issue having to do with insurance was rescinded, it could effectively cut her authority in half. Feeling emasculated, her husband immediately defused the situation by passing on the job to a different agent with a different Insurance firm.

Overnight, Vera's life virtually became divided: the weekend world of family, and her weekday political life in San Rafael. Each day brought a new challenge to the neophyte. All of the problems of her new job seemed to boil down to one of two things— money, or resistance to change. Vera, who considered herself a full time employee of the county, met herself coming and going. There were meetings on top of meetings. Meetings of governmental agencies during the day, meetings at night with citizen groups, meetings that ranged all the way from Grangers to "Mothers against..." or "Mothers for...."

At the second Board meeting, the most persistent battle of all battles was launched when the minutes of the previous meeting were read. There was no mention of the argument over the agent of record, or its resolution. Pre-Schultz minutes had been scant little jots and jittles, more like "Notes to Myself" or "The Way It Should Have Been." They revealed nothing of what had really transpired. Board minutes became the eternal issue because Vera tenaciously insisted on accurate, complete coverage of all discussions, as well as full disclosure of the final actions. Stubbornly, George Jones resisted. For the next eight years, the opening wrangle could take as long as 15 to 20 minutes. Her persistence was a burr under Jones' saddle. His hatred for her increased month by month. She not only quarreled over the minutes, she was always underfoot.

Vera didn't simply attend the Board meetings on Tuesday afternoons, and mind her own business the rest of the time as the other supervisors did. She was a daily presence in the Courthouse and in other government offices around San Rafael. Jones said she was "Snooping around, sticking her nose into things she didn't need to." He let everyone in the courthouse know how much he resented her presence. The stage had been all his before "that woman" burrowed into "my business." Boards of Supervisors, by law, meet once a week but Vera spent five full days every week in San Rafael. She was the county's first full-time supervisor.

To understand exactly what had been mandated and what had been done before she came on Board, she read minutes of committee meetings, annual reports, every document on file in the archives of every department. If a committee was embroiled in a controversy, or contemplating a new program, Vera attended its meetings until the issue was resolved. She met the staff in every county facility so she'd know the conditions under which they worked. She spent hours and hours in the court library researching the law on various issues, and reviewing past rulings of the court. She steeped herself in county government until she was the most informed authority on the subject in Northern California. Soon she was invited to other counties to talk about the creative possibilities of county government, and the limits.

Every commission established by the Board was made up of five members, one from each district. The committee person was appointed by the supervisor from that district. Vera appointed fellow Democrat, Margaret Azevedo, a member of the Marin Conservation League, to the County Planning Commission. Vera had read Margaret's articles on conservation in the *Mill Valley Record* and was impressed. Margaret Azevedo was Vera Schultz's gift to Mary Summers and the County Planning Commission. When interviewed for *The Bridge and The Building*, Margaret said about the years 1952-1960: "There was only one college graduate on the Board. One woman did it."

Did what? The catalog is long. In 1952, Marin County had not one single park, and no recreation program. Other towns in the county followed Mill Valley's lead and created their own, but there were no county programs in place for children's or adults' recreation outside the incorporated areas. Vera moved that the Board create a county parks and recreation commission and appoint citizens to serve on it who would define its goals for the future. The commission would be empowered to draw up a master plan for acquisition of land through condemnation, or by keeping parcels that had been confiscated because of default on taxes. Previously, confiscated parcels had been put on the market at rock-bottom prices for the benefit of developers and their friends who could make a killing from creating subdivisions. Fusselman and Jones opposed creating a new department that could deny the county—and their friends—such windfalls. Vera suspected that many windfalls went indirectly to Jones. From 1952 to 1954 the Board refused to bring her motion to a vote.

Nothing of significance happened until the famous "4-to-1" Board was in place after the 1954 elections. Jim Marshall, representing Point Reyes in the fourth district, was won over to Vera's view of the world as soon as she came on the Board, but William Gnoss, appointed to fill out an unexpired term in 1952, was more cautious. He listened and learned for two years before embracing Vera's ideas on good government. When elected in his own right in 1954, he lined up behind Vera and never deviated from her agenda, even when he and Walter Castro, who was elected for the first time in 1954, were left on the Board in 1960, as the minority opinion. Castro, a quick study, imbibed Vera's "good government" brew and became a stalwart for modernization. Castro, Gnoss, Marshall and Shultz—four solid votes against Fusselman and Jones. "Vera Schultz taught us both (Castro and Gnoss). She gave us vision. She had to change Castro over, but once he saw the need for change, he was the Rock of Gibraltar," Bill Gnoss said in 1971. "We didn't know much about government. We just wanted to do right by the county."

"Four-to-One" rang in Fusselman's ears for six long years.

"Four-To-One" was George Jones' albatross. Together, the two of them plotted and connived to break Vera's hold on the other members of the Board, but Vera was invincible. She had a clear-cut program of improvements that she articulated so cogently that the other three members of the "four" came to believe her program was their own.

Vera's Supervisorial work was not confined to Marin County. In 1953 she became the first woman supervisor to sit on the North Coast Counties Association of Supervisors (NCCA). When she arrived for the first meeting she was confronted by a sign in block letters on a piece of poster board some wag had hung over the entrance. It read, "No Women Allowed." It was obviously intended either to be cute or to intimidate and turn her away. Vera stopped dead in her tracks, retreating to a bench nearby where she sat shaken, talking to herself.

"Damn it! I am an elected official of the people," she scolded. "I am equal to any man in that room and this is my obligation."

Thoroughly aroused, she stormed into the hall and confronted the chairman.

"I'm Vera Schultz, Supervisor from Marin County." she challenged. "There's a sign outside that says 'No women allowed.' I may be a woman but I'm an elected official. Where am I supposed to go?"

"Why," the chairman said blandly, "we thought you'd like to go with the wives to the fashion luncheon. This is a men's club. No women allowed means no women allowed."

Whirling on her heel, Vera went back to the entrance, pulled down the sign, and carried it into the hall. Standing before the head table, Vera wordlessly tore the sign in half and laid it in front of the chairman. Still saying nothing, she spun on her heel and strode through stunned silence to the section of the table marked "Marin County." She sat down and opened her briefcase. "Vera could be feisty when her dander was up," said Ed Ryken about another matter years later.

From that day on, she had no trouble being a political woman among political kingpins. She pitched into the work of the North Coast Counties Supervisors Association with all the zest she brought to any organization. Soon, she was heading committees and making reports, completely at home in this male preserve. The men were learning that sex plays no part in competence. Elected secretary-treasurer for two terms, as well as being appointed a member of the NCCSA's water committee, Vera proved herself superbly.

The men on the Marin County Board of Supervisors were also being taught that competence and persistence, two indispensable qualities of a leader who makes things happen, are gender neutral. All she needed was a majority of votes to legislate her program and after 1954 she had a majority. Two years after it should have happened, a Parks and Recreation Department was established and from then on, great parcels of land were safe-guarded by the county. Land was one of the two thorniest problems of those years, taxes was the other.

In 1956, Vera led the "4-to-1" majority into a battle over land that made Fusselman and Jones foam at the mouth. Well north of downtown Tiburon, the Navy owned a piece of land it wanted to unload. Vera, and the Marin Conservation League, salivated over the prospect. Parks and Recreation and the Conservation League petitioned the Board to buy the Navy's lovely bay front. Vera promptly transformed the petition into a motion that the county not only acquire the Navy's waterfront but also acquire the Muir Woods Overlook that was also on the market at that time. Hoping to block passage of the motion, her opposition labeled her, "Spendthrift." They urged that those prime parcels be acquired, then offered to the private sector as a source of revenue for the county. Vera beat off their attack and, "4-to-1," the county took both treasures of land for parks and open space. Fusselman and Jones added another item to their laundry list of "extravagances" to be used against her when the next election rolled around.

When developers tried to move in on the south and east shores of Richardson Bay, Vera moved that a Richardson Bay Development Plan be drawn up by the county planning commission. As part of a flood control plan, the county could encircle the Bay with recreation space by connecting the south and east shoreline with the shoreline controlled by Mill Valley. Vera envisioned public and private boat harbors ringing the bay in some distant future, and perhaps a return of ferry service from Richardson Bay to communities around San Francisco Bay. The plan was drawn up, the Board of Supervisors voted to approve it, and the State of California allocated $600,000 for the dredging. That $600,000 was the carrot that brought Fusselman in line on a land issue for once. Richardson Bay's shoreline became a lovely oasis in a rapidly developing urban setting. For 25 years, it was protected and none of its shoreline fell into private hands.

But all those acquisitions were expensive. The need for additional revenue brought Vera into conflict with George Hall, the County Assessor. The root cause of the shortage of funds was not the acquisition of land but the low assessments on property belonging to friends of the old guard throughout the unincorporated areas of the county. Assessments on new Marinites who dared to move in and raise their voices in civic affairs were stiff. A mushrooming community is always a cauldron of competing forces, especially as new people want changes older residents don't. A self-satisfied cow county wanted nothing from government except to be let alone. The newcomers wanted modernization, services, and an end to privilege.

Hall penalized the newcomers for their uppity attitudes saying they should be the ones to pay for the improvements they thought they were entitled to. New taxpayers sometimes paid five times as much property tax as older residents though they lived in houses of identical worth. The inmigrants, those settling outside Mill Valley, began demanding equalization in tax rates and an end to the "viewing and assessing" method used by George Hall for establishing their property taxes. Their cry was loud enough for the Grand Jury to hear and take up the issue. Hall knew that "that woman" was behind the Grand Jury probe that burrowed into the assessor's tax rolls. When the Grand Jury censored him, he was furious.

Hall had always been a popular fellow around Marin. A garrulous ham, he showed up at every "opening" from a new Laundromat to a full-blown shopping mall. He arrived with funny hats, lots of balloons and cigars. He shook hands with everyone, kissed the babies, chucked little girls under the chin, and heavy-handedly flattered all the ladies like a vaudeville politician. He attended every school event, clam bake, or garden show around the county and checked all the bulletin boards in the grocery stores for garage sales he might drop in on. So far as anyone knew, he had only one enemy: William Fusselman. Fusselman hated Hall's disdain for the Board and his disregard for the official chain of command, i.e., Chairman Bill Fusselman. Hall felt that having been *elected* assessor, his office was somehow set apart from the supervisors' supervision and censure meant nothing to him. He blithely ignored the Grand Jury intending, as usual, to glad-hand his way out of the mess by going over the heads of the jury to the populace. He reminded taxpayers that they were being threatened with higher taxes. A stalemate ensued which only the Board could break.

By custom, any department head requesting an increase in his department's budget was granted a separate conference with the Board of Supervisors to discuss the request. Those conferences could be held only with the full Board present. All requests had to be accompanied by a letter of justification, backed by facts and figures that substantiated the need for the requested budgetary increases. In 1954, George Hall requested seven additional assessors because of the building boom that had been under way for eight years. With few exceptions, the appraisers already on staff were his friends and relatives. He felt assaulted when he presented what he thought was a routine request for increased staff only to have the one woman—Vera—demand concessions in return for an increase in budget.

If we were to grant you these additional employees would you be willing to use the State's measure of value in assessing?" she asked.

Without pause came a flat, negative response. The "4-to-1" Board, plus William Fusselman who was on Vera's side for a second time, turned down his request.

George Hall again was furious. It was unmitigated gall, he said, for five people elected by the same electorate who elected him to attempt to question the methodology he employed in the administration of his domain. Bursting with indignation, he went to the Grand Jury to demand an inquiry into the legality of interference by one group of elected officials into the work of another elected servant of the people. Each Supervisor was called before the Grand Jury individually to explain her/his objection to the way Hall was assessing property in Marin. When it was Vera's turn to sit down with the Jury she laid out for them what her experience had been with Hall's appraisals in Mill Valley. The Grand Jury found Mr. Hall's refusal to use the state's measure tantamount to insubordination. They directed the District Attorney to ascertain whether there was a legal loophole Hall could slip through or not. There was none. The District Attorney found Hall guilty of refusing to comply with a higher authority.

Now came a Punch and Judy Show of the first order. The Grand Jury ordered that a county-wide reappraisal be carried out immediately. George Hall made no move to do it. Editorials in all the county papers began to take up the issues of equity and change. There were town hall meetings and letter-writing campaigns. Bombarded from all sides, Hall finally agreed to involve the State Board of Equalization in carrying out the directives of the Grand Jury.

The Board of Equalization spent large sums of state funds to set up the mechanism whereby every inch of the county was reassessed. The cost ran into the millions, forced higher by the recalcitrance of some old-time Marinites who resisted signing the reappraisal forms they received. Though they knew they'd been underpaying for years, they resented what was in store for them now. That assessment took over two years and the new rolls were not ready for use in issuing tax bills until January 1958. With the oversight committee keeping the public informed about the current progress of the reappraisal, the spotlight was unrelentingly on Hall.

When the appraisers finished their work, Hall adamantly refused to use the new rolls. The Board of Supervisors threatened him with court action if he didn't. When he still refused, the sheriff was sent to Hall's office to remove the old assessment rolls and replace them with the new ones. When the sheriff entered the assessor's office, Hall could not find the keys to the file cabinets. Neither could his secretary. Disgruntled, the sheriff went back to the supervisors for further instructions.

As the sheriff headed for the Board of Supervisors' chambers, Hall hurriedly appealed to the courts. Judge Martinelli and his cronies could usually find a loophole he could wiggle through when he was in a tight pinch. Martinelli didn't dare help him this time; the county assessor was in defiance of the State of California Board of Equalization. The sheriff's office then made an end run around the scuffle. They walked into the Assessor's Office with a dolly, rolled the locked cabinets out, rolled in others containing the newly prepared assessments, and left the keys to the new file cabinets on Hall's desk. Hall literally wept when he found himself outmaneuvered.

The following June, Hall was voted out of office and Bert Broemmel, a supporter of Vera's, someone who would go to great lengths to support her, was voted in. Broemmel wasted no time in using the new assessment rolls to prepare the 1958 tax bills and get them in the mail. Little could he know that in mailing those revised tax bills he set in motion the demise of Vera Schultz, woman supervisor, agent for change, champion of equity, "good government kook," — and the instigator of many tax bills five times higher than they had been. Outraged cries of "rape" went up. Vera's popularity plummeted. In 1960 they got even with the "Good Government Goddess." Her political career was permanently derailed by reassessment, and by the magnificent architectural triumph designed by Wright which was about to be erected at Santa Venetia.

Because Marin's county government was parceled out to 13 different locations, a county employee could claim mileage to go from one place to another. County records were stored here, there and yonder. Relevant records about an issue involving more than one department were filed in multiple locations. Vera insisted that a county administrator and centralized housing would produce light years of efficiency over the waste in time and money such fragmentation produced. One without the other would be a half solution, she said. Within weeks of being seated Vera submitted solutions to these dual needs in two proposals to the Board. The first of the two ensuing battles waged was over centralization.

Before Vera's election, the County Planning Department was ordered to prepare an analysis of additional space requirements the county needed at that time, and to make projections about future requirements. Apart from the Planning Commission, a group of irate citizens demanded something be done, and formed an ad hoc committee to do it. That committee brought pressure to bear on the Supervisors until the Planning Commission was mandated to hire Louis J. Kroeger & Associates, a San Francisco firm of consultants, to do the needed space study. Their report came in months before the 1952 elections so that Vera was not involved in the issue prior to becoming a supervisor. According to Kroeger & Co., more than twice as much office space as the county was occupying needed to be built.

Kroeger & Associates projected that the population of Marin would double in the next 18 years. That meant that if the needs of a mere two decades of continued growth were met, more than twice the square footage of office space currently in use would be necessary. The consulting firm further advocated finding a building site large enough for a new government center to bring all the parts together, facilitating greater flexibility and efficiency. The piece of land acquired should also be large enough to put in ample parking lots for county employees, the public, and parking space for the county's vehicles. That report had been accepted, but no action had been taken about implementing it or denying it before Mrs. Schultz became Supervisor Schultz.

In addition to land acquisition to meet government needs, the county needed to acquire more acreage for other purposes. Annually, the county leased the Marin Art and Garden Club in Ross for two weeks in order to hold a county fair. The California State Constitution mandates that each county *must* have a County Fair and as the population grew the Marin Art and Garden Center facilities were increasingly too small. Before the Kroeger Report came out advocating a new courthouse site, a Fairgrounds Committee was established to seek a new fairgrounds site. The two needs were in competition with each other for immediate solution. Wherever could the county find two large pieces of ground for two such different uses?

Since the Marin County Fair had always been exclusively about plants and art, food and handicrafts, if the exhibits and scope of the fair were to be expanded—and the growing crowds accommodated—more space was required. The expansion plans did not include a midway or a stadium, so the land area of a typical county fair would not be needed. Therefore, was it possible that the solution to these two needs rested in finding one piece of property large enough for both facilities? A Civic Center-Fairgrounds Site Committee was formed under the aegis of the Planning Commission. The new site committee brought together a powerful triumvirate of women: Caroline Livermore, the transplanted Texan whose position in the county was similar to that of an Adeline Kent clone, Mary

Summers, the planner-conservationist department head, and Vera Schultz, candidate for the Board of Supervisors.

Caroline Livermore had come from Texas as a bride in 1930 and quickly immersed herself in the art and garden world of Marin. In 1943, when an old magnolia tree in Ross, older than the town itself, was threatened with bulldozers, Caroline, in typical Marin fashion, organized a committee to save the tree and the gardens around it. Having saved the tree, its continued protection led to the founding of the Marin Art and Garden Center, one of the county's most treasured organizations. As for Mary Summers, in 1941 Hugh Pomeroy went off to war leaving the brand new post of Director of Planning empty. Across the bay in Contra Costa County they had a woman Planning Director. With men being swallowed up in the Armed Forces, Marin County grudgingly hired its first woman executive, Contra Costa's Mary Summers. Mary headed up the Planning Department for twenty years. In 1961 she resigned rather than be fired by the "Three Caballeros" of the new 3-to-2 Board of Supervisors who cavalierly rode rough-shod over the county after they got rid of George Jones' nemesis, Vera Schultz.

From the hour of its formation, the new site committee was up against an unyielding wall of resistance coming out of the County Clerk's office. Never mind that there wasn't a vacant piece of ground anywhere in San Rafael large enough for the county's dual needs. Never mind that parking was constantly a problem with county offices spread out as they were. Never mind that the county jail was overcrowded and antiquated and also needed to be relocated outside San Rafael. George Jones found the idea of going outside San Rafael, his habitual stomping grounds, to get to work personally insulting and absolutely out of the question. Czars don't move around. People, and the buildings that house them, are put where powerful men want them.

Fusselman was as irritated as Jones about the threatened change of location, but he was aware that things could not continue as they were. He had an idea. Why not build two wings onto the courthouse to rise like towers on either side. The jail could be on the top floors of one of the towers with departments, now scattered willy-nilly wherever empty space could be found, collected and housed under the jail and in the other tower. Then the site committee could look for a smaller parcel of land to solve their remaining land requirements. He even succeeded in getting a special election called so the citizens could approve his idea by voting for the bonds needed to build his fancied additions to the courthouse.

The ballot measure was so constructed that citizens had to choose among three separate courses of action: 1) No bonds, do nothing, let inefficiency reign; 2) Add two wings to the present courthouse thereby reducing the number of scattered offices, but not addressing the problems of parking or the Fairgrounds; and 3) approve bonds for a totally new site away from San Rafael. In that election the citizens thunderously voted for Number One. They still didn't want indebtedness of any kind and they said so loudly and clearly in Letters to the Editor of the *Independent Journal.* To forestall any action at all, the pre-Schultz Board adopted a Pay-As-You-Go plan. They levied a 40 cents per $100 assessed value property tax to accumulate until the funds were in hand for site acquisition and construction. At 40 cents on the hundred, it would take years to accrue the needed sum. Meanwhile, the Clerk and his ally would remain happily ensconced in San Rafael for many moons. What they overlooked was that, at the rate new homes were being built in Marin, those funds would accrue rapidly.

Enter Vera Schultz, the good government kook, the reformer, "That Woman!" She immediately urged that a new site committee, endowed with "teeth," be appointed by the Board. Against the opposition of Jones and Fusselman, 3 to 2 (Schultz, Gnoss and Marshall) the Board voted the new site committee into being, and gave it a definite mandate to recommend a specific property for purchase by the county. That act of defiance should have notified Fusselman and Jones that "the old order passeth, a new order cometh to birth." This time the issue of new housing for county government was going to be bulldogged through.

Once formed, the site committee scoured central Marin for a piece of land close to Highway 101 that would be suitable for a Civic Center. In June of 1953 they came to the Board with their choice: the Scettrini property in Santa Venetia. The Board voted 3 to 2, to offer the Scettrinis $237,000 for the land. Fusselman and Jones were dead set against it. By one frustrating tactic after another Fusselman managed to delay action until the stipulated time set by the Scettrinis for acceptance expired. In 1954, the price of $377,000 was offered, and again obstructionist tactics prevented completion of the purchase. For two years, refusing to accept any conclusion as final, the Daring Duo, in cahoots with the Taxpayer's Association, an exceedingly well-heeled organization with fewer than 12 members, managed to prevent purchase of the property. Finally, in April of 1956, at a cost of $551,416, the County of Marin acquired the 60-acre parcel on which the Marin County Civic Center now stands.

The county bought the adjacent 140 acres as land for the Fairgrounds. Some of the Fairgrounds' purchase price, $233,000, came from the State of California's pari-mutuel fund which had been set aside to be used for county fairgrounds. By then, "Pay As You Go" had produced the purchase price in full. There'd be no bonds. The site committee disbanded, setting the stage for the next act: planning a building and securing an architect. There was no respite from tension, for other problems were brewing which would now take center stage.

Due to the burgeoning exodus of people from America's cities to the suburbs nationally in the 1950s, the immediate rural areas around San Francisco were being overrun. Developers swarmed over Marin's lovely landscape gouging out hills, filling in swamps, bulldozing trees, overburdening the existing utilities and gorging the country roads with traffic, all at county expense and without regard for the environmental hazards they were creating. Any effort by the County Planning Department to curtail their cavalry charge across Marin's hills met with implacable resistance from developers and their henchmen, Fusselman and Jones.

Contractors did not want regulations about soil compacting, septic tanks, adequate drainage, or any of the other restrictions that were good for the county but cut into their profit. Under the callous control of the courthouse by a greedy

156

few, anyone who greased the right palm—and all indications were that that palm belonged to George Jones—could have his way with the land. The old pork barrel politics of the Fourth Street Gang had been made possible mainly through the two juiciest sources of largesse at their disposal: land and roads. When every supervisor was the road commissioner for her or his district, he or she could award contracts, approve new projects, do the district's purchasing and let a little of the fat trickle through his or her own fingers. It was expected. After all, the supervisors weren't paid very much, and one hand rubs the other.

Though Vera worked five days a week and most nights for the same money as the rest, she thought the system corrupt and unacceptable. She began hammering away at the waste, the inefficiency, the inequity, the high-handedness of elected representatives who took their responsibilities too lightly and fed at the trough. She argued for the establishment of a code of ethics, and a public works department which could enforce it. An engineer should be hired, she said, who was qualified to oversee the builders voraciously beetling their way through the woods of Marin and that person must be given the authority to stop any renegade contractor in his tracks. The howl that went up was deafening, but Vera didn't hear it. "Four-to-One," the Board voted to centralize authority over land and roads and take the literal ground out from under Jones and Co.

A public works department was created. Marvin Brigham, who had come to California just before World War II sporting a degree in civil engineering from the University of Nebraska, was hired to be the director. He immediately ruled that when a street was torn up to put in utilities for new subdivisions, that street had to be repaired by the developer with the same materials as those removed. No throwing a little tar and gravel in the trench which of course sank after the first rainy season. For years, Brigham's life was made miserable by contractors who connived to thwart regulations designed to protect the public from their greed. Brigham was an even more determined fighter than Vera. He could not be bribed, cajoled, threatened, browbeaten or intimidated. His obstinacy was somehow laid at the feet of Vera Schultz.

157

Another of Vera's platform planks, which needed to be inaugurated before they moved on to the Civic Center project, was to put the administration of county government into the hands of a professional administrator. Not only did supervisors write contracts for supplies and services in their respective districts, but every department of the government did its own purchasing from paper clips to gasoline for county vehicles. Every little town and every school district went into the market place for what it needed and paid full price at the taxpayer's expense. The plethora of contracts created waste, inefficiency, and, too frequently, corruption.

Still ardent for city managers and county administrators Vera proposed that the county hire a professional to oversee, direct and coordinate the various departments of the government, and to establish centralized purchasing for all. Such rich pork barreling was not to be relinquished without a fight, and fight Jones and Fussselman did. The battle waged over the centralization of authority in the office of an administrator lasted over four long years. Finally, after the 1956 elections failed to unseat any of the four of the "4-to-1" majority, the Board established the office of County Administrator, and young Donald Jensen was hired to fill the position.

Jensen had some of that "vision" Gnoss talked about getting from Vera. Jensen's ideas called for serious surgery on departments, and serious cauterizing of the budget to stop the seepage of funds into private pockets. Fusselman and Jones, intervened to hamstring him by convincing the men on the Board that it was unwise to give one person so much power. They insisted that every decision made be subject to review. In spite of Vera's arguments, the review process was voted into the procedures for overseeing the Administrator. The power the old guard had always exercised over their individual fiefdoms was protected. Sandbagging action through the review process was the instrument with which they tried to guard their self-assigned prerogatives. Jensen, like Brigham, was tough. Despite the foot-dragging and harassment he experienced, most procedures were streamlined, and fat was trimmed off contracts.

One of the juiciest morsels of previous pork barreling was job patronage. Jensen sat down with the new personnel commission to hammer out a method of selecting employees based on merit similar to that used by the national civil service. To that commission, Vera appointed her old League pal, her fellow advocate from League lobbying days in Sacramento, Fern Andrews. A consultant was hired to draw up a questionnaire to be filled out by applicants and a test that would weed out the less qualified among them. Henceforth, anyone going to work for Marin County would be worthy of their hire and obligated to no one. A salaried committee took over the hiring of all non-elective or non-appointive county personnel.

Centralized purchasing came next. Standardized forms for requisitioning supplies through the administrator's office resulted in all departments being supplied with the same items purchased in bulk at wholesale prices. One set of county vehicles, one gasoline storage area, one maintenance shop. It was amazing how much waste had gone unchallenged. As for roads, long paved driveways on private property to houses set far back from county roads were no longer constructed at taxpayers' expense. Roads were repaired where repairs were needed. Centralized purchasing and a public works department made it easier for the citizens of Marin to see where their tax dollars were going. Vera chortled over every success her plan produced.

Some of her ideas about government were too advanced for a county just emerging from the 19th century. One of her ideas, born before its time, is now back for reconsideration in other counties around California, the idea of a County Charter. A charter gives a county self-rule. Mandates from the state are no longer mandates, they are only suggestions. Down in Santa Clara County, Caspar Weinberger, a member of the state legislature when Vera was a League advocate in Sacramento, was touting the charter movement on a local PBS TV program he hosted. Vera consulted with Weinberger who was as Republican as Vera was Democratic. Weinberger was bright, thoughtful, and as addicted to "good government" choices as she was, and that was all that mattered to Vera.

In 1953, Vera presented her Charter ideas to the Board and the Board hired an attorney to assist a "Citizens' Committee for Charter Development." Months of work produced a charter that the National League of Municipalities hailed as the best available at that time. Three men set out to kill the idea, two attorneys and a Realtor. They detonated all hopes for its adoption by going after the support of those who then held offices that would be eliminated if the charter transformed county government as it stood. The charter never reached the voters for their approval. All of her life Vera was certain that charter counties are the most democratic and effective way to govern.

To further block favoritism, she proposed that Marin County have its own legal counselor, not one appointed "case by case" by the courts. The use of the "case by case" method used by the Martinelli court, when the litigant or the defendant was a crony of George Jones or Ed Butler (former county judge and precursor of Jones as county boss) or Bill Fusselman, meant an especially friendly counsel was chosen—friendly to the crony not the county. Grand juries were strait-jacketed by the court before they began deliberation. Vera wanted a permanent county counsel chosen by the Board of Supervisors who could not be dismissed because his decisions were politically incorrect. By a 4 to 1 vote, the independent Office of County Counsel was established and a bright young attorney was hired to fill the post. His head would roll as soon as Vera was defeated for reelection, but, for as long as he served, Leland Jordan, the first county counsel, stood guard over responsible jurisprudence in county affairs.

MARIN CITY

The biggest, sweetest land deal on the horizon in the early '50s was Marin City. It consisted of three hundred and sixty acres of priceless real estate, a beautiful bowl surrounded by steep hills just north of Sausalito. The view from those hill terraces is dazzling. The floor of the bowl is not flat but slightly rolling, making it an attractive setting for a big shopping center, a high school, low-cost public housing, all the things Vera envisioned for it. Before the federal government took it over in 1942, through the instrument of "The Right to Public Domain" laws, the area was occupied by a big dairy operation. In 1943, the Navy needed one more shipyard on the shores of San Francisco Bay to build Liberty Ships for the invasion of Japan. Richardson Bay at Sausalito was the last deep-water waterfront left around San Francisco Bay on which to build. The federal government negotiated with Marin County and with the dairy owners to take over the entire property. The plan was to build temporary housing for shipyard workers coming from the lower midwest and the deep south to build Liberty Ships for the Bechtel Corporation.

Blacks and whites, a potentially explosive mix of people in the Jim Crow climate areas from which they came, during the war years lived peacefully side by side in Marin City. One grocery store, one community center, one school, the same playgrounds, and the same public toilets served all. Almost no visible tension or resentment developed as long as the two races were equal in number and received the same pay for the same civilian war work. When the war ended the whites fled. The blacks couldn't flee. The blacks couldn't go back home because mechanization of agriculture had taken place during the war. Field hands had been replaced by machines. Subrosa community covenants kept the blacks locked in their social and cultural cul de sac. The county faced a dilemma.

Nothing happened for eight long years after war's end as a post-war building boom hit Marin. Neighborhood covenants enforced by real estate agents kept the blacks from benefiting from the increase in available housing. But in 1953, the Department of Defense started closing down World War II

161

facilities all over the country. Land pre-empted for military use was returned to local governments. Developers' most pie-in-the-sky fantasies seemed close to becoming reality. Was Marin City about to go on the block? Fifteen minutes from San Francisco. Five minutes from the Golden Gate Bridge. Three minutes from the Sausalito yacht harbor. Right on Highway 101! Out your door and into the office in 30 minutes or less! Investors drooled over the prospects. However, it would take more than money up front to get all of that land. It would take inside contacts to have a go at it.

The laws of pre-emption required that pre-empted land first be offered to the people from whom it had been taken. If original owners wanted to buy it back, they had first option. If the original owners no longer lived, didn't want it, or had "gone to Hawaii," the local government would be next in line. If the local government didn't want it, then, and only then, would it be thrown onto the open market. The original owner was Golden Gate Farms. Relocated over 13 years earlier, the dairy was not interested in buying back land that would have to be cleared, then left fallow for at least a year in order for meadows to be reestablished. Furthermore, Marin City would be reassessed at much higher tax rates. Golden Gate Farms said, "No, thank you." The federal government moved to step two, Marin County.

Notified that Marin City was to be returned to them if they wanted it, the Board of Supervisors established a Marin City committee to draw up proposals for its development. Though the land lay in Vera's district, Fusselman wanted another member of the Board to be the chairman. Vera protested. Annoyed at being challenged, he grudgingly conceded. But it was another nail in Vera's coffin. Jones told the Board he had buyers in the offing prepared to purchase the entire property. The sale would be a financial windfall for the county, he argued. Vera had other ideas, big ideas that would keep the people already in Marin City where they were and in much improved circumstances. She wanted an integrated city built there, a town about which Marin County could take pride. She insisted that the Board create guidelines governing the platting and selling of lots, and allow for competitive bidding for construction. When the Marin City committee began to meet, it was quickly apparent that some of the people who had volunteered to serve on that committee had done so in order to quash any plan that required racial integration, at least in their world.

Ignoring the public outcry, the committee, under Vera's leadership, drew up a plan that would provide low cost housing on the disputed land to replace the decaying wartime housing. Tiers of lots rising above the valley floor would be platted so that elevation determined size and cost. The topmost lots, those with panoramic views of both the Pacific Ocean and San Francisco Bay, would necessarily go to the wealthiest buyers. She hoped the middle tiers of lots, those with bay side views only, would be sold to salaried professionals and managerial types. On the lowest tier of the hillsides she envisioned homes modest enough in price to offer housing for blue collar wage-earners. Vera wanted integration of class as well as race, a microcosm of American society. The disgruntled members of the committee who opposed integration left, but other members of the committee, charmed by her notions, wanted to buy in Marin City themselves and be part of an experiment in interracial living.

For weeks, Vera's letters to Housing and Home Finance in Washington D.C. to expedite the transference of Marin City to the county went unanswered. Jones kept talking about how much money these grandiose plans would cost the county, money out of the taxpayers' wallets. He droned on and on about "great profits" if the county put it on the market. Impatient with deleterious paper shuffling, Vera put in a call to the chairman of Housing and Home Finance in Washington.

"If you are not going to relinquish Marin City to the County of Marin would you tell me so?" she asked.

"You had better come to Washington," was the reply.

At her own expense, Vera caught a flight out that night. Next morning, when she appeared at the Housing and Home Finance Office to remind the agency of its obligation to turn over the land to the County of Marin, she was politely waved aside, dismissed. They had dismissed the wrong lady. Furious, Vera headed directly for Estes Kefauver's office. Ushered into his presence, she threw her problem into his lap. "I need your help," she fumed. "We can't let this happen."

Kefauver reached for the phone. He made one call and Vera got a lesson in how people in Washington respond to a voice from the Hill. Doors to Housing and Home Finance opened like magic. The next day, Vera attended a meeting of the full membership of HHF. Loaded with copies of all her own letters, copies of official communications from the Board of Supervisors to Housing and Home Finance, and committee reports from the Marin County Planning Commission, Vera arrived early. She sat down at the highly polished table next to HHF's attorney and the invisible thread of circumstance, which Vera believed works in most human affairs, took over.

Members lolled around the highly polished table, waiting in silence for the meeting to begin. Spread out before the Housing and Home Finance attorney was a series of letters from George Jones written on county stationery. Without a by-your-leave, Vera picked up one after another and read them all as the attorney silently watched. Those letters requested that HHF ignore any communications from the Board of Supervisors. Jones assured them he had a buyer for the land who would pay the government above current value for the whole of Marin City. Such a sale, he argued, would be a boon both to the federal government and for Marin County.

What current value? Who was to establish that value? With Jones determining through George Hall what that current price would be, it was going to be a rip-off for the federal government and Marin County. If the government yielded to his seduction, Jones would be on his way to a bonanza land deal like none before. There never was an inquiry into George Jones' manipulation of county lands for his own profit, but if there had been, Vera was sure Jones would have gone to prison.

When she read the last letter, Vera went through the ceiling. She upbraided and educated the officials present about the law governing returns of government property to the private sector. Home and Housing relinquished the problematic cul-

164

de-sac and its circle of protective hills to Marin County without further delay.

In all the accolades showered on Vera over the ensuing years, this incredible achievement has rarely been mentioned.

Still smoldering when she got back to Marin, she couldn't wait to confront Jones at the next Board meeting. As soon as the minutes were read and approved, she angrily laid copies of the letters Jones had written to Washington on the table before the other Board members. With all the fiery eloquence at her command, she blisteringly castigated the county clerk. She stormed at him for going over the heads of the Supervisors, usurping their authority. She berated him for even considering a land deal to which the Board had not given sanction. She didn't stop until Jones was beet red and the rest of the Board was fidgeting in their chairs. When she finally finished, Jones sat silent saying nothing in his own defense. Instead of the censure she'd expected, the men merely scolded him for using official county stationery for his private correspondence.

In 1956, the newly-acquired community was turned over to the newly-created Marin County Redevelopment Foundation, the first such county agency linking redevelopment with housing authority to be established in the state of California. The people of Marin City were invited to sit down with the new agency and the County Planning Commission to create their new town. Three thousand people were still living in wartime housing that was falling down around their ears. They spent their money in Marin, sent their children to Marin schools, were the county's house cleaners, gardeners, bottle washers, janitors, maids, chauffeurs, delivery men—the help for families and businesses alike. Certainly, they shouldn't be evicted and pushed out of the county. Housing shortages still existed all over the Bay Area and rents were sky high. Though covenants were illegal after 1948, discrimination nevertheless prevailed. Real estate agencies had their own sub rosa convenants from Maine to California.

Aaron Green, of the Frank Lloyd Wright Foundation in San Francisco, was contracted to design eight multiple-resident units for public housing. Those apartment buildings have been occupied continuously since their initial occupancy with less vandalism than public housing usually suffers. The town plans, wonderful in concept, were based on misguided assumptions about the willingness of people to integrate. Though very little of that plan was developed it was awarded the seventh Annual Design Award for Community Planning by *Progressive Architecture.* When Vera left the Board of Supervisors in 1960, she was named to the Marin County Redevelopment Foundation Board and continued to struggle with Marin City's problems for many years. Aside from the eight low-cost housing apartments that Aaron Green designed, only 200 units of the plan were built and none of the community buildings. While Vera and her colleagues might be ready for an integrated future, Marin was stuck in the segregated past.

VERA AND RONALD REAGAN

In 1958, a Democrat ran for the office of governor and won. Pat Brown had charisma and made promises. His personality and his post-war progressive program elected him. One of the things he promised was to establish a Consumer's Advocate Department. No state agency existed to protect customers from the incomprehensible fine print of purchase agreements. The law in California stated that if a consumer fell behind in his/her payments, the object purchased, whether it be a car or a casserole, could be repossessed and resold. Though someone else now possessed the object and was also paying for it, the original buyer had to pay off the balance of his indebtedness. Brown wooed Helen Nelson from Marin to become the states' Consumer Counsel under the new industrial relations department, the first such official in the entire United States. As Consumer Counsel, Helen wrote the "four rights of consumers" now known as the Consumer's Bill of Rights. Under her leadership, a law was passed nullifying the practice of double billing for returned goods. A faulty piece of merchandise could be returned and the customer's money refunded.

When Ronald Reagan ran for governor in 1968, he promised that, if elected, the first thing he'd do would be to "fire Helen Nelson." Elected, he did just that. From the moment they were first introduced, Vera and Reagan had clashed. When he fired Helen, Vera headed for Sacramento. She cornered him in the hallway of the capitol before he could take to his heels and cried: "Governor, what have you done? For shame! After all Helen Nelson has done for the people of California!" Reagan walked away stony-faced without answering. Years later, when he was president of the United States and she was at the White House to attend a meeting of the National Council on Aging, Reagan didn't recognize her presence. He never forgot and neither did she.

MARIN HIRES FRANK LLOYD WRIGHT

In spite of the plethora of issues before the Board in the mid '50s, the biggest issue of all during Vera's second term was the long-delayed development of the Scettrini property. A Civic Center Committee made up of employees of the County was established by the Board in 1956. Mary Summers, head of the Planning Commission; Leon de Lisle, County Auditor; Donald Jensen, County Administrator; and Leland Jordan, County Counsel, made up the membership. The CCC was empowered to select an architect. For almost two years, 1956 and well into 1957, with their county credit cards in hand, the Civic Center Committee traveled around the state looking at government buildings and office complexes in search of a style that would fit their community, as well as an architect to design it. Twenty-six different architects were screened and sent on to the Board of Supervisors for their consideration.

Bill Fusselman insisted the architect be a home-grown product, even some new hotshot architect residing in the county would do. Architectural fees should be kept at home. George Jones wanted someone who would design a no-nonsense, no-frills, low cost, square building, plain, severe and what he called "governmental looking." Mary Summers, Planning Commission chairman, favored a cluster of buildings like a campus to be spread out over the property. At the end of a year and a half, they were no closer to a decision than they had been when they started.

Richard Neutra, southern California architect, who was putting up spare, square, igloo-white Santa Barbara-style homes along the coast from Laguna Beach to Newport Beach and whose hospitals and government buildings were being tagged "modern architecture," brought a model to San Rafael that pleased Jones and Fusselman. Vera stared glassy-eyed at its impersonal stark lines. Whose idea was it to invite Frank Lloyd Wright to submit a plan was a matter of controversy then, and has never been resolved. Mary Summers? Engineer Harold Summers, Mary's husband? Vera Schultz? Every written account agrees with Vera and says the idea came on an idle New Year's Day when Vera sat reading *House Beautiful.*

House Beautiful carried an article about some of Frank Lloyd Wright's newest designs and the impact they were having on other architects. The article dealt with his ideas about organic architecture and its relationship to the physical environment. Vera's imagination was ignited. Why not bring America's foremost architect to Marin to create something uniquely "organic" on the Scettrini property. Excited by the idea, she hurried to the phone to call Mary Summers.

"Mary!" she exclaimed when she heard Summers' voice, "Why can't we have Frank Lloyd Wright for our building?"

Why not indeed. Vera wrote to Taliesin West laying out the county's needs and inviting him to come to Marin to see their piece of prime property for himself. If he agreed that this acreage was a most unique parcel to be found so close to a major city, one he could work with, they could negotiate a contract. Wright was elusive. He would not come hat in hand as Fusselman thought he should. Instead, he arranged a meeting on his own turf in the Frank Lloyd Wright Foundation offices in San Francisco. On the afternoon of April 26, 1957, four went to the meeting, one stayed home sulking over the great man's refusal to come to them. Gnoss, Castro, Marshall and Schultz, with the entire Civic Center committee, spent most of the afternoon with Wright and Aaron Green, Wright's San Francisco CEO. Wright spun out his visionary theories about the elevation of ethics in governmental operations when said government is housed in good architecture. He left them breathless.

That night, Wright was the Bernard Maybeck lecturer at the University of California School of Architecture, so Wright's Marin devotees had dinner together before crossing the Bay to Berkeley to listen to more of his ideas on organic architecture and inspired esthetics. They came away burning with evangelistic zeal for his imprint on their county. Wright had suggested that afternoon that the design of their building should reflect the personality of their piece of paradise. They, the inhabitants of that paradise, were part of that personality as well as the physical setting. For Fusselman, Neutra's admonition to reflect the urbanization going on in Marin County made more sense than ethereal rhetoric about something "rising out of the natural environment." Those crazy environmentalists, moving into the county by droves, building their expensive tree houses on the hillsides of Marin, bought into that slushy "id and ego" stuff, but not practical realists like himself.

For almost two decades, solid citizens engaged in business and ranching had been pestered beyond reason by babblings about "respecting nature." Now this. Frills and folderol had no place in the practice of government. What should be the cardinal rule was getting the most for the taxpayers' dollar. Neutra wanted an eight-percent fee; Wright demanded ten-percent. Frightened by the euphoria that gripped the rest of the Board after their meeting with Wright, Fusselman and Jones urged Neutra to return to Marin to address a joint meeting of the service clubs of San Rafael. It was one last attempt to bring public pressure to bear on a practical problem, not a "singular opportunity" to create something that spoke of "the soul of Marin." Neutra came but to no avail. Four to one, June 27, 1957, the Board voted to open negotiations with Frank Lloyd Wright. A contract was drawn up June 28 to be signed by Wright, and the Board, at San Rafael High School on June 29th.

Late in the afternoon of the 29th, Vera overheard Jones speaking to a county employee about the contract being mislaid somewhere. Smelling a hog-sized rat, Vera called Walter Castro to see if he had a duplicate. Fortunately he did. That night the four supervisors present for the meeting, with Wright in tow, found a table in a hallway providing a semblance of privacy and signed the contract before going into the auditorium. Over 700 people awaited them. The great architect was going to meet some of the citizens whose lives made up the personality of Marin that Wright intended to reflect in his drawings. From all over the county they came, except William Fusselman. Chairs for the supervisors had been set up on the stage. One remained empty, loudly proclaiming its absent occupant's disapproval of the whole affair.

Margaret Azevedo, who is always worth a quote, said about the event: "He talked for one and a half hours. He insulted everybody and they ate it up."

The man's electrifying panache, plus his mastery of oratory, set off a wave of hero worship unusual in Marin whose sophisticated citizenry is used to celebrities. From that night on, so many people became Wright worshippers that Vera's insistence that Wright was right for Marin echoed from every hill. The opposition, however, was determined and organized, even if outnumbered. That opposition showed its collective willingness to be militant as well as insulting. Wright remained in Marin County overnight to be on hand the next morning for the formal Board meeting. After the presentation of the contract, time was to be set aside for him to answer questions. The Board was seated on a rostrum above him while Wright stood on the floor below facing the audience. On an easel beside him were some rough drawings and a few enlarged photographs with which to illustrate some of his ideas.

Not more than 10 feet away, in the front row, sat members of the American Legion wearing Legion caps and post insignia. As soon as the meeting opened, circumventing any speech by Wright or any questions to the architect, Old Guard Bryson Reinhardt, opponent of all these pesky inmigrants and their fancy pansy ideas, rose and began reading a seven-page letter to the Board which accused Wright of being pro-Communist during World War II. Four were stunned, one showed no sign of surprise. Wright shook his fist and shouted angrily "I don't have to listen to this rot! There's no substance in that. I am a loyal American citizen. Look at the record!"

Amid gasps of horror, he stormed out leaving a shocked audience behind. Vera bounded out of her chair furiously demanding an apology from Reinhardt. He had humiliated the whole county, she cried. It was not the province of the Board to investigate the political beliefs of anyone. Political belief was a personal matter protected by the Constitution. Unfounded and unsubstantiated accusations had no place in Board Meetings. "Doc" Duhammel bounced to his feet shaking his fist at Vera, friendship forgotten, civility out the window. He denounced her for being a soft-headed woman trying to make Marin

County into something it wasn't. Voices crying "for shame!" were answered with "He's a Commie! No matter what he says, he's a Commie!" Tumult reigned. The Board meeting was over.

When Wright stormed out, Mary Summers ran after him and stuffed him into Castro's car. She then ran back and motioned to the Board to hurry out to mollify their incensed architect. Four left the meeting hurriedly, one remained behind to face a most satisfying shouting match. Wright was whisked off to the mellow atmosphere of the Meadow Club high on Mount Tamalpais for lunch. They hoped soothing words of praise and appreciation in such a delightful setting would be balm for his wounded ego. Their blandishments had the hoped for effect, and, once the delicious luncheon was consumed, Wright sat down at a grand piano in the dining room to entertain them with his fine musicianship.

From the Meadow Club, they took him to tour the site for which he was to create a great masterpiece. Three knolls rose at the south end of the Scettrini ranch and Wright wanted to go to the top of the middle one. Riding with Marvin Brigham who seemed uncertain as to where the best point of ascent lay, Wright took charge and navigated.

"See where cows have gone up?" he said. "Just follow their trail. Animals are the best road engineers there are." Marvin Brigham was duly impressed. Never in engineering school had that proposition been laid out for him.

From the top of that knoll a gem of unspoiled earth stretched out before them. Squinting, Wright threw back his head and let his eyes graze thoughtfully over the scene.

"We can level anything you want leveled." Brigham assured him.

"Don't you level anything!" snapped Wright. "I need it all. I'm going to use these knolls just the way they are. I can see it now."

Wright went back to Taliesin to start drawing and Fusselman began writing— writing to every critic Wright had ever had, trying to unearth something really substantial with which to undermine the man and woo the citizenry away from the contract already signed and duly recorded. "Old Fussy," as some now called Fusselman behind his back, hoped to get the issue of scrapping the work of the "4-to-I" Board put to the people for a vote. Once Wright had drawings ready to submit, the fees would have to be paid. In response to Fusselman's letters, Representative Carrol E. Metzner of Madison, Wisconsin came out to California to lay before the supervisors and the *Independent Journal*, and anyone else who would listen, a long litany of sins he laid at Wright's feet. Of the many diatribes Metzner leveled at the man he thoroughly hated, one was useful to Fusselman who'd already tried the Communist gambit and failed. When Metzner said he didn't think Wright could stay within a budget, Fusselman seized on it.

Wright returned March 25, 1958, to present his preliminary drawings to the Board of Supervisors and to the public at a meeting in the San Rafael High School auditorium. His drawings were hung in the cafeteria, and after his rhetoric had soared over their heads for almost an hour, a recess was called so that all could see with their own eyes what he had been seeing in his head. Such a vision! A 10-story office building laying on its side reaching from the southern-most knoll to the middle one with a future Hall of Justice faintly sketched in, stretching from the middle knoll to the northernmost little hill. His daring concepts swept up the 700-plus people present in a euphoria of delight. Delight with Wright, delight with their lovely landscape, and delight with themselves for being worthy of such a building. Vera went home too elated to sleep.

The next day the starry-eyed devotees of the Wright design were plummeted back to earth by the Marin County Taxpayers' Association. The MCTA, defunct for many years, was resuscitated overnight to stop what threatened to burden the county with a building that would be expensive to maintain. The new president, elected minutes before the meeting, began without preliminary discussion from the floor. He announced that he had already made arrangements with an attorney and with Fusselman to draw up a petition for a referendum to allow the populace to vote on Wright's plans. The next day the

I.J. carried an account of the taxpayers association meeting. As soon as the paper came out, county-wide citizen protest groups sprang up like mushrooms.

Harold Stockstad, Hartley Sater and William Steward put together a slide show called "Marin's Greatest Hour," produced by a San Francisco advertising firm. For weeks, night after night, they trundled the slide show around Marin County in a school bus, showing it to as few as five or as many as a hundred. Two hundred Marinites organized a protective association called the Citizen's Committee for the County Center and elected Harold Stockstad president. Letters to the editor about the arrogance of the MCTA flooded the *I.J.*, letters so inflammatory they almost curled the edges of the editorial page. The opposition responded in kind. Ads appeared in the *Independent Journal* soliciting members for the Taxpayers' Association. Even Fusselman wrote letters to the Editor urging defiance of the majority of the Board. Never before had the *Independent Journal* enjoyed such wide circulation or had such a daily soap opera to report.

Oddly, in the middle of the ferment, the Fireman's Fund Insurance Agency of San Francisco became political and joined their voices to the MCTA chorus. How this issue presented a problem for Fireman's Fund was bewildering. What difference did it make to a San Francisco-based Insurance Company whom Marin County hired to design their civic center? A contingent of Firemen's agents, nevertheless, went to Sacramento to solicit the aid of the governor in this purely local free-for-all. It was unclear as to where the governor could obtain the power to contravene a contract made by a duly-elected body of County supervisors. Pat Brown was coming soon to Marin for a Democratic club progressive dinner, and he promised to look into the problem then. At the hors d'oeuvres stop of that moving feast, he met Vera Schultz. She smiled, held out her hand, introduced herself, and Brown said later he knew he was in for a stimulating evening.

The Meadow Club was *the* place in the county where Marin displays itself best to VIPs passing through. The entree for the Brown dinner would be served there. For the ride to the Meadow Club, the governor and Vera were assigned to the same car. From Ross to the Meadow Club was a long ride, time for lots of discourse. When Brown told Vera that the Fireman's Fund wanted the contract with Wright canceled, she demanded to know why an insurance company cared about an architect. "Well," he replied," they must have their reasons." To tell Vera Schultz that a tight-knit group of male brokers of power need not explain their reasons for a position or action they took was incautious and incendiary.

Vera began talking. By the time she was through castigating the Fireman's Fund chauvinists, the MCTA, and by implication, the governor for his interference in something that was none of his business, Brown was subdued. She enumerated all of Wright's many architectural innovations, including the design of the Imperial Hotel in Tokyo that had weathered a series of major earthquakes since being built in 1923. By the time she finished Brown was educated, flattened and silent. He never mentioned cancellation of the contract again. Vera thereafter said that Pat Brown was a "darned good fellow. Not a great man, but a good man."

News coverage of the taxpayers association and their bond with Mr. Fusselman at last aroused the less hot-blooded, more sober citizens who until then had stood above the fray. It was time for the majority of taxpayers to speak out against a high-handed clique of tight-fisted ideologues who were trying to override the decisions made by officials elected by the majority to make those decisions. So eloquently did they speak their displeasure through the editorial page of the *Independent Journal,* that nothing came of the call for a referendum. On April 28, 1958, before a packed house, the majority of the Board re-avowed their commitment to the Wright contract and voted to authorize the acceptance of bids for construction.

In June, the Board requested the Wright Foundation to prepare a model of the master plan to be displayed in the county. September 3rd the model arrived and, at last, those who could not visualize from drawings could see the model and know what the finished product would look like. That model traveled to Italy for a great international fair and today stands in the lower floor hallway of the administration wing of the civic center. People still pause to study it and compare it with the finished product.

The arrival of the model did not abate the controversy; it ignited the conflagration all over again. This was a government building? Fusselman fumed and snorted. Ten stories of office building lying on its side anchored between two knolls? You'd need roller skates to get around inside the darned thing. Two stories high under a space-ship roof, circles within circles adorning the eaves. The carping was an endless, monotonous dirge. The loyalists, on the other hand, those whose hearts filled at the lyrical beauty of the design, thought this was the type of cultural statement they wanted made about their county. Vera spent hours poring over the model, admiring it, proudly loving it.

Any new plots on the part of Fusselman and his cohorts against the Frank Lloyd Wright contract were abruptly sabotaged in April of 1959. America's foremost architect died. Now the maneuvering shifted from trying to renege on the contract to trying to re-negotiate it at the standard architectural fee rate of 8 percent. Refusing to even discuss renewed negotiation, the rest of the Board unanimously decided to continue the scheduled construction of the civic center. They paused only for a moment of respectful silence honoring the architect's death. Olgivanna Wright took her husband's place at the head of the firm and any effort to alter anything with Wright's imprint on it met her unsheathed talons. Fusselman might be willing to brawl with her, but no one else on the Board cared to challenge the lady.

In September, the supervisors received the blueprints, along with Aaron Green's report of the foundation's estimate of cost— $3,379,000 plus a five-percent contingency allowance. November 10, 1959, after every department had reviewed the plans, the county announced it was ready to receive bids from contractors. The date set for the opening of bids was December 22. The Board waited with bated breath and crossed fingers, four of them praying that the bids would be less than opponents prophesied. One was praying for a figure out of the wild blue. Six bids came in, and four of them were *under* the architect's estimate. Whoops of surprised joy filled the supervisors' chamber. It was vindication for all the players in the game who had kept the faith and believed that Wright's estimates were on track. Lowest bid of all came from Rothschild, Raffin and Weirick Inc., of San Francisco.

Most Marinites were delighted by the news. Said the *I.J.* "...the people who have had the vision of this government center for Marin County were standing on firm ground, even though their heads may have been in the clouds at times. They have come through with a realistic program, based on solid estimates and planned in a substantial pay-as-you-go way that makes it possible to finance the structure without a bond issue and its extra cost." "It's the best Christmas present we could have had!" Vera exulted to a reporter from the *I.J.* She practically salivated at the thought of sitting in the handsome Supervisors' Chambers while conducting the business of the county. Such surroundings demanded wise judgments and sensible solutions. Sadly, by the time the supervisors took their seats behind that long polished bench, she had been out of office for over two years.

Groundbreaking ceremonies were scheduled for February 15, 1960. Mrs. Wright, as heroine of the hour, not Vera, would represent her husband at the ceremonies and share the podium with Walter Castro, now Chairman of the Board. Vera's earned curtain call was denied her again, as it had been when she should have been the first woman mayor of Mill Valley. She had not had a glorious installation as the first woman supervisor in Northern California. Now, as she had done twice before, she would have to smile and step aside for someone who had had nothing to do with bringing about this moment.

If the weather was kind, if it didn't rain, it would be a lovely time of the year for an outdoor event. Along the roof line of the civic center, Wright had drawn in a row of round balls dripping from the bottom of the ever-circling circles that adorn the eaves. Those balls represented raindrops, symbolic metaphors for Marin's wet winters. February 15th dawned bright and clear, no hint of a cloud anywhere. Low acacia trees, cloaked in shawls of yellow blossoms, rising out of carpets of California's ubiquitous golden spring mustard, seemed to be vying with the winter sun to throw a golden haze over the proceedings.

The golden haze harmonized with the gilt shovels lined up for the turning of the earth. Each Supervisor had her/his own shovel with which to do the ritual lifting of dirt, already dug by someone else, then throwing it somewhere where it wasn't needed. Olgivanna Wright, Vera Schultz and Walter Castro were photographed perched atop a giant earth mover as the festivities began. When it came Vera's turn to speak, she told the enthusiastic audience, "This is the second happiest day of my life. The first was when Frank Lloyd Wright presented the plans for this incomparable site. The third will be that day two years hence when we move in." She meant what she said.

Four shovels were used while one remained clean and shiny, untouched, unclaimed, as the crowd of 500 departed. No one could sulk like Bill Fusselman. From that day forward, Vera's shovel, bedecked with its dull gold bow, stood in her front hall under the bookshelf that held the great array of books about Frank Lloyd Wright she had collected. Many a visitor to the Schultz home asked, "What's the story of the shovel?" Vera loved to tell them. When Vera's house was dismantled following her death, Vera's daughter gave the shovel to Jody Becker. When the Marin Museum is open, Jody plans to give the shovel to the museum which will be a perfect repository for such a memento from the ground-breaking ceremony. While the other four supervisors were participating in ritual celebration of the beginning of Marin's grand new administrative offices, Fusselman was busily formulating a plot. Unable to stop the hated building from going up, he plotted to find a way to politically bring down the woman whose brainchild it had been.

In June, three members of the Board were up for reelection: Fusselman, Jim Marshall, and Vera Schultz. Forces were gathering to unseat Marshall and Schultz and make way for the second phase of what Fusselman had in mind. At that juncture, as though fate was his co-conspirator, the State of California initiated an action against Marin County that ignited a burst of public indignation. The county hospital out in Lucas Valley was condemned. It was ironic timing. A few weeks before, the county had been honored by the National Municipal League for its forward-looking political reorganization. *Look Magazine* had come out with a feature story on the "avant-garde" county government that had been created in Marin County under the leadership of Supervisor Vera Schultz. As though to bat down the national acclaim Vera was receiving, the county was censored for not having addressed major problems out on their county poor farm.

By the beginning of the 20th century, every county in the U.S. had a Poor Farm. Poor Farms were America's answer to homelessness, care for the indigent poor, and a way to support the "old folks" who were unable to care for themselves. All three categories of citizens—the homeless, the poor sick, and the poor elderly—could be collected onto one property and housed under one roof. With few exceptions, Poor Farm dormitories were cheerless barn-like structures equipped with little infirmaries and central dining rooms. Personal quarters were plain little cells for sleeping. Local missionary societies provided some socialization for the residents, but for the most part poor farms were "homes for the disinherited," isolated places poor people dreaded.

One of Marin's poor farm residents, one of those buried in the county's "Potters' Field" for the unclaimed dead, was Seldon Connor Gile. Gile was a member of the "Society of Six," a group of renowned painters, most of whom lived in Oakland. They painted the landscapes of the Bay Area in superlative impressionistic style. His use of color was reminiscent of Renoir's palette: bold, evocative, reflecting California's brilliant sunlight. When Gile died, a San Francisco art critic wrote a long article extolling his genius, and at long last the Public's interest caught fire. His canvasses began to bring incredible prices, and those who had had the foresight to buy his paintings when they were cheap made small fortunes. Fame and fortune, however, came too late to rescue Gile from his residence and death at Marin County's facility for the forgettable.

Social Security legislation of 1933 began emptying America's Poor Farms before World War II and Lucas Valley was no exception. By 1960 no one was living on the county's property in the valley except young delinquents housed in Juvenile Hall, and frail, forgotten old folks in the county hospital. The question of the hospital and the reformatory, shabby old buildings occupying prime acreage no longer being tilled, was forced onto the agenda of the Board of Supervisors by the state. Developers, interested in acquiring a portion of the farm, had nudged the state into action that resulted in a public debate. Properly orchestrated by the developers, such a debate should result in some of the land being put up for auction in order to raise funds for the renovation of the condemned buildings.

Out of sight, out of mind. It had been easy for Marinites to ignore the facilities and their problems. The State of California rudely forced Marin's attention to turn to their embarrassing problem. The state ordered the county to bring the hospital up to state standards or close it down. Closing down the county hospital would mean swamping Marin's handsome new Marin General Hospital with charity cases. For solvent citizens, it was unthinkable to have wings of their proud new hospital transformed into charity wards. As for Juvenile Hall, if the state chose to mandate a major overhaul or a new facility, the costs would be almost as much as the price of a new hospital.

Juvenile Hall, built originally to serve a rural, sparsely populated county, was bulging at the seams with the sons and daughters of the new residents pouring into Marin. In the utopian decade of the 50's, laws were passed that made misdemeanors out of what had been considered naughty pranks in an earlier day. The new laws sent kids to jail rather than to the woodshed. Measures to improve or replace both facilities had been defeated at the polls numerous times during the past ten years. In the charged political climate of 1960, Vera was accused of being so absorbed in the art and esthetics of the Civic Center that she had failed to take an interest in the two unglamorous and glaringly ugly buildings which should have had the Supervisors' attention. Under the gun to do something fast, the Board proposed a bond issue for hospital renovation. Foolishly, they proposed that the bond issue appear on the November ballot. No one seemed aware of the bond issue's potential boomerang on Vera's reelection campaign. As for the Juvenile Hall, the "4-to-1" Board proposed a five cent rate hike on every $100 of assessed property values.

Fusselman fought for a 10-cent reduction in the 42-cent rate levied for the Civic Center, the ten cents to go for renovating the detention center. The Civic Center fund would be reduced to spartan levels in order to provide the needed monies for the Lucas Valley facilities without additional strain on taxpayers' patience. Touted by Fusselman and company as an extravagant, artsy architectural wonder foisted onto a "Just-Plain-Bill's" county by "Mama-knows-best" Vera Schultz, the Civic Center would be stripped of its circles-within-circles and extravagant landscaping, and the county would have the money for stout jails and a no-frills, charity hospital. Many alarmed voices were heard demanding Vera's head.

Jim Marshall, as well as Vera, was on the rack that year. The ranchers out in West Marin were up in arms over the proposed Point Reyes Seashore. On the public dole themselves, the cattlemen were leasing public lands at rates insulting to other taxpayers. The National Park Service did not begin to acquire land for the Point Reyes National Seashore until 1962, but the handwriting was on the wall by 1960. Fearing their palmy days might be ending, that dispossession lay ahead, the ranchers went gunning for their supervisor who favored the Seashore. Jim Marshall had to be thrown out. The ranchers were not alone in their resentment. When Jim went on the Board, there were more cows than people in West Marin. By 1960, suburbanites had spilled out along county roads expanding suburbia into the open spaces of cattle country. Job-oriented to San Francisco, as a rule the invaders were on the side of the environmentalists and enthusiastically in favor of the Seashore. Those positions put them on the ranchers' enemy's list. However, the suburbanites were bedfellows of the ranchers over reassessments.

The new tax bills arrived in early June, just before the primary. Fourth District handily voted Jim out and a new man in, conservative grocerman George Ludy. Fusselman's seat in the Second District was secure. He was pristine pure for he had opposed everything anybody was upset about. Schultz, the nemesis of all the malcontents, became the target for a massive assault. The reappraisal process had begun in the second and third districts where more property had changed hands since the opening of the Golden Gate Bridge than in other districts, where more new housing had gone up, where many of George Hall's under-appraised friends lived. Third District folks, outside Mill Valley, were facing double or triple rate increases. Suddenly, in Southern Marin, the civic center became "Taj Mahal," and was blamed for the whole tax increase. There is nothing like a tax increase to raise the hackles of citizens who rely on government for services, order and stability, but don't want to pay for it. Instead of being a matter of equity, equalization became Vera's recklessness with other people's money.

Campaign season, 1960, Vera Schultz faced the political battle of her life. That year, the Kennedy family from Cape Cod, MA. took over the presidential race, en masse. For many across the nation, it seemed ludicrous to think that a 43-year-old upstart from a Catholic background could become president of the United States. To many in Marin, a Catholic president seemed no more ludicrous than scuttling the recent remodeling of their county government. Ludicrous or not, both outcomes came to pass that fall. Reaction to reappraisal in Southern Marin and the establishment of the National Seashore in West Marin gave the Courthouse Gang the openings they needed to start dismantling all the edifices of good government that had been erected in the county under Vera's leadership.

Vera didn't see the steamroller headed her way in time. She campaigned vigorously for the young Massachusetts senator. She should have walked the hills of Mill Valley in her own behalf as she did in 1952. She should have taken the taxpayer's association seriously and aggressively fought back. Above all she should *not* have assumed that a politically sophisticated electorate would weigh her achievements against the charges being levied against her by Marin County Taxpayers Association's, (MCTA) propaganda and realize what her defeat would mean. "Should have" becomes clear with hindsight. For once, Vera was blinded by her own success.

One of the most difficult aspects of leadership is to march ahead in cadence with the people following you. Keeping in touch with the grapevine, paying attention to innuendoes, being aware of the inattention of your supporters—all are necessary for continued tenure in public office. Because Vera had put Marin County on the Bay Area leadership honor roll with her work on Bay Area environmental projects, she thought environmentally-minded Marinites were pleased with all her achievements. To the contrary, most Marinites were unaware of what she'd done outside their county, and didn't care. They were too myopic to see beyond their own shores, too localized in their interests to care about the larger landscape. Not until the late 60's would protecting America's other natural resources become a Holy Grail in Marin.

Vera should have touted her record as a way of educating Marinites about the world outside their little Eden. She should have touted what she'd done to stop the damage being done to that world: 1) six years as treasurer of the 13-county Bay Counties Water Problems Committee; 2) member of the water committee of the North Coast Counties Supervisors Association; 3) two terms as secretary-treasurer of that association; and 4) one of four Marin members on the Eel River Flood Control and Water Conservation Association.

The "good government kook" had made Marin's reputation in Bay Area progressive legislation. She had: 1) been a member of the Government Operations Committee and Urban Problems Committee of the State Supervisors Association; 2) been twice chosen by the National Association of County Officials to serve on special committees, one on taxing districts and one on Bonds; and 3) helped author and sponsor a work furlough program for jail inmates that was adopted Bay Area-wide. Vera had become a major figure on the Board of Directors of the Association of Bay Area Governments (ABAG). ABAG is an organization of the 82 cities and nine counties that make up the Bay Area. It was established under the State of California Joint Exercise of Powers Act, passed to deal with the area-wide problems of rapid transit, air-and-water-pollution, recreation, planning, and other matters of mutual concern. In 1955, while she was a member of ABAG, the state of California established an area-wide Air Pollution Control District. Vera had been in her element--- conferring, planning, struggling with California's most perennial political hot potatoes, particularly water. She had done meritorious work for the whole Bay Area, work that had redounded to Marin's stature among the counties of California as a leader in Conservation programs.

None of these accomplishments would have helped her cause with old-timers in Marin who loved their own preciousness and were willing to let the wider world take care of itself, but it would have gone down well with the new folks in town. Seeming blissfully ignorant of the amount of amassed anger eating at those who wanted her out, Vera failed to protect her flank. Instead of single-mindedly running for reelection, she found time that fateful season to be chairman of the committee to reelect Clem Miller to the House of Representatives, to be chairman of the women's committee for the reelection of State Controller Alan Cranston, and to be Mill Valley campaign coordinator for Robert D. Carrow running for the State Assembly. She served on the Speakers Panel for the reelection of "Pat" Brown for Governor, and spoke at rallies for him across the state.

If she had spent her time shaking hands in shopping malls, taking her message door to door, earnestly extolling her record to people on the street, campaigning in her familiar personal style, maybe, just maybe, she might have won a third term on the Board of Supervisors. From there she could have ascended to state, perhaps national office as she longed to do. She didn't do any of those things. She was too busy helping put others into office to invest her time and talent in working for herself. Swept out of local office, Vera was swept out of the political mainstream leading to membership in the circles of power-brokers outside Marin.

Her opponent was J. Walter Blair, owner of a string of Laundromats in Mill Valley, a "wannabe" fringe member of the inner circle of the good-old-boy network. Vera didn't really run against Blair. She ran against Reappraisal and against George Jones. J. Walter Blair's candidacy was announced at a dinner given by Jones in Sausalito in late spring. At that dinner, Vera was mocked for "mother knows best" coercion of the Board. In ads supporting Blair, Jones called the Civic Center a "Monument to ego" —Vera's. Blair's great battle cry was, "Look at your tax bill!" All the cannons were lined up with her in the cross hairs and in November they shot her down. It was the worst day of Vera's long life.

Vera had done more to enhance the quality of life in the county and to put Marin on the map than any supervisor in memory. When she lost the 1960 Supervisorial election, Marin lost its most influential voice at every level of government all the way to Washington. Never again would one supervisor hold so many different offices at so many different levels of government, all at one time or even spread over a lifetime career. Cast out by a fickle electorate, Vera had no platform for further service. Not having a crystal ball through which she could glimpse all that still lay ahead, Vera firmly believed she'd lost her place in history.

AFTERMATH

When the new Board was seated in January, the Taxpayer's Association and George Jones gleefully made public their plans to dynamite everything Vera had wrought: the County Administrator, the Civic Center, perhaps even the Commission on Personnel that had done away with treasured nepotism. The first target was to reestablish the old committee system of supervision of the county's finances. Walter Blair and George Ludy were assigned the task of scrutinizing all financial transactions of every department of county government. That step was followed by placing the data processing center under the direct control of the Board. Skillfully, the county administrator was being expunged. The citizenry had barely begun to see the strategy of the "3-to-2" shift before the conspirators threw a bomb that opened a political crater in Marin County.

January 10, 1961, on a three-to-two vote, the Board issued the infamous "Stop-Work Order" on the Marin County Civic Center and dismissed the Civic Center Committee. Shock waves, so forceful they created fusion of very disparate groups within the county, rocked the complacency the electorate had produced. The "three" of the new Board were instantly assaulted. Their telephones rang incessantly. Telegrams arrived at their homes at all hours. Their mails were filled with hate letters, hate letters from the very people who had voted Schultz and Marshall out, and Blair and Ludy in. Fusselman, their favorite target, put his phone in a closet and covered it with pillows. There was no peace.

The Stop-Work Order had been issued, Mr. Fusselman said, to give architects time to determine what it would cost to convert the half-finished building into a hospital. Changing that bilious bauble into a hospital would save the county money, he insisted. Save the county money? One hundred and twenty-five men were instantly out of work while subcontractors in the county were facing disaster because of materials already ordered. As for the building itself, it was said that unsupported retaining walls were in danger of buckling if construction didn't proceed on schedule. Workmen had to be paid while the

189

Stop-Work Order was in force and damages to the building would cost money. Vengeance is expensive, Fusselman discovered. The county could be in for increased costs of $1,000,000 if work was halted for long.

Taxpayers, who were not members of MCTA, were outraged. They had voted for more responsible government, not less. Nothing Vera had ever done approached the high-handedness of this. There had been no public hearings, no prior cost analysis, no warning. At the January 11 meeting of the Civic Center Committee, (CCC), the planned agenda became confetti and bedlam took over. Over 200 angry Marinites had come to protest the Stop-Work Order and damn the newly constituted Board. Pandemonium reigned. Petitions were in hand to curb the authoritarian excess of Fusselman & Co. Leon de Lisle, County Auditor, poured gasoline on the gathering when he announced that he'd been fired that day. Furthermore, he'd been told that the Civic Center Committee was now an ad hoc gaggle of political illiterates. Fury mounted with every further revelation of Board arrogance. Jack Bissinger presented a petition demanding a grand jury investigation to determine if Jones and his buddies were guilty of malfeasance in office. When that petition started its journey around the room, it was almost torn to shreds by those trying to get their "John Henry" on it.

With the meeting completely out of order, Chairman Helen Nelson adjourned the formal proceedings and turned the gavel over to Harold Stockstad. Something new in Marin politics was about to be born. That night, the newly-defunct Civic Center Committee became the Marin Committee for Civic Affairs to be known in the future as the MCCA, a powerful citizens' lobby which determinedly watchdogged the Supervisors until the entire building was complete. Harold Stockstad was unanimously elected president, and one-hundred-dollars-per-person present was collected on the spot to overturn the hated Stop-Work Order, and possibly recall J. Walter Blair. It was after midnight when the meeting broke up. Those in attendance were eager to take on the Board the next day.

Vera was in Salt Lake City when the world turned upside down in Marin. Before the election, she and Don Jensen were invited by the Utah State Association of County Officials to be part of a symposium on county government. Vera's expertise had not been voted out of existence when she was voted out of office. Don Jensen was to speak about what had been accomplished during his brief tenure as county administrator. No one knew when they left for Utah that the office of county administrator was about to be abolished. As they had done earlier for the Humboldt County Institute on Local Government Problems, Vera and Don lauded efficiencies achievable when government is elevated to the status of a corporation belonging to the people, not a clubby affair controlled by an inner circle playing a game called "governing." At the end of the day, the Association presented Vera with a complete set of pots and pans. Pots and pans? For a housewife returning to the kitchen after a fling in politics! Vera didn't know whether to laugh or cry. All she could do was turn on that dazzling smile, laugh that infectious laugh, and thank them for their kindness. Peter Behr, who was about to become a supervisor in the first recall election in California, said it best: "Vera never has defeats. She only has setbacks."

As she walked into the San Francisco airport that night, she was greeted with news of the volcanic eruption of Fusselman's long-planned gutting of the "good government" changes she had made in the county. She'd known he and Jones would launch a frontal assault as soon as they dared, but she hadn't expected such a surprise attack. Now the people of Marin, who should have been awake to the possibilities of again surrendering the county to the suzerainty of George Jones, were up in arms. The Schultzes' phone was ringing when Vera walked in the front door and it didn't stop ringing for days. "What are we going to do?" was the constant cry. Besieged, she even felt a little sympathy for Fusselman who pleaded through the *Independent Journal* for calm.

Calm? How could there be calm when the Board continued unchecked on its mad course? Still in love with their own wisdom, and feeling smugly secure in their belief that the opposition's fires would die down as quickly as they'd burst into flames, the "3-to-2" Board, in spite of public outcries, refused to back off. Ludy told the *San Francisco Examiner* that if the building couldn't be used for a hospital, the Board would find another use for it. It would never be a civic center. Blair publicly avowed that the people of Marin would be better served with any change in purpose and design, than with this extravagant, architectural blunder. Leon de Lisle, having refused to be fired, said that if one cent set aside for a government office building was used for any other purpose, he would freeze the Civic Center funds and no one would be paid. The contractors and the workers sought legal beagles who could tell them how much power over a contract already let by a duly constituted government (established by Fletcher vs. Peck, 1810), this bumptious trio of self-inflated potentates, and their Godfather, had assumed.

Every word uttered in San Rafael took on invidious meaning as it traveled on the wings of anger. The stop-work Order had come on Tuesday. By Thursday there was even a fanciful move under way to recall William Fusselman who, though in no real danger, had thought his own district solidly behind him. Now he found himself vilified in his own bailiwick.

Fateful Thursday of that week, the *Independent Journal* threw its staff into the fray and printed a ballot by which its readers could cast straw votes in an extra-legal referendum on whether to block the stop-work order and continue with the construction of the building, or not. The strictest legal procedures were followed to prevent charges of rigging the outcome. Names and addresses were required on the ballots mailed in which were checked against the registration rolls to prevent ballot stuffing. Fusselman, trying to thwart independent citizen action, suggested that the Board of Supervisors print a ballot of their own to be mailed to the voters that would be returned to the County Clerk's office for counting. The MCCA hooted at the idea. They said a ballot needed to be clearly stated with no ambiguity worked into it and they didn't trust the dandy candy maker and the real estate king to be unambiguous about anything they were bent on manipulating.

A volunteer committee of attorneys worked right up to press time creating the single question on the *I.J.* Ballot, "Do you approve the Supervisors' order to stop work on the County Civic Center? ( ) No, I do not approve ( ) Yes, I approve."

Ballots had to be returned by midnight Saturday, January 14. By five o'clock that Thursday, the *I.J.* was sold out and the switchboard blazed like a Christmas tree. Frantic calls reached members of the MCCA from commuters who had returned from San Francisco too late to get a paper. The *I.J.* kept printers working that night turning out 5,000 more ballots to be distributed Friday morning. The ballot reappeared in the paper Friday afternoon and on Saturday.

Dalton, Graupner and Barber, an auditing firm, was engaged to count the ballots and by mid-morning on the 13th, their mail chute was stuffed. By mid afternoon, Dalton, et al, employees estimated the response was running about 18 to 1 against the stop-work order. Every columnist in the Bay Area had something to say about the idiocy of a candy maker, a Laundromat owner, and a grocer thinking they knew enough about architecture to believe it possible to make a hospital out of an office building. The plumbing alone presented insoluble problems. Herb Caen entitled his verbal lance, "*Kiddin' on the Keys.*"

On Saturday, 6,000 ballots were mailed. Dalton, Graupner and Barber had to call in volunteers for the whole weekend to help with the counting in order to meet the 1 p.m. Monday deadline. Saturday and Sunday, the county sprouted placards and posters that were posted on fences, taped to car windows, nailed to telephone poles, stuck on store fronts, put wherever one could be affixed. They all said "NO!" By 9 a.m. Monday morning pickets of all sizes and ages and of both sexes conga-lined up and down the courthouse steps waving signs. Employees, leaving the building on coffee breaks, were handed placards to carry with them. By 1 p.m. the Supervisors' chamber was packed to overflowing; people were spilling out into the hallway. The meeting was moved to a courtroom. The result of the balloting came first. Yes, I approve—1,225. No, I don't approve—8,152. A first class rout! Only the most stubborn blockhead would hold out, but Fusselman would not stop the proceedings and concede. He insisted on receiving the architect's report.

Crawford and Banning said that conversion of the building to a hospital would add $1 1/2-to-2 million to the original cost.

For $2,000,000, an efficient hospital could be built from scratch out in Lucas Valley. Before Fusselman and Blair could gather their wits to tack against the wind, Ludy moved resumption of construction on the building and the reinstatement of the Civic Center Committee. Walter Castro seconded and 3 to 2 it passed! After six wild days, the county was right back where it had started, except the political landscape had been irrevocably changed. Never again would a Board of Supervisors be able to sit in isolated splendor outside the public's purview.

Charles H. Schneider of the *San Francisco Call-Bulletin* wrote: "The proposal that the partially completed center at the whisk of a hat and magic words muttered over the architectural plans be transformed into a hospital confirms our estimate that a Wonderland to dazzle Alice herself lies to the north of the Golden Gate Bridge." Work on the Civic Center resumed January 17. The Center was safe at last from the miserly, aesthetically limited San Rafael boys, but not safe from Oligvanna Wright. When it proved impossible to find a paint for the roof to match the brown hills of Marin, a paint that would hold its color under California's brilliant sunlight, she imperiously declared the roof would be sky-blue and the walls pinkie-beige. Vera was insulted. When people referred to her beloved building as "The Big Pink," she winced, but secretly she agreed with them.

INTERMISSION

Following the emotional tension of January's political firestorm came February, the month of love. Marin flooded Vera with valentines. The Northgate Merchants Association found a way to say "I love you," to the lady they admired extravagantly though they'd thrown her out of office. A radio promotional called "The Northgate Valentine Mystery" was a contest. A mystery voice was to be heard coming over the air several times a day at odd intervals. The first person to identify the voice would be awarded a prize. Vera went to a studio in San Rafael as directed and made a recording for the merchant's project. She looked forward to the suspense that could go on for days. To her disappointment and the merchants' chagrin, it was over the first time the recording was played. Like the voice of the turtle, the voice of Vera Schultz had been heard across the land and was identified immediately.

The merchants weren't the only group in the county to say "I love you" that month. The 14th district of the California Congress of Parents and Teachers Association chose February 1st as the date for a gorgeous gala to be held at the Meadow Club where Vera would be awarded a life membership in the PTA. The event was planned as a big splash to recognize someone who had given unstintingly of herself to the children of Marin. Added to her work as assistant to the superintendent of schools of Mill Valley and Sausalito, and as a headmistress of her own school for two years-1935 to 1937* (see Appendix)-as a supervisor, she had been instrumental in solving the housing needs for a special education program for the cerebral palsied.

Cerebral palsied students required specialized space as well as specialized instruction. Soon after she was voted into office, Vera was approached by County Superintendent of Schools Wallace Hall. Hall needed funds to replace the space that had been made available in the basement of Marin General Hospital. The Hospital was expanding more rapidly than expected and needed the basement. State instructional funds were available for special education, but not for building costs. Hall secured a grant of land from the Dixie School

District on the same campus as the Dixie Elementary School where some of the costs—school nurse and school psychologist—could be shared. He found matching state construction funds for handicapped programs up to $50,000, but they were available only on a matched fund basis. Hat in hand, he approached the most approachable of the county supervisors.

Vera dug in, did her homework, and found a fund established in Marin some time in the past for child welfare that could be used for this. The Marindale School for the Education of The Handicapped was born. All the handicapped could be housed under one roof, integrally linked to a mainstream school so the handicapped would not be isolated. Those children had already fallen down a "glory hole," Vera thought. They deserved the best assistance the county could provide. Once the program was in operation, Vera "stopped by" again and again to encourage and support teachers and students alike.

A lifetime membership in the PTA was not only merited, it was an excuse to throw a bash to honor someone they truly appreciated, and to say "Thank You." The testimonial dinner was held at the Meadow Club. All her fans in the county, and from far beyond, who were there that night signed a parchment scroll longer than she was tall to present to her after dinner. They didn't limit their recognition to her unstinting public service to education. They lavished praise on her for her work on the Board of Directors of the Senior Citizens of Marin organization, for her work as a member of Zonta International Service Club, for her role in helping to found the Marin League of Women Voters, for her leadership in the creation of the Marin Branch of the American Association of University Women, for her active role in the Outdoor Art Club, for her establishment of the Marin City Community Council, and for her elections to the Boards of Directors of: the Red Cross, the Family Service Agency, the Community Chest and the YMCA. All these activities were cited as being tangentialy related to her dedication to education.

Leland Jordan, about to be ex-County Counsel, was master of ceremonies. In his remarks he dubbed her "Marin's First Lady," a title that thereafter always meant Vera Schultz. From all quarters of California, and from as far away as Washington, D.C., came messages of congratulations. Among the sheaf of communications handed to her after dinner was a letter from Governor Edmund "Pat" Brown urging her to keep up the good work of reformer as a private citizen. Bill Gnoss and Jim Marshall stood before the crowd to acknowledge their debt to her for the education she had given them in good government. Neighbors, friends, fellow club members, dignitaries from every major organization in the county feted her joyously. A good dance band struck up after the formal program was over and Vera danced her feet off. She chuckled, "I had just said no to Walter Castro when Leland Jordan asked me to dance. Walter was the dearest man, but he just moved around the floor, he didn't dance. But Leland and I had a wonderful time. He was a very good dancer." The little girl from Tonopah could still cut a rug after all those years.

The February love feast was a heart-warming interlude before the next storm. Throughout February, March, April and until the Board meeting of May 24, the politically-minded watched and waited for the next attack on county government. As they expected, it happened. At 3:00 p.m., May 24, Walter Blair moved to abolish the Office of County Administrator. George Ludy, having returned to the shelter of Fusselman's wing, joined the chorus and 3 to 2 they passed it. The fires of wrath that had been banked in January erupted all over again, and spewed out of the MCCA onto the front pages and into editorial columns of every county newspaper. Retaliation came instantly and MCCA members circulated petitions in every shopping mall in Marin for a referendum on the June ballot to reinstate the Office of County Administrator.

Petitions, carrying far more than the required number of signatures, were turned in June 23 to Jones' office. *The San Francisco Examiner* reported that 10,788 signatures had been collected while only 5,319 were needed. Surely no one could claim a margin of error of that magnitude. Nonetheless, there was silence in San Rafael. Why, the papers asked, didn't the supervisors declare the results now? By law, the county clerk was allowed 10 days for the counting and he took them all. When the 10 days were up, he cryptically announced that the referendum would be put before the voters.

The County Administrator was not the only juicy issue on that ballot. The third district had a bone in its craw that could be excised only by getting rid of J. Walter Blair. July 16, 1961, Mill Valleyites fired a salvo at the courthouse and destroyed Fusselman's majority. When the third district dumped Vera the previous year they had not voted for a return to 1952 personal patronage. They'd had a family fight with their own "First Lady" and nothing more, a tiff that had been completely misunderstood by Jones and Gang. Spokesmen for the third district announced a "Recall Blair" campaign.

Though the process for recalling a county supervisor was written into the California constitution adopted in 1879, it had never before been used. Marin was about to have another "first." The voltage of public outrage was so high, 153 petitions were presented to County Clerk, George Jones by, among others, Mrs. Franklin McClain of Altos, John F. O'Brien of Sausalito, and wonder of wonders, the Chairman of the Republican Party, David Winslow of Belvedere, and the vice-chairman of the Marin Democrat Party, Gerald Hill, of Mill Valley. For the first time in Marin history, Republicans and Democrats forgot their antagonisms and became bedfellows.

Everyone wanted to know who Vera thought should be offered as replacement for Blair. The law requires that an election be held in conjunction with a Recall. Unable to say what she felt without sounding vindictive, petulant, or triumphant, Vera dreaded answering the phone. When, at last, someone suggested Peter Behr, she heartily endorsed him. Though they disagreed about many political issues--he was as committed a Republican as she was a Democrat--he was bright, he was moderate, he was honest, he was eloquent. He was a courteous gentleman, he had the respect of the community, and what's more he was for the Wright-designed Civic Center. Endorsing Behr couldn't be viewed as partisan-politics on her part. Neither could it be seen as helping to bring in someone whom she could easily defeat should she choose to come back into the fray in '64.

Peter was the ideal candidate to replace Blair. Ideal candidate or not, having served on the Mill Valley City Council, a non-partisan office, he had no desire to become a public servant again. Peter was not well and his wife Sally didn't want him to run. Those were respectable arguments, but so far as the third district was concerned, irrelevant. Marin County government needed Peter Behr. Vera went to see him and, supported by the swelling chorus of pleadings from many other quarters, persuaded him.

Once Peter consented to take on Blair, Vera determined to get out of town. If she hung around, she'd get drawn into the conflict, and her presence could impact either for good or for ill. Best to leave Mill Valley for a season. A question that had bothered her for years was: How did the state of Alaska come into the union without counties? It was the only state in the union that didn't share political power between the state legislature and county government. Forty nine other states had counties, why not Alaska? She decided to go to see for herself how their county-less government worked.

With an absolutely empty agenda for the first time since she started baby-sitting at the age of ten, she approached Zetta and Mae about taking the trip with her. They were enthusiastic. Along with Zetta's two children, they piled everything they'd need for a long summer trip into Vera's station wagon and headed out. That trip to Alaska was a great adventure, an interlude never to be forgotten. In late August, after Behr's campaign was fully formed and in capable hands, the Smith girls returned to Marin in time for Vera to breathlessly watch Peter Behr take on J. Walter Blair.

Behr's campaign manager orchestrated and scheduled his public appearances, almost told him when to breathe. Every prominent person in the county was brought into the fray—but Vera. Vera knew she dared not make public appearances in his behalf. It could be the kiss of death. Blair's transgressions had not wiped out lingering resentment in the third district over reappraisal. Vera could only work behind the scenes. In November, another "good government kook" became the new supervisor from the third district, and Vera was off the stage of elected county politics forever. When asked if she'd ever been sorry she'd fought so hard to have Wright design the Civic Center that had inadvertently contributed to her downfall, she said, "That building cost me my political career, but every time I drive by it I know it was worth it."

When interviewers asked personal questions she didn't want to answer, wily-as-a-fox Vera could skillfully shift the focus of discussion without seeming to. Her personal life, as well as most of her personal opinions, was off limits as much as she, and her devoted public, could keep it. She believed that all women must stand alone before the public. Never should they seem to be encumbered with familial responsibilities, or tainted by the acts of their relatives. More than men, she said, women must be seen as strong, independent activists, freely engaging in the political process without restraint or hint of scandal.

While Behr and Blair fought it out in 1961, Vera had plenty of time for introspection. She had to come to grips with the vacuity that swallowed up her days. Forced into inactivity, sorrowing over her lost world, she pondered alone on her mountain side about what she could do with her life now. Slowly, as events unfolded without her, she reawakened to the power the private citizen could wield. Vera reminded herself that one didn't have to hold elected office to affect the course of reform and the contours of community building. The watchdog MCCA was doing it. The League of Women Voters was doing it. Carrie Chapman Catt and that whole phalanx of women reformers had done it. She herself had done it. She needed to give herself a good shaking, she told herself, and look around to find a non-elective way back into the centers of action.

In the late summer of 1961, she learned of a projected community to be called Marincello that was being planned to go in near the headlands of the Golden Gate out in Rodeo Valley. She heard about it through Curt Heath, a former neighbor. One night, Curt invited himself and a man named Tom Frouge over to the Schultzes so she could meet the man from Connecticut who wanted to build a planned community in a valley high above the mouth of San Francisco Bay. Frouge had secured a lease on the valley from Gulf Oil Company, the owner. "Planned from the sewers to the church steeples. The guy's a real visionary," Curt boasted on the phone. "Bad thing is, he's from back east which makes him suspect out here before he unpacks his brief case."

They came, and Vera learned that Curt had told Frouge she was the one person in the county who knew where all the bodies were, who understood all the interrelationships among the various governmental agencies that Frouge would have to deal with—sanitation, roads, etc. If, as an outsider, he was going to pull this project off, he needed Vera Schultz. Not only did she know all the players, he further boasted, she was a spellbinder. When they spread Frouge's plans out on her dining table that night, it was Frouge who was the spellbinder. He spun out his philosophies about town planning, about careful use of land, about social usage wedded to physical setting, about disciplined investment in the quality of life, which included the environment. Vera couldn't believe that this man and this idea had walked through her front door to invite her to be part of something so exciting. He was talking about all the things Wright had talked about: organic planning as well as social architecture.

If Frouge's ideas could be transformed into reality, Marincello promised to be a splendid demonstration of town planning at its best. Rodeo Valley was bare of people and pre-existing buildings. Site preparation would cost almost nothing. Frouge planned to put in all the utilities himself without installment or maintenance costs to the county. The community was to be self-sufficient and self-supporting. Nothing was to be built until the whole concept was rendered into a working model to be studied thoroughly, and until investment capital for the entire project had been raised. Vera's mouth watered to be part of an enterprise beginning with nothing and ending with a marvel in social engineering. Tom Frouge offered her a job as consultant and promoter at a salary of $l,000 a month. Vera jumped at it. She felt reborn. Other prominent Marinites also came on board as consultants, many of them ardent environmentalists.

Marincello would need a phalanx of credentialed sorcerers to overcome resistance from hard-rock preservationists bent on keeping the headlands pristine. Pristine? Can any urban area providing campers, hikers and sunbathers, be kept pristine? Preservation and urbanization are antithetical, Vera thought. She had never been for preservation, i.e., nature left untouched by man. Nor had she extolled the virtues of keeping Marin's population small, and the county rural. People were moving in, like it or not. With no regulations in place, they were building anywhere and everywhere without restraint. What she abhorred, and tried to stop, was exploitative development of beautiful open space into grid-pattern towns, towns that stretched out along the existing thoroughfares of the county without regard for availability of utilities, roads or schools. She had always been for good planning and intelligent acceptance of the inevitable.

Demographic forecasters predicted that, by 1985, Southern Marin would have to absorb from 100,000 to 115,000 people. If all those people built single family dwellings wherever they found an available lot, there would be a sea of houses in low-lying areas, and an extensive denuding to make room for development on the hills above. Across a landscape now virgin and untouched, blacktop roads would snake sinuously along paths of easiest accessibility. The impact of indiscriminate building on the charm of Marin was already devastating. When complete, Marincello would be able to accommodate about a quarter of the expected influx. Hidden away in a valley all its own, a well-planned community of single family dwellings, townhouses, condominiums, and apartment buildings, would provide homes for a diverse group of families, i.e., single people, married couples, and families with children. All buildings would be limited in height to well below the crests of the surrounding hills. Marincello would be a demonstration of intelligent development.

To those who protested that any development at all in that area would be a blight on the landscape, Frouge pointed out that the new town would be visible only from the headlands of San Francisco, and then only on clear days. As for the cry that existing water supplies were inadequate for such a concentration of people, wells were already being dug to supply water for human consumption, and a sewage treatment plant was being built to care for the town's waste. Comprehensive planning in the present prevented environmental problems in the future. The Frouge Corporation had a solid plan and Vera was thrilled to be part of it.

From the time Vera announced she was going to work promoting the Frouge plan for Rodeo Valley, some who had been her most devoted fans saw her as an opportunistic turncoat. At a Board of Supervisors' hearing on Marincello's application for permits, protesters attended in number and frigidly ignored Vera's presence. She sat alone, waiting to testify. The charged atmosphere felt like a trial rather than a hearing. When she rose to speak, subdued but audible hissing greeted her. The *Pacific Sun* tried to defuse the situation with a laudatory article about Vera and her past heroic achievements on behalf of conservation, but few would listen.

The animosity her advocacy of Marincello created has never entirely spent itself. Today, when her name is enough to turn political tides of action into proper channels, there are those who freeze when Vera is mentioned.

A full scale model of the proposed town was on display at 3030 Bridgeway in a suite of rooms Frouge rented to serve as headquarters and sales offices. At catered private group dinner parties held in the Frouge suite on Bridgeway, Vera acted as hostess and fielded questions. Tom hired a film company to make a promotional piece called "The New Town" that was shot out in the valley. Vera, dressed in a green Italian knit suit to contrast with the sandy setting, narrated the film, walking through the landscape describing where everything would go. That film and the model were shown to chambers of commerce, town councils, county agencies, whatever group had been invited for dinner. As a ground swell began to build in support of the project, opposition mounted. Marin seems always to need a good fight to keep her citizens energized.

SPUR, a San Francisco based organization studying town planning, was sending its Board to Europe on a tour of new towns built in eight countries to replace bombed out villages. The purpose of the trip was to bring back ideas that could be incorporated into redevelopment of neighborhoods in the Bay Area. Frouge sent Vera and her husband along on the SPUR trip. Finland, Holland, France, Sweden, Switzerland, Germany, Denmark and England, wherever they went, they were treated like VIPs. It was the other trip of Vera's life, her only trip abroad. If Tom Frouge hadn't sent her, she would never have seen Europe. Europe, according to Vera's husband, wasn't worth the money it took to get there, but he enjoyed the trip at someone else's expense.

They were gone for four months, and all 60 of those people came back on fire for town planning. In the fall of 1965, exactly one year to the month from the supervisors meeting where the proposal had first been laid before the Board, 3 to 2, the permits were all granted. The two who voted against the project were Peter Behr and Byron Leydecker. Those who approved it were Tom Storer from West Marin, Ernest Kettenhofen from Ross Valley and William "Bill" Gnoss from

Novato. Besieged from both sides, Gnoss was the swing vote. When he came down on the side of Marincello, the search for investment money began. Tom Frouge wasn't big enough to do it all on his own.

The catered dinners continued as the focus shifted to prospective investors. Frouge wooed people the length of California, wining and dining corporate investors in his Sausalito offices, and in San Francisco restaurants like Alexis, his favorite haunt on Nob Hill. He scoured the land for money. He turned to labor unions and their fat pension funds, even to the Vatican. Frouge, always a union contract labor developer, would have preferred Pension money, but if it wasn't forthcoming, then perhaps the Vatican's investment funds could be tapped. The big problem was that Frouge said he had to retain 51 percent control in order to protect the design and the concept of Marincello. Sources of the kind of money he needed wanted control as a guarantee of a return. When Lyndon Johnson was elected to the presidency in his own right in 1964, and the U.S. expanded the Viet Nam war, investment capital became scarce at any terms. The war siphoned off funds from private projects, and inflation set in making money tight in all quarters of the economy. For seven long years, Frouge pursued his dream and for all that time Vera was part of the Marincello organization in Marin.

What might have happened in Marin can only be surmised. What did happen was that in July of 1972, without warning, Tom Frouge died of a heart attack. None of the Frouge sons wanted to continue the battle. Marincello became a lost opportunity. After Frouge's death, Gulf Oil Company gave the land to what is now The Golden Gate National Recreation Area and took a huge tax write-off in return for its bequest to the public. Today Rodeo Valley is empty, wind-swept, and natural. But beautiful as it is, it is not pristine. Though many sigh rapturously over the wonderfully empty landscape, sandy hollows provide shelter for love-making, smoking a little pot, or camping out. Here and there, in spite of Park employees' vigilance, can be found traces of man's presence which remind nature that human beings remain Lords of this planet. The people who lay their weary bodies down behind the headlands are trespassers who should spread their bedding elsewhere.

One last footnote. Vera's vision of what Marincello could have accomplished became a moot question when the Park Service took control of the land. The 20,000 people she imagined in Rodeo Valley moved farther up Highway 101. As she envisioned it, they would have accessed the highway at the Richardson Bay bridge, and perhaps she was right in projecting that 5,000 fewer cars would clog the freeway north of that point. Five thousand cars would use less gasoline than they do now, 5,000 drivers would suffer less commuter frustration once past Richardson Bay bridge. 5,000 people would have more time for family and community. For Vera, that would have been a healthy bonus to come from the project. It is true that the demand for more and more housing in Marin continues, and is now causing storms in Novato over the same issues the conservationists raised over Marincello.

Every Marin community has expanded; there is no reason to believe that any community can long be contained, not even a mythical Marincello. The 5,000 cars she estimated for the projected Marincello population could, in today's figures, be well over 10,000 cars off the road just a few miles into Marin. Ten thousand fewer cars to clog the corridor to Novato could relieve the need for more highway construction. In Vera's view of a well-ordered world, it was axiomatic that planned communities are far better than unfettered sprawl. Unfettered sprawl, she believed, resulted in unnecessary social problems. To quote Elizabeth Ann, Vera's mother, "Every little cause has a consequence."

Marincello was heady stuff but it wasn't policy making. Still unconvinced that her yearning for political office was hopeless, Vera plunged into the 1964 state Senate race even before Marincello folded. Jack McCarthy, figurehead senator put into office by his developer father, rarely bothered to show up for debates, or votes when bills came to the floor of the Senate. It was widely felt that McCarthy was not serving his district and it was rumored that he needed to join Alcoholics Anonymous. Vera was indignant that an inadequate man sat in the State Senate while she was politically idle. She handily won the Democratic primary, for no one wanted to buck the formidable Republican McCarthy money and power.

Peter Allen Smith, Democratic Central Committee chairman, later named to the municipal court bench, headed up her campaign. Jody Anne Becker, long-time friend, headed up the women's committee. When campaigning began that fall it became apparent that only Vera's most devoted friends would contribute funds to her campaign, and even they offered token support. She was only able to put up one billboard ad showing an empty chair with the simple statement across the bottom, "Vera Schultz will fill it." The first woman to sit in the halls of government in Sacramento had not yet been elected. Vera's bid, a woman's bid, for the Senate was greeted with the same derision that her bid for the Assembly had been 12 years before. Still, she was opening doors. Though being the "first" eluded her, like the lead goose in a migrating flight, her two candidacies made it easier for other women to fly in her wake. By 1968, just four years later, two women were members of the legislature.

Her defeat was the third time in four years she had been humbled, and she felt it keenly. If the '50s had been her decade of success, the '60s were her decade of almost unremitting failure. Sensitive to her despair, Peter Behr attempted to rescue her by appointing her to the Grand Jury. The Grand Jury had power second only to that held by the Supervisors. It was the '60s, and Marin was plagued with the ubiquitous drug problem. A rash of new hallucinogens, reality-altering substances, was hitting the market—synthetic drugs people didn't know how to pronounce, let alone spell. The stuff was finding its way through the woods of Marin County as freely as Prohibition whiskey had come off the boat at Point Reyes in the 1920s. Bootleg hooch never created more wealth in the wrong hands, or more crime in the streets, than the Magic Dragon created in the 1960s, all over the country. "Too bad you can't tax the stuff, "Vera said. "We'd have all the money we needed for everything." For the two years she served on the grand jury, almost the entire agenda was taken up with the drug issue. Sadly, the jurors could find no better solutions to the problem than the police methods in use.

By 1966, Vera felt as though she'd been pointlessly slogging along through heavy mud for what felt like an eternity. Marincello had failed; she'd failed as a candidate for state office for the second time; the grand jury had been futile in its efforts. She reminded herself that picking oneself up, dusting oneself off, and going back into the fray were a matter of character, and faith in oneself. Her attempts at reviving her love for life were ineffectual. Her spirits didn't lift. In her dark mood, Vera lost sight of all she'd accomplished as a volunteer activist. When her spirits hit their lowest point, it's too bad she couldn't get a tiny glimpse of all the challenges to come.

Life wouldn't have seemed so bleak if she could have seen that she was on the brink of bringing about a major social change in Marin that would restore public appreciation of all she had accomplished in the past. She would find herself again in the forefront of the county's affections. Vera was about to take a leading role in a project that would put Marin in the forefront of experimentation in social engineering. For several years she had been engaged in a field of social change that was going to grow dramatically in the next 20 years, and carry her with it. On the national stage, it was referred to as Senior Citizen legislation. In Marin, its final form would be, "Whistlestop."

The plight of the elderly became an area of concern for Vera back in the '40s, while she was still on the City Council of Mill Valley. She was approached by seven or eight concerned citizens who felt that one of the most glaring inequities in society was the plight of "the elderly." A new term, "Senior

Citizen," referred to a new phenomenon. Miracle drugs were extending life. Social Security, and other pension funds inaugurated during the war years, were relieving younger families of having to house the elderly members of their families in their spare bedrooms. Mobility, brought on by corporate shifting of people around the country, was breaking up extended families.

A whole segment of the population was being ignored by the post-war focus on youth. Vera's sisters fell into that category and they made her sensitive to the problems this new Senior Citizen population faced. Vera urged the little group who came to her in search of a solution, to go to the Board of Supervisors to secure funds to carry out a study on aging. Always in Marin, any new project begins with a study. For many proposals, the study ends the project. Both study and project are shelved when the report comes in.

The last thing men who are focused on roads and bridges want to do is take on social problems that families and churches ought to handle. The Board tried to ignore the issue, but advocates for the elderly wouldn't go away. Grudgingly, the Supervisors allocated a few thousand dollars to hire Louis Caplan to do an in-depth study on the "Aging of America." As of then, Aging was as yet an unexplored field. Caplan's study was a blockbuster. Lacking Vera's finesse, too abrasive to sell an idea, Louie Caplan prepared a "paper" for the supervisors that contained long-term projections that scared the Board out of their collective pants. Caplan's study revealed that though Marin might be an affluent, upscale place in which most of its citizens lived the good life, the elderly were more numerous and more seriously neglected than anyone had known. Some of his case studies were horrifying. What to do?

Just as Vera was elected supervisor in 1952, The National Council on Aging was established. Clem Miller, U.S. House of Representatives, appointed Vera delegate from his district. The first conference was to be exploratory only, not directive. Much was revealed at that conference that had gone unnoticed in the boom times following the war. As corporations shunted their employees around the nation like freight cars, they left old people stranded. Left behind by the generation that traditionally had assumed responsibility for them, with no one to turn to for help at the time in life when energy flagged, poor pensions forced the poor elderly to rely on almost non-existent public transportation. Even shopping for groceries was a monumental challenge to the hesitant infirm. Everyone wanted to live longer, but society wasn't prepared to accommodate the problems longer life presented: adequate shelter, medical care, and transportation. The increasing number of old people, increasing in big spurts with each new medical discovery, voted in greater percentages than other age groups. Papers read at the conference revealed a web of changes in society that ensnared the elderly and impacted on the world of politics. Senior Citizens could no longer be ignored, or sent to Poor Farms which no longer existed.

Vera returned from Washington filled with ideas. She called a meeting of those seven or eight people already incoherently wrestling with the problem. She urged them to invite the presidents of all the women's clubs in the county to join them in a meeting modeled on the Washington conference. They should focus on what, if anything, was Marin going to do about any of the issues revealed by Caplan, or discussed at the White House. Another study of Marin's elderly was launched, and when the results were tabulated, it was revealed that Marin had no program of any kind for her elderly—not by a church, not by a club, not by a governmental agency. No one attended to the special needs of senior citizens, unless they were on welfare or in the county hospital. Only one man, working in only one area, was engaged in doing anything at all to relieve the loneliness and isolation of pensioners, and the worse plights of those older people not lucky enough to have pensions.

That man was Manny Charnow, retired San Rafael real estate agent who, struggling with his own retirement, looked about for something to do. The bleak landscape was daunting. He began chartering trips for old people, planning parties for them, gathering them together for meetings. In collaboration with Wishard Brown, in May, 1954, he signed papers of incorporation for an organization he called The Marin Senior Coordinating Council. Once he had the charter in hand, he put together a Board of Directors that read like a who's who of older citizens of Marin County.

Rose Paul, a real estate agent in San Anselmo, agreed to serve as a director and offered the new organization a telephone, plus office space until better housing could be found. She leased an old house that stood on a corner in San Rafael where two street car lines crossed, a perfect location for Seniors who could take public transportation to and from on their own. The Marin Senior Coordinating Council, the first such organization in California, went to work on the old house, cleaning, painting, and refurbishing it. When the place was in order, the coordinating council began inviting other older people to come by to play cards, to enjoy coffee and cookies, to chat. Such simple activities relieved the monotony of their days. Those who came felt rejuvenated in the company of other people with whom they shared the same problems, the same worries, the same memories.

People came from all over San Rafael, and all the surrounding communities that could be reached by public transportation. It was cheering to watch them make new friends among their own generation, to hear them laugh when they had been so silent, to see them smile when they'd looked so sad, and above all to see their steps lighten and their health improve. Obviously, Charnow and his Board were on to something. A clubhouse involves costs, such as utilities. Someone came up with the brilliant idea of opening a second-hand store named Trade Whims. People "making do" could buy clothing and odds and ends, dirt cheap. The store was a smashing success.

Tom Campanella, future county administrator in Marin, offered to keep the books and deal with the IRS. Many talented people got involved in raising money to expand the program. Members, wearing clothes donated to Trade Whims, put on fashion shows which were riotous good fun. Bridge tournaments, book reviews, bingo - they did anything older people could enjoy. They charged a small entrance fee, and every dollar went toward paying the rent. For five years they supported that house without receiving one penny from the county, the state, or the federal government. Vera, meanwhile, became president of the Coordinating Council, putting in all the hours she could spare from the long days she invested in being a conscientious Supervisor. Six years after that first

White House conference, the rising national interest in older citizens' welfare resulted in the passage of the Older Americans Act.

The Marin Senior Coordinating Council had no support from the Board of Supervisors until the passage of the Older Americans Act. To receive funds this new federal legislation made available, the Coordinating Council needed extensive documentation. The Board of Supervisors coughed up $20,000 for a one-year study, and when the time ran out, they coughed up another $20,000 for a second year. When even more time was needed, an additional $25,000 was allocated. A total of $65,000 went into the final document, the *Master Plan for Older Adults in Marin County* published in 1965. Vera, still a member of the National Council on Aging, played a leading role in creating that Master Plan. Her political acumen was being used as a private citizen just as Pat Brown had wished. Thanks to Vera, Marin was the first county in the state to receive funds under the Older Americans Act, California Grant # I.

Then three things happened almost simultaneously: 1)The Pancake House chain bought the old building that Rose Paul had leased for the Coordinating Council. Meetings and programs had to be shifted to church halls and school rooms until new space could be found; 2) The supervisors designated the Marin Senior Coordinating Council as the official aging agency of the county to receive the federal grants; and 3) With money in hand for salary, the council went in search of a full-time director. Vera was again president of the Marin Senior Coordinating Council, (MSCC), and she and the other members of the Board set out to find this qualified person.

Throughout the state, there were only three programs for the elderly in operation at that time and none of their leaders had been specifically trained to work with seniors. There was: 1) Little House in Menlo Park; 2) Aquatic Park in San Francisco; and 3) the Marin program. A job announcement went out across the state in vain. The MSCC then went nationwide in their search, again to no avail. In desperation, the rest of the council threw up its hands and turned the search over to its in-house miracle-worker, ex-Supervisor Vera Schultz. In her usual approach to a thorny problem, she sat down alone at home to think it through. Then she got on the phone with colleges and universities in the Bay Area talking to sociology departments, recreation departments, public administration departments, every field that might be producing people who could do for Marin what Vera thought should be done.

By chance, she called the Department of Leisure Science at San Jose State. Mary Wiley, head of the department, immediately shot back, "You need to talk to Ed Ryken." Ed Ryken was midway through a graduate program in recreation at San Jose. More important, he was head of the Neighborhood Youth Corp in San Mateo County. Vera called Ed and a few minutes into the conversation she knew she wanted to see this man, and she wanted the rest of the Board to see him too.

The following Saturday morning, when Ed left home to go to Marin, he told his wife he'd be back for lunch. He didn't make it back for lunch; he stayed in Marin all day. For hours, Vera probed and posed "what if" situations for him to solve while the other Board members listened attentively. As he fielded her questions it became apparent to all that they'd found their director. It became equally apparent to Ed that this job had potential for a rich experience in a new field just opening up. Such an experience could put him in the forefront of a rapidly expanding profession. Ed Ryken, tall, blond, energetic, full of ideas of his own, took a reduction in income and came to Marin on February 1, 1966, just as Vera was winding down her tenure on the Grand Jury. He thought he'd come for five or six years. To date he's logged well over 30.

The second White House Conference on Aging was held in 1971 when Richard Nixon "owned" the White House. Vera, with Ed Ryken in tow, was again a delegate. For Ed, trailing in Vera's wake, the conference was an eye-opener. He was amazed at whom she knew and who knew her. She showed him how to get around Washington, and how to make the wheels of politics turn. Ten years later, in 1981, when Ronald Reagan was in the White House, Vera attended her third meeting of the National Council on Aging, this time as a guest of the Council. Upon Reagan's election, Vera had been dropped from the National Council. Guest or council member, she constantly huddled with someone or some committee as much at work as ever. Title and salary were all that were missing from her public life.

White House conferences stoke the fires of commitment, but they don't put "bread on the table." The Marin Senior Coordinating Council had much to do, and too little money with which to do it. That meant brainstorming for hours on end about ways and means. The adrenaline flowed and the coffee pot drained. Vera was always on hand to be used as a lightning rod, a friend, a mentor, or a liaison with the county agencies they had to deal with. Above all, she was a guide, someone who could walk them through every new idea looking for pitfalls, wrinkles, flaws, and help them find all the gold nuggets. If they became cautious, she started prodding. If they became too fat and happy, she deflated them. Her fertile brain never stopped.

Lu Hodgen, second in command under Ryken, suggested they lease the old Southern Pacific Railroad station down on Third Street in San Rafael, and convert it into a center. They'd call it "The Whistlestop." Ed, and some of the members of the Board, panicked. Where were the funds? Vera calmed the waters, stiffened spines, and the quivering doubters believed. They leased part of the railroad station, then more of it, and finally the whole building. Whistlestop opened its doors February 1, 1982, with a big celebration at which Vera, then 80 years-old and again president of the Board, accepted a plaque denoting the transfer of the property from a representative of the S.P. A picture of Vera striding toward the podium in her spike heels, the famous smile blazing away, was on the front page of the *I.J.*

Leasing a building gives the lessee the right of occupancy, but a lease doesn't carry with it the right to remodel extensively, or alter the physical structure. Whistlestop needed to be remodeled if the building was to serve their purposes. In order to remodel, they needed title to the building. Vera teamed up with her old friend, Ernest Kettenhofen, another ex-Supervisor, and the two of them made trip after trip to the S.P. Offices in San Francisco trying to work out a deal. The S.P. asked $206,000. It was a good price and everyone knew it, but, short of winning the Lottery, where would that kind of money come from? Vera thought she knew where to go treasure hunting. She and "Kett" went again to the San Francisco Foundation.

In the late '70's, the U. S. Government decided to move the main post office out of downtown Mill Valley. Vera and Kett had made their first appeal to the San Francisco Foundation for Buck money then. The old downtown post office building was for sale and the price was right. A group of imaginative people had plans for taking over the building to convert it into the long-awaited Mill Valley community center. The San Francisco Foundation controlled the enormous fortune left by Mrs. Buck for the benefit of Marin County. Vera thought the foundation would give Mill Valley the money to acquire the post office when so many citizen groups would be using the building. She was wrong. The San Francisco Foundation parted with only enough money for a cost analysis of conversion.

To buy the S.P. Station, Kett and Vera made a second attempt to wrest money from the Foundation. This time Vera and Kettenhofen hit the jackpot. San Francisco Foundation money was forthcoming for the full amount of S.P.'s $206,000 asking price. The building became the property of a private, non-profit organization, not a government agency. Title to the building was the first hurdle. The second hurdle was transportation. If seniors, county-wide, were going to use the center they had to be able to get there.

The Redwoods, the first housing in California built for seniors, opened in Marin County in 1965. Two Hundred units were built in 5 different locations. Vera was chairman of the Benecia Oaks Committee of the Housing Authority that developed the first of these sites. After the units were up, she supervised the establishment of services for the residents. Meal service, counseling, and transportation were the three most pressing problems the Benecia Oaks committee faced. The Redwoods, however, was a residential project so the only persons to be served were the residents. Whistlestop was established to serve the older population of the entire county. Urged on by Vera to provide door-to-door service from wherever the elderly lived in the county, the Marin Senior Coordinating Council became a transportation company. Up and down the streets of Marin go their 52 vehicles. Over 25,000 people are shuttled somewhere by Whistlestop every month. Whistlestop's ambitious transportation project grew out of Vera's experience on the Benecia Oaks committee.

When Congress expanded the scope of the Older Americans Act with a program called Meals on Wheels, Vera quickly involved the Marin Senior Coordinating Council in establishing that service in Marin, as well. The staff at Whistlestop was too small and too busy with existing programs to take on still another program; certainly not one requiring such disciplined and constant coordination as the preparation and dispersion of hot meals. Vera organized a subsidiary committee responsible to the staff of Whistlestop that took on the responsibility. Nothing was ever too inconsequential or too overwhelming for her to handle if it meant the improvement of life for any disadvantaged segment of the population. Until she lost her sight, the coordinating council knew that whatever was needed or had to be faced, Vera would be ready with the solution. Also, whenever they ran out of presidents they could always call her back into harness.

To say thank you to the Godmother of the program, on its 20th anniversary in 1972, the Whistlestop staff put on a gala luncheon for 200 people. They created a special award for "20 years or more of dedicated service to programs on aging on behalf of Marin's elderly." They called it the Distinguished Service Honor Award, and in the history of the Senior Coordinating Council, only one person other than Vera has received it. Not since the Lifetime PTA membership given her at the Meadow Club in 1961 had Vera been so touched. They thought they were also saying good-bye to her but they were more than a decade too early with their farewell. At 70 years of age, she was just steamed up. Her last stint as president was from 1975 through 1982. On August 23, 1977, the Senior Coordinating Council celebrated its Silver Anniversary. Again, Vera was honored and received a plaque she proudly displayed in her dining room as long as she was allowed to remain in her house.

About a decade before her death, after her vision became so poor she wouldn't go out to eat with anyone else, she went to lunch with Ed Ryken and Lu Hodgen one day. They did the clock meal for her. "The meat is right in front of you at 6 o'clock, the bread is at 12 o'clock, the potatoes are at 3 o'clock,"— something she wouldn't let many people do for her. These three had been together so long, and been through so much, she could accept being handled like a baby by them. At that lunch, she asked Ed where he had all those Whistlestop vehicles serviced.

"Oh, here and there," he said.

"You can't do that," she said. "You're too big. You should have your own service center, hire your own mechanic, maintain the quality of your own service and save money for other things." And so he did. Vera never stopped thinking, and never stopped amazing the staff by the things she thought about.

Ed says, "I'm here today because of Vera. Of all my early colleagues I'm the only one to stay in the same job these many years. We were trained to move.... But Vera kept thinking of new opportunities, new projects, that kept me excited about being here. I feel as if I've had 14 or 15 different jobs." Almost like a benediction, he said that it didn't make any difference whether a person was on the same side of a controversy with Vera or not. They wound up liking and respecting her. "She never walked away with an enemy she could possibly change into a friend." Quite an accomplishment for someone as convinced of the merit of her own ideas as Vera was.

In reviewing Vera's life after she left office, the observer who didn't know how keenly she missed the political hustings would be puzzled by her statement that her career ended in 1960. Marin didn't allow her to be idle, nor did the Democratic Party, nor did Vera herself. On invitation, she went to the White House for Democratic party functions many times. One event she loved to chuckle over was the tea "Lady Bird" Johnson gave for prominent Democratic women at which her husband, Lyndon Baines Johnson, president of the United States, insisted on showing all present the scar from his recent appendectomy. At another gathering in Washington, this one to begin the 1968 campaign, each attendee received a handkerchief from Hubert Humphrey with his monogram on it. Vera had met the Humphreys many times before, beginning with the Council on Aging conference in 1952, and admired them both. She thought Muriel Humphrey one of the brightest, most charming, well-rounded women she ever met. As for Hubert, "He was a thinker," she said. Too many politicians thought in the same clichés they used in speeches. Not Hubert. For Vera, he was a breath of fresh air. That fall of 1968, she campaigned untiringly for Hubert and for Peter Behr who was running for the State Senate. When the final results were known, Behr was in, but Hubert was as out as she was.

In 1968, after six years on the Board of Supervisors, Peter Behr was ready to move on to a larger stage, a senatorial seat in Sacramento. Aline McClain, aided by dozens of devoted supporters, headed up his campaign committee. One of the most ardent campaigners was Trubee Schock, Republican whiz lady, whose organizing skills are prodigious. Trubee pleaded with Vera to come out of retirement and campaign for Behr. A prominent Democrat working for a Republican candidate to fill a partisan seat in the senate of the state of California could happen, couldn't it? Vera was more than a prominent Democrat. She was first and foremost a prominent citizen who happened to be a prominent Democrat. For the first and only time in her life, Vera switched parties for the primary and voted for Peter Behr, making speeches in his behalf with all the ardor she'd poured into her own campaigns.

In 1970, the Marin County Hall of Justice, the second phase of Wright's wondrous work, opened to the public and Vera was not only present for the dedication, but this time was seated on the dais. Fusselman had not even sent her an invitation to the dedication of the administration building in 1962. His name was on the brass plaque as one the supervisors credited with having built it but hers was not. In 1970, as she sat looking out at the crowd she thought that in this place justice would not be blind. This place, the Hall of Justice, called for dignity and decency. The judicial process would be removed from the control of a small group of self-serving henchmen bent on protecting each other. So much for fancy. She, the county, and the nation, learned one August day that year that idealism in architecture does not give birth to civility.

Today, persons taking the guided tour through the Hall of Justice are shown the leg irons installed in 1970 to keep the notorious "San Quentin Seven" in check. They are told afresh the story of Angela Davis and the shoot-out that killed a judge. Vera was in the Supervisors' Chambers that day as a Marin Committee for Civic Affairs watchdog when shots were heard, followed by confused shouting, and the sound of racing feet. In the background could also be heard the strident wailing of police sirens. An officer rushed to the door of the Chamber shouting, "Out, Out! Walk, do not run. Out of the building, now!" Not knowing who was shooting at whom or why, Vera hurried to her car as fast as her knocking knees would carry her. She was so frightened she had to use both hands, one to steady the other, to insert the key in the ignition.

Once out of the Civic Center grounds, Vera made a mad dash for home and the television set. All channels were reporting live "from the Marin County Civic Center outside San Rafael, California, where this day, a black woman radical named Angela Davis..." Vera was furious. How dare she! How dare she scorn the legal process that way and play the vigilante? How dare she betray women by behaving like a gangster? Later Vera would laugh about her initial reaction to one of the most violent episodes in a volatile, violent decade. What should have made her more indignant, she later thought, was to have her beloved building become a symbol of an old order under attack by a new generation.

In 1974, though the Hall of Justice had been completed, the Veterans' Memorial Auditorium and the Exhibition Hall for the county fair were still on the drawing board. Vera was appointed to the Committee established to oversee the construction of these two remaining buildings. For two years she hovered over the site like a brooding hen over an egg to be hatched. In 1976, when the Veterans' Memorial Auditorium was completed, and the third big celebration to honor the opening of another Wright-inspired building was held, she, Bill Gnoss and Jim Marshall, all of the surviving members of the "4-to-1" Board, were on hand to cut ribbons and allow the public inside to view their latest Civic Center triumph.

When Vera ran for the Mill Valley council back in '46, she doggedly muscled her way into the male bastions of politics. It wasn't easy. She determined then that women had to band together, work together, fight together, and support each other if they were ever to achieve the status they deserved and aspired to. Organizational support would make it so much easier to scale the walls. In her heirarchy of women's organizations that prepared women for the public arena, two shared top honors: the League of Women Voters and the American Association of University Women. The League, once it was formed in Marin in 1936, never flagged in its pursuit of the public's common weal. Not a single bill in Sacramento or Washington, D.C. escaped its scrutiny. After leaving the Board of Supervisors, Vera became the ex-officio grand dame of the LWV of Marin. Her advice and wisdom were sought about every issue. On February 6,1969, at her mountain aerie, a "Heritage Tea" was held where past presidents and founding members were honored. Vera placed in both categories.

As for the AAUW, she did not withdraw from the original group and become a member of the Southern Marin Branch for several years after its formation. Her focus trended toward San Rafael rather than Mill Valley in those years. Nevertheless, she was always available for committee work, as an adviser, as a resource, as a speaker.

221

A Mervyn Field California Poll, in 1970, reported that only 35 percent of the population in this "radical feminist state" supported the women's liberation movement. Thirty-eight percent of the population opposed it. Twenty-seven percent were neutral. Men were more neutral than women. More women than men supported equality and more women than men opposed it. Conclusion? On the average, men were indifferent to Feminism while women were energized by the issue. Those who supported the Equal Rights Amendment, which was before the U.S. Congress, were 38 percent Protestant, 26 percent Roman Catholic and 52 percent Jewish. Opponents were 36 percent Protestant, 41 percent Roman Catholic, and 19 percent Jewish. March 1972, the U.S. Congress mustered the necessary two-thirds vote and passed the Equal Rights Amendment. The California assembly quickly ratified in April and in November so did the state senate. Nationally, jubilation among advocates ran high.

Marin County women enthusiastically launched into a county-wide effort of their own. The LWV, the AAUW, and the Business and Professional Women's Club united with a small group of independent female movers and shakers to form an ad hoc committee for the purpose of establishing a Commission on the Status of Women. To go armed for battle to the Board of Supervisors to petition for enactment of their proposal, they needed the cavalry, i.e., they needed Vera. They needed her help in getting their request onto the agenda of the Board, and to make their presentation. Santa Clara County was the only other county in California with such a commission at that time. To be fully prepared, Vera suggested meeting with some of the Santa Clara leaders to learn the secrets of their success. Also, she warned, it meant instant defeat to go to the Board without two things in hand: 1) a precis of exactly what the proscribed duties of such a Commission would be; and 2) a detailed analysis of how much it would cost.

With the Santa Clara women in attendance at their second meeting, committees were formed to work on the two aspects of the proposal Vera had suggested: program and estimated cost. Vera attended every meeting of both committees. A list of responsibilities was drawn up to lay before the Board. Included were: 1) watchdog the county to make sure women were given equal consideration with men for public employment; 2) be advocates for women as consumers, clients and investors; and 3) gather statistics and initiate programs to liberate women from the oppressive limitations second class citizenship imposes on people in the work place. In Vera's view, the foremost responsibility of this newly established commission was to urge women to run for public office, any office, from dog catcher to president of the United States.

Vera made the proposal to the Board for a Commission on the Status of Women, and to her surprise there was no resistance. No resistance to their proposed advocacy of women in the realm of politics. No resistance to county funding for their Commission on the Status of Women. The Budget, of course, consumed mind-numbing time but in the end the supervisors voted unanimously to establish the new Commission and place it under the civil service department. It was the easiest victory of her career. Vera was a member of the governing board of the commission during its first year of operation, and an Emeritus member for years thereafter.

Over a decade later, the Commission on the Status of Women spawned the Marin Women's Hall of Fame. The Hall of Fame was established to honor women for outstanding achievements in public service. To prevent the award from ever becoming trivial, criteria for what constituted contributions worthy of recognition were drawn up. Induction into the Hall of Fame should never be based on a popularity contest, they decided, or be tailored to support historically applauded attributes of exemplary womanhood: "charitable, gracious, sensible, industrious, modest, etc." Women inducted into this roll call of the best and the brightest had to have given of themselves far beyond the call of duty, or the public's expectations. Marin had more than its share of such women. So numerous were the Athenas whose position on Mount Olympus should be eulogized, the commission had some catching up to do. They chose eight women to be the honorees that year. March 24, 1988, at a special dinner, Vera, 85 years old and very much alive, headed the list. One woman was inducted posthumously. The party was grand, the festivities gala, the elan glorious, and Vera was proud.

Beth Ashley conducted an hour's "conversation" with each of the recipients for local television. The interviews were taped, and each honoree was given a copy of her "conversation." During her interview, Vera's age received special mention. She was a little over four years away from being 90. She repeatedly made mention of the blindness that so dreadfully restricted her life. Vera seemed repentant for growing old, apologetic for having dropped out, but the timber of that vibrant voice belied her avowed surrender to age. Her mind was still percolating ideas for others to carry out in her stead; she was still marshaling the forces.

A HAND UP TO OTHER WOMEN

Vera's dedication to advancing the status of women was a lifelong commitment. Her mother's response to widowhood, Patty's devotion to education, Zetta's acumen for business, Mae's resilience, Vera had grown up with confident, competent women who were too proud to hide behind the men in their lives, or to surrender their independence to any circumstance, or any person. She'd modeled her own life after other women she admired, women also in reform movements or politics. Her major icon was Carrie Chapman Catt, someone who had made her great contribution as a Suffragist while Vera was a schoolgirl. Several women whom she had admired almost as greatly were more contemporaneous. She had watched them stride across the national stage, proud of their accomplishments but envious at the same time. Second to Catt in her hierarchy of heroines was Eleanor Roosevelt who died in 1962.

Another of the women whose mental gymnastics delighted her was Alice Paul. Paul formed the famous National Women's Party, and not only wrote the Equal Rights Amendment in 1923, she continued to push for its adoption through the '50s and '60s. In 1974, Paul had a stroke and her voice was stilled at a time when women still believed in the inevitability of the passage of the ERA. Vera felt that the ratio of men to women in the Congress will have to equalize to a greater extent than is presently the case before Paul's dreams for women will come true. The Religious Right will have to become more amenable to gender equality before there can be any serious hope that women are protected by law as fully as men are in the United States. It is being done piece-meal, Vera noted shortly before her death, but not with the forceful declaration an amendment to the constitution would make.

As her models died, one by one, it was painful for Vera to have the familiar faces disappear, but she had an unfaltering faith in the young women she saw coming up behind her. There were many other admirable women who were exemplars of courage and intelligence. In the early '70's, Barbara and Stewart Boxer moved to Marin. Barbara began writing on a "per-line" basis for *The Pacific Sun* as Vera had done for the *Mill Valley Record* 40 years before. Fred Drexler said he paid Vera five cents an inch for copy in the late '30s. Barbara's instinctive grasp of local issues so impressed Vera that she wrote to Boxer to express her admiration. The Boxers joined the Marin Democratic Party and, as Vera told it, Stewart confided to her that though he'd like to make a run for the Board of Supervisors, he might be too new in the county, not well enough known, to be elected. Vera wondered aloud why his wife didn't take a flyer at it. The next day Barbara Boxer called to ask if they could get together some place to talk.

Over a glass of wine in the late afternoon, Barbara quizzed Vera about her possibilities as a candidate. Vera said, "You have the assets needed for the job. You're very attractive and very bright. You're a facile speaker, quick on your feet. You can write. You have all the attributes of a good politician. It's time we had another woman on that Board."

Barbara leaned closer, "If I ran would you endorse me?"

"You get in there and stir things up! I'll endorse you, I'll put money in your campaign, I'll pass out circulars, I'll write letters. Lots of us will. What we need is a young woman like you right now."

Vera was as good as her word. She did write letters, she did make phone calls, she did send money, she did endorse her. Barbara campaigned her heart out, but the county wasn't yet ready for another woman supervisor. Four years later Barbara proved she had the stuff that makes politicians, the pluck to rise from the ashes of defeat and run again. The onus against women and their confounded notions was finally broken for the second time in 1976 by Barbara Boxer. Boxer was the first woman to sit behind the supervisors' table in the Frank Lloyd Wright Marin County Civic Center. The rest is history.

Barbara Boxer was not the only young woman to enter the world of politics wearing a mantle of association with Vera Schultz around her shoulders. Lynn Woolsey received financial support from Vera, who, though already blind, appeared on stage with Lynn at one of Lynn's rallies. The newspaper in

Santa Rosa played up Vera's appearance with Lynn, and quoted Vera's comments made on Lynn's behalf. Congresswoman Woolsey remembers. Vera kept every note she received from Lynn, and until her death, she admired the spunk of a woman who had so capably taken her own life into her own hands.

Vera's interest in the advancement of women was not limited to the arena of politics. In 1978, Jody Becker and her neighbor, Kit Cole, launched a project that would captivate Vera and harness her energies for the next two years. Jody and Vera were old friends by that time, but Kit was a new person in Vera's life. In 1978, 99.6 percent of all financial institutions' Boards of Directors were made up of white males.

Kit Cole had been a stock broker and was trying to establish herself as a financial consultant. Jody was the North Bay correspondent for the *San Francisco Business Journal.* Both felt that if women in Marin were going to be urged to invest in a financial institution, it should be in a Marin-based bank or savings and loan association. They agreed to meet for breakfast the next morning to gnaw over this big, new, novel idea. By the time breakfast was over, and they'd drunk enough coffee to propel them into space, they had decided to start a savings and loan association in central Marin. They determined they needed 23 other people to join them in becoming founders. Nineteen women and four men were recruited. Founders put up $1,500 each to launch the enterprise, and set out to sell shares at $12.50 per share. They could not begin operations until they had accumulated $2,000,000 for capital. All of their choices of Founders were shrewdly evaluated. Vera was invited to be a founder for several reasons. Her name on the letterhead would add to the impact of their prospectus. She could persuade others to invest, and finally, they could use her enthusiasm.

Kit Cole, who left the S&L after two proxy fights, was the First Chair of the Board and Jody was the vice chair. Nothing could be more certain to hike the voltage on Vera's enthusiasm than a call for "Women to Rise" and stride out on a new trail as challenging as this one. She not only sold shares, and solicited accounts, she became a leading spokeswoman for New Horizons Savings and Loan. When Vera's husband learned she was buying shares in a "misbegotten play bank founded by women," he was dismayed. He tried to put the brakes on, but his protests were in vain. Vera bought a large bloc of shares.

When the stock rose in value Ray became expansive about the sound investment his wife had made. After he was dead, and Vera's scrambled financial situation threatened to force her out of her home, "New Horizons" came to her rescue with a loan against her house that guaranteed her a monthly income so that she could stay in her home. Earlier, Vera and Ray had made a colossal mess of their affairs when they enthusiastically put their faith in a "con man" who came to live with them in the mid-'80s. He served as chauffeur, friend, confidant, the son they'd never had. By the time the extent of his misadventures came home to haunt them, Ray was incapacitated by his stroke. Their daughter from Texas came home to rout the entrenched manipulator, and New Horizons restructured her financial affairs. The "misbegotten play bank" saved her from ruin.

Sixteen years after its founding, New Horizons was sold to Luther Burbank Savings, a savings and loan association owned by the well-respected Trioni family of Santa Rosa. The original investors made a handsome profit from the transaction. Vera rejoiced over the vindication of her investment in and enthusiasm for New Horizons, but the larger fact remains, there is now no other financial institution in the Bay Area whose Board of Directors numbers 50 percent or more of women.

THE VERA L. SCHULTZ/MARIN COUNTY AAUW FELLOWSHIP
OR
MARIN SALUTES VERA SCHULTZ

In 1963, Trubee Schock joined the Southern Marin AAUW Branch and became involved in a political awareness interest group just being formed. Claudia O'Connor, who had moved to Marin in the '40s, suggested they have "Bobbie" (Vera) come to speak to them as their opening program for the fall. Trubee had heard about the remarkable career of this woman who was becoming an icon in her own time. Would a woman of such stature, she asked, come to a little group like theirs? Not in the least impressed with her own success, Vera's focus was on good government, not Vera Schultz. She came and she inspired everyone present. That fortuitous meeting later led to *the* high point of Vera's life.

In 1981, the American Association of University Women was 100 years old. The Marin County AAUW Branches decided to celebrate. What could they do that was big enough, splashy enough, important enough to honor a full century of the Association's existence? Additionally, they were again asking, "How can we honor Vera Schultz, and tell her what we think of her?" Put the two questions together and the result was a never-to-be-forgotten party the size of which Marin County rarely sees. Almost a coronation, the party was a heart-warming, laughter-filled, shimmering affair billed as "Marin Salutes Vera Schultz." One hundred and fifty people gathered at the Exhibiton Hall for a banquet. People from far and wide, all across the nation, came to be part of the schmaltzy soiree filled with love and appreciation for their gallant, "First Lady of Marin."

Appropriately, they were gathered in the last of the buildings to be built that was designed in 1959 by Frank Lloyd Wright. "The Big Pink" was now listed on the National Heritage register. A monument to many things, including Vera, her beloved Civic Center had achieved the status she always knew it would. Any party to honor her would have to be held on the Civic Center Grounds. A cocktail party was held in the Exhibition Hall amid a display of photos, plaques, resolutions, telegrams and messages that came from everywhere, which could be perused while the guests warmed up for the main event. The crowd reminisced, and schmoozed, and noshed until, by the time the gathering of Schultz fans moved into the dining room, they were fizzed up and ready to pour themselves into speeches and music and even a hokie little (not so little, it took almost an hour) spoof of her years on the Board of Supervisors.

The honorary chairman of the event was her old friend, Bill Gavin. Bill was an honorary member of AAUW. His membership dated back to a gift of $10,000 he made to their Fellowship fund after his wife Janet, who was the first president of the Marin AAUW Branch, died. He set the tone for the gathering by saying, "We are all here to pay honor to a very great lady." Betty Deedy was a long time friend of Vera's, and a long-time leader in AAUW. After an overview of the raison d'être for AAUW's Fellowship program, Deedy said: "In this centennial year of AAUW, the three Marin branches decided there was no better way to mark the recognition of growth in AAUW than to establish a Fellowship Endowment in the name of a person who has always been, in her public activities and in her life, the epitome of AAUW." People were instantly on their feet joyfully applauding their very own Vera Schultz. The passage of time had all but eliminated old antagonisms, only love and respect remained.

Senator Peter Behr was emcee that night, and, in his usual droll way recalled some of Vera's major achievements and triumphs. Pointing out all the ways Vera had left her fingerprints on the county he said, "To count you've got to be persistent, and persistence is the hallmark of persons who count...you've got to triumph over disappointments...being more interested in what you're doing than in whom you are. Tonight there is an up welling of love...for Vera..." A bit farther on in his remarks he made his famous assessment of her. "Vera never suffered defeats, she merely suffered setbacks."

Ernest Kettenhofen, former Supervisor, former president of the Marin Senior Coordinating Council, long-time friend and admirer, retired sea captain, dairy rancher out in the open sweeps of West Marin, told of the time when he was working stock and a very lovely lady he had never seen before, climbed through his barbed wire fence. Walking across the field with outstretched hand she said, "Hi! I'm Vera Schultz and I'm running for the Board of Supervisors." "I said to myself" Kett remembered, "My God, if she'll do that, she'll do anything. I was for her then, and I've been for her ever since." When he himself was supervisor along with Peter Behr, Vera appeared before the supervisors to champion the Marin Master Plan for Seniors. He turned to Peter and said, "I think Vera is the Queen Mother of Marin." Telling the story that night he added, "to this day, I still respect her as the Queen Mother of Marin."

The Tamalpais High School madrigal singers performed a "Vera Schultz Medley" with new words for old favorites. The music was followed by a wonderfully-hammy, memory-provoking performance of "The Princess and the Supes," written by long time friend, County Counsel Douglas Maloney. It was a satire about five members of an imaginary 1660s governing body dealing with the events in Marin that had occurred on Vera's watch. It was a romping recap of the years when Supervisor Vera molded the county like clay. Every major conflict of those eight years was replayed in mangled Elizabethan English that left the captivated audience sometimes bewildered. They loved it, though many of the newer Marinites didn't understand a great number of the references that left other members of the audience howling. When the catcalling, the laughter, the cheers, the clapping ceased, Vera was presented with an incredible little work of art, done by Betsy Debs. It was a miniature statuette of herself, gavel in hand, seated behind a desk on whose top were representative objects of all the offices she had held.

Supervisor Gary Giacomini, Chairman of the Board, ended his introductory remarks with, "Thank God you were so far ahead of your time." He then read the notes the other members of the Board had written for the occasion. One eloquently said, "Most of us affect events for a moment. Vera affected Marin forever." Another, "Much of the best quality of life in Marin County's government, environment and culture is attributable in large part to this beloved and extraordinary leader." Barbara Boxer, Supervisor Boxer then, wrote and Giacomini read: "When I ran

Vera was my only role model. She illuminated the path for every woman who followed." The rest of the letters contained the same abundant praise and gratitude for her legacy. Every note, every telegram, every speech was gathered into a scrapbook that they presented to her so she could remember this night of nights long after the ball was over.

Vera took the podium and her fans surged to their feet again, and stayed on their feet, beaming up at her as she beamed back. More than one admirer was seen surreptitiously wiping away a tear. When at last they subsided and let her speak, she inspired the faithful, and re-inspired the disenchanted, speaking without notes as was her wont. When she finished they stood again, deafeningly applauding, as they cheered themselves hoarse. Then came the biggest moment of all, the announcement of the establishment, by all three Marin branches of the AAUW, of the Vera L. Shultz/Marin County Fellowship Fund .

To begin, a pot of $10,000 to qualify the project is raised and an honoree chosen. The branch, or branches, files a petition with the national organization to establish a Fellowship Fund in that woman's name. The nominating group has 20 years to raise the (then $80,000) $100,000 needed to inaugurate a Fellowship and make it operational. Vera's Fellowship was the fourth AAUW Fellowship to be fully funded in California.

Money began to flow in far ahead of schedule. When Gen Bryant, Vera's childless niece, died in 1987, leaving her estate to the fund, they were well over the top. Except for one little glitch. Gen hadn't bothered to pay income taxes for a number of years; she hadn't even filed. It took more than a year to sort it all out but there was about $25,000 left, enough to put them over the $80,000 hurdle. Instead of 20 years it had taken seven. The first Vera L. Schultz/Marin County Fellow, Margaret Myers, was chosen in 1989. To date there have been five and there will be Vera L. Schultz Fellows in a long continuous line for years to come. No recognition, no award, no honor ever came Vera's way that meant so much to her. As for Trubee Schock, in retrospect she says, "That banquet was the high point of my life. I'm proud of the fact that we did that."

WINDING DOWN IN FITS AND STARTS

Vera's brothers fell by the wayside, one by one, from 1938 TO 1966, but her sisters lived on into the 1970s, '80's and '90s. As long as her sisters, "Pooh Bear," "Maynie" and "Miss Patty," surrounded her, Vera felt loved and secure, regardless of other adversities. In 1966 Patty had a stroke, broke her hip and lay absolutely mute for 7 long years. Her reprieve came October 14, 1972. Vera's life-long teacher, her constant mentor, her beloved Miss Patty, slipped away in her sleep. Maynie suffered most from Patty's death. Except for the short years when she had lived with Ross in Washington and Colorado, and the few years after Patty first came to The Coast, she and Patty had either lived in the same house or next door to each other all their lives. With Patty gone, Maynie's interest in life began to close down. She suffered from a hiatic hernia for seven years before she died in 1978, at the age of 94. Only Zetta was left. She went to live in Sebastopol near her daughter.

Meanwhile Maynie's daughter, Gen, was making a poor adjustment to widowhood. She wasn't eating properly and she was becoming reclusive; her old joie d' vivre was gone. Vera brought Gen home to her middle bedroom. The Schultz household of two people, husband and wife, both of whom had been free to come and go without consultation, became a family of three. A regular routine was established. Nightly, they lined up in the living room in front of the Schultz's only television set. Ray began to feel stifled. They were too cramped. There was no place to go to get away from the women. The thing to do, he decided, was to build an addition onto the house, something he'd been hankering to do for some time. Semi-retired with too much time on his hands, he needed a project.

The neighborhood was changing. Many of his early neighbors had expanded their 1940s houses, why not he? Ray itched to elevate 26 Ralston Avenue again to being one of the largest and finest houses on the street. It would make Gen more comfortable, he explained. With space of her own she wouldn't leave. Gen was a good listener and he needed a compliant audience. Also, her presence in the house couldn't have come at a more opportune moment. Due to failing eyesight, Vera had lost her driver's license and having Gen there provided Vera with a live-in companion and a chauffeur. Ray was again free from running errands and being tied down. If the addition was planned well, not only would Gen have her own quarters but so could he. He determined to increase the size of the main house by almost half.

The addition to the house in 1982 brought the Schultzes to loggerheads. How to connect a square two-storied frame box onto a one-storied, stone-faced rambler, particularly, when the lot sloped so precipitously downward? Years before, they'd added a big deck to the back of the house in order to enlarge the infinitesimal amount of level area for lawn chairs and a picnic table. That deck had been tied into the house at the basement sill. Ray decided to tear down the deck and use its foundations to support the addition he was planning.

Vera was on the now Marin County Housing and Redevelopment Foundation for the third time when Gen moved in in 1982. Charles McDonald, the architect engaged by the housing commission to work on the reconstruction of Marin City, let Vera persuade him to come around to look over Ray's rough drawings. Immediately, McDonald questioned the feasibility of using the existing deck foundations. McDonald felt they were not strong enough to support four rooms and three baths. Putting down additional footings, as Ray wanted to do, wouldn't be enough. When the deck was built by a gaggle of guys, hired and supervised by the master of the house, a big rock about four feet from the basement was used as one of the supports. At the time, a few exploratory probes into the thin soil showed the rock to be either a large boulder or an outcropping of the mountain itself. Boulder or mountain, it would cost more to break up and remove the offending rock than Ray was willing to pay. It couldn't be blasted out for it lay too close to the house.

Boulder or mountain? The rock was humongous. Ray insisted it could support a whole house if need be, McDonald felt it was too risky. After many heated exchanges, McDonald threw in the sponge, bowed to Ray's intransigence, and moved on to the problem of connecting the old structure to the new addition. It was a problem because the house sat close to the north lot line. Finally, they used Vera's dressing room as a connecting hallway into the new wing, with no regard for her privacy. For the rest of her life, traffic from the addition funneled through Vera's bedroom and on out into the front hall of the main house. Delighted with the solution, Ray moved himself into the front upstairs bedroom in the new addition that sported a private bath and afforded the same splendid views as the former master bedroom. Gen moved into the apartment below. After her death that area, with its own front entrance, became a rental unit.

During the fateful winter of 1982-83, the Bay Area lived through a virtual deluge. It rained day in and day out from November through February. Shallow-rooted trees fell onto houses and blocked streets, smashing parked cars in their path. Mud slides overflowed freeways, whole hillsides oozed down slope carrying houses off their foundations. Every little crevice became a rill, every little rill became a torrent, every slope a slide. Boulder or Mountain? The big rock imperceptibly began to move. The creeping was enough to pull the foundation sills of the old deck loose from the main house. The addition separated from the main house by several inches. Gen had to be evacuated back into the middle bedroom and her furniture went into storage. Water from leaks along the connecting wall was carried across the ceiling of the new master bedroom and dripped onto Ray's bed. The creaking and groaning of the addition as it pulled loose from the solid old foundation was enough to make a grown man cry.

A long hard bruising battle ensued with the insurance companies who were loath of pay for inadequate engineering and circumvention of building codes. It cost just under $100,000 to put the house back together again, and to join it with such care that a similar catastrophe could never happen again. After a tedious lawsuit came a rather generous refund of 88 cents on the dollar. Ray felt vindicated.

To comfort Vera during all the turmoil, a little Chihuahua Vera named Missile came to live with the Schultzes that year. She was irresistible when she wriggled about begging to be picked up. After giving her host a good licking Missile snuggled into a lap, any lap, preferably Vera's, to be stroked. Deer came often to the back lawn to lie in the sun on the grass near the verandah. Vera could walk out onto the verandah without the creatures doing more than glance curiously in her direction. Vera's love for animals was sated by the raccoons. Below, on Summit Avenue, June Bonnard fed a little band of the "masked critters." At sunset she'd put out food, then ring a bell hanging outside her kitchen door to call them to dinner.

One day when Vera was there, a raccoon came along the kitchen porch and rang the dinner bell itself. So enthralled was she with the performance of the little bell ringer Vera decided she, too, would feed the raccoons. She set out her own bait, a dish of kibble. Several days went by before the first coon chanced on the repast and, nervously keeping one eye on Vera, ate her offering daintily and quickly. After dinner, he licked himself like a cat and sauntered off across the lawn. The same lone coon came again and again, so trusting Vera could almost touch it. One day she left the door from the dining room to the verandah slightly ajar to see what the raccoon would do. Though the opening was no wider than three inches, the raccoon pushed its way right in. Before long, whenever it chanced by and found the door open, the raccoon came in and curled up on a footstool in front of the fireplace.

Vera was ecstatic. Her enthusiasm was not shared. To keep peace, it was decided she would keep the animal outside, feed it at the kitchen door, or not at all. The kibble bowl was shifted to the end of the house. Once, when she forgot to leave any food in the bowl, the raccoon, finding the living room door ajar again, traversed the full length of the house to find her to let her know it was time to eat. As soon as the coon had her attention, it turned and walked purposefully back the length of the house to the empty bowl at the kitchen door, uttering scolding sounds as it went. Vera didn't forget again.

Before long her first boarder returned with a lady friend. Soon after, little kits came with them. Once assured that the food supply increased in ratio to the number of beggars, numerous raccoons began to converge on her back stoop. To train the coons to come at supper time when she knew she'd be home to watch, Vera began setting out the bowl (now bowls) promptly at six every night. In the beginning six raccoons were lined up along the sliding glass door, their bright eyes reflecting the light from inside as they peered into the kitchen. They developed a cunning habit of standing on their hind legs, front paws on the glass, scratching to let her know they were waiting. As word spread through the coon community, Vera found herself knee-deep in raccoons, and buying kibble by the bushel. One night she took a picture of them and the snapshot revealed that her little masked band numbered over 40. Sadly, the torrential rains of 1982-83 ended the coon interlude. A leaking heavenly plug allowed the river Styx to cascade down onto Marin. Runoff scoured out the gully below the garage where the coons lived. Whether they drowned, or left for higher and drier areas, Vera didn't know. They never came back.

PROPOSITION 13 AND THE COUNTY LIBRARY

In 1983, the rains subsided, California dried out, and life moved on. As the sun came out, so did Vera. The library system was being decimated by Proposition 13. Not just Mental Health, not just the schools, not just parks and open space, not just a myriad of other social graces society had acquired, but the libraries of California, too, were dealt a cruel blow by that taxpayers' revolt. Vera insisted that libraries, all the way back to ancient Greece and Rome, had been the font from which flowed mankind's accumulated knowledge, from one generation to another. They had to be preserved. Libraries cost money, taxpayers' money. Five years of under-funding had brought the libraries of Marin to the point of closings. Proposition 13 was making life brutal and cheap.

Marin's incorporated towns supported their own libraries but branch libraries in the unincorporated areas served over half the population of the county. All of Marin's libraries were starved for funds. Proposition 13 had cost them $200,000 annually. Trying to staunch the mortal bleeding, County Administrator, John F. Barrows and county librarian, Mary Lou Rowe, proposed closing the Central Library at the Civic Center, dividing library services coming out of Central Library among the branches. Library users would have to hoof it from one location to another in order to receive full library service. In May, librarian Rowe proposed a $5 charge for a library card. May 17, Administrator Barrows proposed closing three libraries: Central Library, Marin City library and Bolinas library. Nothing came of any of their proposals but each was a reminder of how desperate things were.

In December of 1982, the Board of Supervisors appealed to the San Francisco Foundation for a bailout, but the Foundation wisely refused. Marin County could have shifted the whole burden of social services to Buck if the Foundation had allowed it. In January 1983, the Board asked the State of California to pass a law making it possible to charge library user fees of $10.00 annually. The Assembly refused to alter the state constitution which mandated "free" libraries for all Californians. On her own, Jacquelyn Mollenkopf, a former reference librarian at Central Library, carried out a straw poll asking Marinites whether or not they were in favor of closing Central Library in exchange for one third the space in an as-yet-to-be-named new location. That move would have broken up Marin's most complete reference collection. She mailed out a double post card, half of which could be returned to the Board of Supervisors. The results were astonishing. Because of the intense interest in the issue, more cards were returned than expected. Very few wanted the library to leave the Civic Center. That mailing had touched the right nerve. Supporters of the library, including Vera Schultz, became more vocal and more insistent that the library system be preserved the way it was.

In response to library lobbyists from all over the state, a bill was passed by the legislature in 1983 allocating an annual outlay of $18,000,000 in State funds for the support of all of California's troubled libraries. Governor Jerry Brown, son of liberal Pat Brown, vetoed the bill and killed hope that California's residents would be allowed to circumvent Proposition 13 and vote for themselves what they bloody well pleased. It seemed ironic that one of the main supporters of the ad hoc committee and its findings was Marin Supervisor Harold Brown, cousin of Jerry Brown.

The mounting crisis elicited a Buck Fund grant of $92,000 to pay for a county-wide needs assessment and a sound, cost-analysis justification for maintaining and expanding the libraries. That study took over a year to complete. Meanwhile, in March, 1983, alarm over the possibility of losing the central library and its multiple services sent concerned library users to their typewriters. A constant flow of letters to the editor kept the issue before the public. On March 23rd, at a crowded hearing at the Civic Center, the Board of Supervisors was petitioned not to close the Civic Center Library and dismantle the reference collection. An ad hoc citizens' committee called the "Save Our County Libraries Committee," (SOCL), was founded and Vera was invited to be chairman. Vera could think and speak even if she couldn't read. "Jackie" Mollenkopf, as executive secretary of the committee, had to be Vera's eyes. Within weeks SOCL was recommending a $22 tax override to be put on the November, 1984, ballot.

Berkeley had successfully gone through such a ballot effort. Speakers were brought over to the College of Marin where, in a meeting in Olney Hall on May 25, 1983, they told SOCL how Berkeley had secured the passage of successful library tax measures. The Board of Supervisors then decided to put the tax override measure on the June ballot in 1984 instead of waiting for November. Six other county districts, under-funded because of Prop 13, also needed relief through initiatives placed on that ballot. The total amount of all initiatives would be too high to expect passage of any of the funds if they were all thrown at the taxpayers at the same time. SOCL decided to scale back to $18 per household, which would be only 77 percent of the 1978 budget.

In May, in a "Campaign '84" feature in the *I.J.* just before the June election, Vera responded to the anti-tax group's comparison of 1968 costs with those of 1984. She pointed out that in those 16 years, because of population growth, regional, full-service libraries had opened in Novato, Corte Madera and Fairfax. Each offered a full range of library and information services, including reference and children's programming.

Thinking Vera's point of view too conservative, without Board approval, a much more zealous leadership took over. Vera's name remained on the Committee's letterheads and the newspapers continued to cite her opinions when writing about the issue, unaware of the behind-the-scenes power struggle that had unseated her. The public was not aware of her displacement, but Vera was humiliated. She had been judged inadequate.

In June 1984, Measure A, a tax override which required a two-thirds voter approval, went down to defeat. The vote had been premature. The assessment report did not come out until six months after the election. That report solidly affirmed the judgment of SOCL. The staff was almost down to using library paste to keep the system afloat when finally in August 1984, the county loaned the library $68,716 at 11.9 percent. It was enough to tide the system over until a new measure could go to the voters.

Following publication of the results of the Buck-financed study, separate ballot measures were drawn up in different parts of the county. In 1986 and 1988, those ballot measures resulted in special assessments of $36 per parcel. The increase in inflation since 1978 made the $36 rate equal to the proposed $18 of a decade earlier. It had taken seven years to hammer out a solution once the problems of the Library became a thorn in the body politic of Marin. The "Save Our County Libraries" campaign was Vera's last great crusade on behalf of "the people," and she almost missed seeing the victory.

There was more on Vera's plate than the Redevelopment Foundation, SOCL, and Whistlestop in the '80's. The Community Health Center of Marin needed guidance and historical perspective. Marin was in the process of defining the goals for the new community health center that had just opened in Fairfax. Vera was invited to join the Board. Formerly called Medical Contact Services, the agency operated out of two clinics, one at Novato and one at Fairfax. Both offered a wider range of health services for the poor than had been available before Medical Contact Services came into existence. However, what was offered at one clinic, both in quality of care and per capita cost, was not necessarily available at the other. There needed to be uniformity so that all the poor of the county were treated equally.

Vera wanted the new agency to become a model of geriatric care for other agencies to emulate in the future. In addition, she felt it imperative that the agency be commissioned to oversee clinics for the poor of all ages. Expansion was a keynote of Vera's approach to reform when already-existing agencies could be expanded. Expansion is cheaper. In the end, she firmly established the axiom that geriatric care is special care that requires special programs. She not only knew what the problems of aging were from her work with Whistlestop but also was beginning to know from her own personal experience.

Her eyes were giving her fits, constantly weeping and blurring over. Vera wanted a miracle, she wanted her eyesight back. She wanted her driver's license restored, her mobility returned. She knew all the frustrations of the elderly. In January and February of 1984, she had two different back-to-back surgeries that produced slight, temporary improvement in her vision, but not enough. She was told she was too old for the kind of redemption she longed for. All those fabled cures she'd heard were what happened to younger people. Unable to accept the results of her first surgeries, she had back-to-back operations on first one eye, then the other in 1985 and 1986. After the second operation, she abruptly lost 80 percent of her remaining eyesight. Overnight, she could no longer read even the headlines in the newspaper. She was frantic. Luckily, Gen was there to see her through the despair that filled her as the impending blackness, not too gradually, blotted out the world and left her helpless.

Blindness, for a voracious reader like Vera, was a calamity of horrific dimensions. She and Zetta talked by phone every day, since they could no longer get together physically, and the telephone kept her in touch with her friends, but she felt intellectually shipwrecked. Books on tape, condensed as they are, and radio for the blind helped to ameliorate the full impact of her isolation, but inadequately. The books she wanted to read were not popular literary fare so they had not been recorded. Radio for the Blind had to provide pleasure for a vast array of people and much of its programming seemed trivial to Vera. Searching in vain for the silver linings her predicament must yield, she futilely tried to talk her way out of the worst of her depression. No tack was effective against the slough of frustration in which she was mired. Friends who called heard the despair in her voice and began to talk about what could be done.

Josette Gavin, Bill Gavin's new wife, followed the footsteps of first wife Janet Gavin who had been the first AAUW president in Marin County. She was now president of the Southern Marin Branch. Josette came up with the solution that rescued Vera. Why not have members who had the time take turns going to Vera's to read to her from 2 o'clock until 4 in the afternoon, five days a week. Someone could go to read to her what Vera wanted read. It was a brilliant idea that worked magically. Vera sat in her little rocker stroking the coat of her little one-eyed Chihuahua, listening so intently she never missed a word. She loved biographies. Sometimes she'd interrupt the reading to comment. "I remember when I was in Washington back in 19__," or "I met her or him at a meeting..." "Reader" and "Read-To" spent wonderful afternoons together. Vera had as many as five different books on five different subjects going at once, all stacked within reach beside the couch.

Dorothy Killion, the first of the readers to sign up, took Monday afternoons. Her ulterior motive in volunteering to read to Vera was to compile a story of Vera's life. The problem was that Vera was more interested in other people's biographies than her own. So, Dorothy read biographies of 20th century people whose lives had been invested in politics: books on the Roosevelts, every word of McCullough's *TRUMAN*, the latest biography of the man from Texas, LBJ. Books on the Kennedys, Jimmy Carter's own book, everything that came out in that genre was grist for Vera's mill. One of the last books Dorothy read to her in the fall of 1994 was Betty Friedan's, *THE FOUNTAIN OF AGE.* Friedan's ideas helped Vera accept what was happening in her own life.

At the foot of Vera's mountain, a young, enthusiastic, female attorney named Kathleen Foote ran for a seat on the Mill Valley City Council in 1984. When she announced her candidacy, she heard from Vera. First she received a letter of congratulations, then came checks. Kathleen began to ask questions about this donor, this Vera Schultz, and was embarrassed to learn that her benefactress was the first woman to serve on the council. Vera was losing her place in history a second time. A new generation didn't know her.

Kathleen won the election, served for eight years, and was Mayor of Mill Valley several times. She is now a trustee of the Marin Community Foundation (the Buck money is at last housed in Marin and controlled by Marinites). Shortly after meeting Vera, Kathleen became a regular visitor and talked to her on the phone when she couldn't find time to drive up the mountain. Kathleen scoured the newspapers for news items about issues before the county supervisors, articles about the Civic Center, treatises on government, anything current and vital in Marin to bring with her and leave behind for someone to read to Vera later.

Sally Hauser moved to Marin in 1972. The Civic Center drew her like a magnet the first time she saw it. Sally arrived in the county just as the Civic Center Docents' Organization decided to create a conservancy to protect the building from any architectural change. Sally became a member of the Conservancy Board of Directors. In 1987, as the Board of Supervisors and the Conservancy began planning for the 25th anniversary of the administration building, she began compiling a brochure for that stellar event. She'd never met

Vera, but she wanted to video-tape an interview with her to be shown on the big day. Vera, of course, was delighted to be the subject of the tape, and thereby part of the program. Out of that interview came Sally's commitment to be a reader. Who learned more from the sessions, Sally or Vera? Sally thinks she did. "I never ceased to be amazed at the breadth of her acquaintance with all the current issues, or at her vocabulary," she said. Vera had an incredible stock of words to dip into. The readings continued until the last two months of Vera's life.

When the Board of Supervisors approved the docents' resolution giving the new organization full authority to oversee the building in the future, there were stipulations attached to their charter. One frustrating limitation was that the Board gagged the docents' organization in regard to a proposal then before the Board to build a new jail. Within one decade, the jail, buried under the north knoll at the end of the Hall of Justice wing of the Civic Center, was too crowded. The supervisors were planning to build a free-standing structure at the western edge of the property up against the freeway. Shades of George Jones! His ghost must have guided the hand that wrote the proposal which said that a jail should look like a jail. Never mind that the four-square fortress the Supervisors wanted would block the public's view of those magnificent buildings and the three knolls that enhanced and bracketed them.

Sightless, Vera quit letting people take her for outings, but she could be blasted out by events. In 1989, the jail issue finally reached boiling point. Only the threat of demolition of the Civic Center itself would have caused Vera more anxiety. The Board's proposed free standing jail, in full view of the public, was about to be voted into existence. In the Frank Lloyd Wright plan, only the exercise yard of the existing jail was above ground. That exercise yard was visible only from the air. The supervisors were about to take bids for a stark, spare, four-storied, highly-visible building to be erected on the drive below the Civic Center. Construction had to be stopped before it began! Vera went to work.

Being the careful technician as always, Vera made sure she understood all the ramifications that would accrue to the county if she had it her way before she raised her voice in protest. If she stopped this monstrous defilement of her precious building, would it place an unconscionable burden on the county? She talked Margaret Azevedo into reading the E. I. R. (Environmental Impact Report) legalese and explain to her what all the various regulations meant. Margaret, a graduate of the county planning commission, could read the fine print well. Once Vera was sure she could work within federal and state regulations, she contacted attorneys to ground herself thoroughly in the law about how "breach of intent" could be used to stop this defacement of a National Heritage Property.

As a last check on the infallibility of her position, she asked her readers to read the letters to the editors about the issue in every paper in the county. She wanted to take the public's pulse. There had to be a reasonable number of equally incensed people if she had any hope of success. When she had all her ducks lined up, she began her campaign to kill the project before any money could be spent.

Equally indignant, Aaron Green had a solution to the problem that even Frank Lloyd Wright would have approved. Bury a new jail next to the existing one, connect them and double the space horizontally. February 7, 1990, 88-year-old Vera went on Aaron's arm to the Supervisors' meeting where a public hearing on the matter was underway. Though his health was little better than Vera's, Peter Behr was also there to help defend the building. There was a buzz of murmuring when Vera was led in. The hearing came to a halt. No one had expected her or been warned that either she or Peter would appear. The two beloved, old political giants had come to support Aaron's plan and their appearance almost stopped the meeting.

When Vera rose to speak, the chamber erupted in a din of spontaneous cheering. Outfoxed, the Board had to give her the podium. As eloquent as ever, as persuasive as ever, without histrionics, she succinctly stated her case. Many other people had come to defend the purity of the Civic Center design and, empowered by Vera's presence, they too were granted audience. They averred that what Ann Kent, sister-in-law of Roger Kent, had once called a gaudy piece of lawn decoration was now universally recognized as Art with a capital A. Together with the Olympian triumvirate—Behr, Green and Schultz—they urged the Board to put beauty before bucks. The speech that carried the day however was delivered by the Founding Mother.

She said, "Aaron and I look back down on the vestige of another time when there was much opposition to the Frank Lloyd Wright concept. You know it's appreciated by the world, not just Marin. We must preserve it." A new Board in a new day was humbled. They buried the jail in the north knoll as Aaron envisioned it. Ominously, however, it is full to overflowing a half decade later. Unless society finds its way back to a more civilized state of being, the jail question will come again before long. Whatever the solution, the integrity of the design of the Civic Center is sure to again be a major issue. Next time, someone other than Vera will have to protect it, someone who loves magnificence more than expediency as she did.

RETREAT

Three years into Vera's blindness, Ray had a stroke. Though he regained his speech and could walk haltingly with a cane, his driving days were over. They had to have live-in help. A series of caretakers followed each other through the house. A few were good, some pretty good, and a few were excellent, but none were permanent. Then Ray had a second stroke in 1990, a stroke from which he never recovered. Their daughter flew in from Texas. The apple of his eye was at his bedside when he died and it was she who told Vera the next morning that her husband of 64 years was dead. In the tradition of Vera's family, there was no memorial service. Ray's ashes were buried without fanfare under his favorite bush in the backyard.

Left now to the care of live-in help, Vera was helpless to control the flow of people through her house. Victimized, poorly attended in the beginning, Vera was at last lucky when Karen Swarm moved in. Under her supervision the house became orderly, visitors were screened and scheduled, meals were prepared when Vera wanted to eat, not according to the clock or to the whims of others, and Karen made no presumptions about what Vera should or should not hear, think or do. A quality of contentment and serenity settled over the house.

In 1992, on her 90th birthday, Marin County decided to tell Vera Schultz one more time how much they loved her. By now she was indeed an icon in her own time, a prized in-house, genuine gold symbol of what the Women's Movement had always been about. August 26, 1920, the Constitution of the United States of America was amended to give women the right to vote. The suffragists had carried the day in state after state until 36 states had approved the amendment that had been 72 years aborning. A second 72 years after the 1848 Seneca Falls meeting, August 26, 1992, the anniversary date of the 19th Amendment, was used to honor the woman who had become an example for other women of what the amendment had made possible.

Even though her birthday was not until the 31st, when told of the proposed celebration, Vera asked that the observation of her four score and ten be held on the anniversary date of the passage of the 19th Amendment. It shifted the focus from one woman's longevity to something more significant, something she wanted one last chance to hammer home--the need for women to go into politics.

Wearing a lovely dress Sally Hauser had chosen for her--a dress beflowered in bright red poppies against a rich green background--her wig on straight, her smile radiant, Vera was excited. The committee sent a white orchid corsage for her to wear. She could still walk, if the distance was not too great, the path smooth, and somebody led her. It had been some time since she'd been out for a gala of any kind and Vera did love a party. Seated on the dais in the Supervisors' Chamber, people could approach and greet her. If she had not heard their voices for some time, they had to tell her who they were as they took her outstretched hand.

She gave her well-wishers the usual heart-warming experience of watching a master in human relations at work. As person after person approached and was identified, she called upon her prodigious memory to respond skillfully and appropriately with anecdotes from the past that involved that person. Two young girls, ages 12 and 13, Caysea Dawson, daughter of Mill Valley city manager, Doug Dawson, and Kathleen Foote's daughter, Grace Rubenstein, were there. When they were propelled forward to meet the great woman Vera pulled each of them to her in turn and said, "I want you to listen carefully to what I say this afternoon because my remarks are directed to you." Somewhat unnerved, the girls took their seats and paid rapt attention when she spoke. The future was present and Vera still had a word for it.

A number of people spoke that afternoon, all eloquent in their almost reverential love for her. Al Aramburu, former chairman of the Board of Supervisors, in extolling her wisdom in selecting Frank Lloyd Wright as architect for the Civic Center, said: "Without Vera there would be no here here." When the eulogizing was done, Vera took over. Clearly, articulately, in full sentences and complete paragraphs, Vera reiterated much of what she'd said to a previous generation. She went back over the history of the women's movement, stressing the fact that British and American female delegates who had gone to London to attend the anti-slavery conference in 1840 had not been allowed to participate because they were women.

Moving from the past to the present, she eloquently spoke of three women who were running for office that fall. The women in question had not only overcome the handicap of being women, they had overcome obstacles of race and poverty to present themselves to the people of their respective states as candidates for national office. Carol Mosely-Braun, an Afro-American woman from Chicago, was running as the first female black candidate for the United States Senate. Lynn Woolsey from Santa Rosa, single parent of two children, who had gone to college while on welfare, was running for Congress from Vera's own district. The third woman was the first Native American woman to make a race for national office. She was also seeking election to the House of Representatives. If such women could stand before the electorate in 1992 and offer themselves as viable candidates, competing with white men, then indeed the aspirations of Elizabeth Cady Stanton, Susan B. Anthony, Lucretia Mott, Carrie Chapman Catt—and Vera Schultz—had been realized. She closed her speech that night with the same quote she'd used twice before at events honoring her, Carrie Chapman Catt's words to the new League of Women Voters in 1920:

> "Women have suffered agony of soul that you can never comprehend in order that you and your daughters may inherit political freedom. Our hope has been that you will aim higher than your own selfish ambition to serve the common good."

Paul Peterzell, long time reporter for the *Independent Journal,* who in earlier days had not always been enamored with Vera's determined persistence, was inspired to say, "This is one of the golden events of my life." He spoke for everyone present.

LADY BIRD, LADY BIRD, FLY AWAY HOME

The party over, a tired but happy Vera was delivered into Karen's capable hands with nothing to do now but live to be 100 and have another party. Karen kept the calendar, scheduled the readers, oversaw the medication, cooked, and supervised the cleaning woman and the gardener. Karen read Vera's mail to her, every single piece of it. Since they were politically kindred spirits, and since Karen was bright and gentle and close to being family, the hours they spent together were comfortable and easy. A friend, or friends, visited Vera every day, and a reader showed up five days a week. For a whole year she drifted contentedly down the stream of her life toward the sea, planning for her centurian celebration. Then the winter of 1993-1994 brought Vera into the rough waters that ended her journey short of 2002.

Her heart began giving her fits. There was no cure. For a whole year, with the help of hospice and the loving care of Karen, she remained in the home she loved. People streamed through her house as constantly as they had since Ray's death. Her readers came on "good" days when her heart was behaving and there was no pain medication to dull her mind. She dictated all the memories she could dredge up of the 92 years of her life for her biographer. She listened to her radio. Even Caysea Dawson and Grace Rubenstein, the young girls who had listened at her 90th birthday party, came to call. Led to where she reclined, they took turns perching on a chair facing her. Vera and Grace had a long talk about losing elections. Grace had just lost a school election and expressed her disappointment to Vera, as though talking to a peer. In exchange, Vera told Grace what it felt like to lose the election of 1960. She admonished Grace that the merit of a winner is to be able to go on from there, to assess losses as carefully as wins, and learn from the process.

Grace's visit came close to the end of Vera's days in Marin. Talk of moving Vera to Texas was already in the air. When he heard of it, Doug Dawson said, "Taking Vera to Texas is like putting a magic bird in a cage." Most of her friends agreed. All through November and December Vera stoutly insisted she was not going to Texas. In November she wouldn't even consider a trip for the holidays. In December she yielded and said she'd go sometime after the holidays for two or three weeks, but no longer. At last, in January, 1995, she capitulated and said she'd try it for one year. The house would be left in the hands of her daughter's friend so it would be there for her if she decided to return. The last day of January, 1995, on a makeshift bed in the back of a big battered yellow van bearing Texas license plates, Vera left on the arduous journey, wedged in with two cats, two dogs, a huge bird cage holding the well-traveled Texas parrot that had been resident in her house for over two months, her recliner chair, and the traveling paraphernalia of a fragile, heart patient. Suffering from a heavy cold, Vera was wafted off to a little ranch in east Texas. She was leaving behind her precious aerie in which she would never nest again. The First Lady of Marin's departure from her realm was a dolorous, rain-soaked trek begun before dawn, a journey of 2,000 miles which was accomplished in three-and-a-half days.

For three months, trying to make her friends feel better about her going, she told everyone who called her in Texas that she was "thriving." Then May 1, 1995, she told Kathleen Foote she was "enduring." May 3, 1995, Vera Lucille Klingensmith Schultz died in her sleep. One of the greatest public servants Northern California has ever known was gone. One of the most effective women politicians in the 20th century left the stage to other, younger women who will follow in her footsteps. A life-time of activism was over and the social-political landscape of Marin had been irrevocably changed by her sculpting. Vera was the model citizen, the model activist, the model politician. Since her death, she has become almost heroic in stature in the county she loved so much. As someone said two weeks after her death at the memorial service held in the supervisor's chambers: "The world needs many Veras and we were lucky to have the original."

APPENDIX

THE MOUNTAIN MEADOW MASSACRE AND OTHER STORIES

Long before Vera's birth in 1902, her grandmother truncated the family name from Klingensmith to Smith, disavowing her husband and all he stood for. Klingensmith was a foremost name among the Mormon "Saints" until 1857 when the Mountain Meadow Massacre made it synonymous with "outcast." Vera was forever indignant about the events of 1857 and the years that followed. She needed, or seemed to need, to reestablish the family's lost status. Even at age 92 she was still indignant over the turn of events that left her with a pedestrian surname like Smith. Over the years she constantly sought historians, researchers, anyone willing to take on the Mormon Church and plow through their archives to find information that would clear her grandfather's reputation and give the family back its dignity. She pressed Wallace Stegner to take on the task but he ducked her request as he is reported to have ducked similar requests from the Babbitts of Arizona. Stegner insisted that nothing worth knowing about the Mountain Meadow Massacre would result from new research.

To the end, Vera stubbornly refused to believe that information of importance no longer existed or was forever hidden away. She didn't believe there was little merit in opening up the old story. She clung tenaciously to the notion that someone could unlock the secrets of the past if only the right source—the hidden trunk, the secret diary, the crumbled letter, the confession—was found. She was very sure that "history" would be well served by "the truth."

In 1857, eastern papers carried stories of a cold-blooded attack by 20 Mormon men and a small tribe of local Indians on a disarmed wagon train of Missourians headed for California. They called it "The Mountain Meadow Massacre." "Gentiles" poured through Mormon territory on their way to California that year and plenty of money was made from provisioning westering pioneers. On the other side of the equation, the federal government was demanding that "The Kingdom of Deseret," i.e., the Mormon Church, acknowledge the

255

supremacy of territorial laws passed by Congress over Mormon law promulgated in Salt Lake City by The Prophet, Brigham Young. Young refused to acknowledge U. S. sovereignty and began to stockpile weapons. All wagon trains were, henceforth, to bypass Mormon Territory.

Most settlers coming west that year were ignorant of the ban and the rest ignored it until armed "Mormon Battalions" began to block their path. Those already en route, ignorant of the edict or willing to chalk it up to rumors, followed the California Trail across Mormon territory. The Fancher party out of Missouri had come through Salt Lake City without incident. Farther into Utah, they encountered some heckling as they passed through small enclaves of Mormons living away from the Temple city, but nothing portended danger. Cedar City, the seat of Bishop Philip Klingensmith's authority, lay on the southwestern end of the well-worn trail that led ultimately to southern California. That trail had been cut more than a decade before the Mormon show-down with the U.S. government.

Perhaps if the Fancher party had not stopped to rest their stock and fatten them on Mormon grass before heading out across the Nevada desert there might have been no violence. But violence erupted as soon as the Fancher party made camp. Whether acting on their own or inflamed by the "Saints," a band of Indians living nearby attacked the encampment. The Missourians immediately circled their wagons and drove their livestock into the enclosure. From this improvised fortress they returned the Indians' fire for three days without a single death on either side. On the third day 20 armed Mormon men appeared, led by their elected militia leader, John D. Lee, and by Philip Klingensmith, the bishop of Cedar City.

The Indians withdrew behind rolling hills to the north. The men of the Fancher party were persuaded to lay down their arms and walk out of the enclosure under Mormon protection, paired one Mormon to one Gentile. The women and the children of both sexes, accompanied by three Mormon guards, were sent well ahead of their men to return to Cedar City. When the two groups were out of sight of each other, the Indians fell on the women and children and, as though by script, the Mormon "protectors" immediately gunned down the Fancher men, each Mormon killing the Gentile beside him.

When the fury was spent that grisly day, the air hung still and heavy over the meadow where tomahawks had gleamed in the sunlight and pistol shots had echoed off the hills. Only the soughing of the wind stilled the echoes of curdling screams from people scattering helter skelter in all directions trying to escape. Caught out in the open with no means of self defense, the Missourians were butchered in their tracks. Stunned by their own violence, horrified at what had been done, sickened by the carnage they'd created, the "Saints" stood mute in the thick silence, unbroken by bird call or the sound of any living thing. They were young Mormon men who had been eager to serve a holy cause but nothing was holy about the gory corpses strewn over the meadow, crumpled where they fell.

Horrified at the harvest they'd reaped, the Mormons pledged to each other before God that no one would ever tell what happened that day in that place. It was an empty pledge. News of the massacre could not be suppressed by a compact made by guilty men of heavy conscience. Within days, newspapers in the East carried stories of the body-strewn field where dogs roamed and the curious came among the unburied dead. Every man, woman and child in that wagon train, all 126 of them, had been killed except for two little girls who disappeared.

Did Philip Klingensmith order that massacre? All documentary evidence that could prove that Vera's grandfather did not participate nor in any way goad the Indians to bloodshed has disappeared. The question of who ordered the slaughter remains. Many Mormons today "know" that the men who were accused and the men who went to trial acted under direct orders from Brigham Young. Within two years, Philip Klingensmith himself broke the vow he'd imposed on the others and openly put the blame on Prophet Young. Brigham Young loudly accused Klingensmith of lying and threatened him with excommunication if he did not retract the charge. In 1864 the bishop gave an affidavit to the "truth" of what had happened to U.S. government marshals who were investigating the atrocity. In that affidavit he again asserted that Young had given the order. The gauntlet was down.

Young retaliated by carrying out the threat of excommunication. He not only threw Klingensmith out of the church but stripped him of all his lands. Fearful that excommunication and expropriation would not satisfy the "Lion of Judah" in Salt Lake City, and fearing that his life was in danger, the ex-bishop went into hiding with John D. Lee at Pocketville in the mountains near the Utah border. Klingensmith was hunted by the church and Lee was hunted by the United States Government.

When finally they stood trial in federal court in 1881, ex-bishop Philip Klingensmith testified under oath that it had been Prophet Brigham Young who had planned the massacre and by secret messenger sent the order to carry it out. To confuse the proceedings thoroughly, a courageous (or mad) few took the stand and swore they saw the 20 Mormon men kill many of the women and children themselves after the men of the Fancher party were all down. Out of a welter of conflicting testimony the truth became thoroughly obfuscated. In defiance of the church, a jury of his peers found Philip Klingensmith "not guilty." Lee was found guilty and executed by U.S. Marshals. The United States was appeased but the church was not.

Klingensmith fled to Sonora, Mexico where he set to work developing mining claims he held down there. He hoped that in time tempers would cool and he might one day return to Utah. That was not to be. As he worked at the bottom of a shaft of one of his claims, two men approached the mouth of the shaft and, without preliminaries, fired straight down into the pit, killing him instantly. Many watched the pair of executioners walk proudly away making no effort to hide their identity. Vera's family was convinced that those two men were members of The Avenging Angels, a unit of the Mormon church that administered justice as the Mormons saw fit.

Philip Klingensmith's murder aroused in Vera's family an aggrieved sense of righteous indignation over the loss of name and place. The children of the bishop passed on to their children a hatred for organized religion so strong that the antipathy survived the second generation to be passed on into the third. It kept them away from clergymen, even for marriages and funerals. If Ray Schultz had not made all the arrangements for their wedding without consulting Vera, no minister, no matter how casually he practiced his calling, would have officiated at their nuptials. "You can see why I detest organized religion, can't you?" Vera asked when she told the story of her grandfather. Her scorn for religious orthodoxy knew no bounds and she seemed obsessed by a need to exonerate her grandfather.

VERA GOES TO A PARTY

Life in the mining towns of the West was hard on women and children. In most mining towns there was nothing for women and children to do but gossip and fight. Tonopah's mine owners tried to provide enough entertainment of the right sort to keep their miners' families happy and content. One of the highlights of every year for the children was The Tonopah Miners Association Christmas Party. The association hired a traveling troop of entertainers to provide a rollicking afternoon of fun. The children sat on the floor before the raised dais watching some of the same people perform they'd seen come through with the carnival the summer before. Once the performance was over, food was laid out for all, and Santa Claus himself appeared with a bag of treats: candy canes, gingerbread men, red licorice sticks, and a toy for each child to take home.

The year Vera was 10 Charles told his mother to get "Bobbie" all dressed up because he was going to take her to the Christmas party. Vera was overjoyed. She shivered with delight. It had never occurred to anyone before that a miner brother was as good as a miner father as an escort to the big event. The night before she excitedly laid out her best clothes and had her mother put her hair put up on rags. Putting one's hair up on rags produced Shirley Temple corkscrew curls long before Shirley Temple was born. The little hard spindles were agony to sleep on, but what price beauty? Her shiny black hair becurled, Vera felt like the fairest child in the land. Dressed in her best, she walked proudly and demurely down the street beside Charles, hanging onto his hand. Her beautiful coiffure bounced up and down as she walked.

When they arrived, there was a jam of children in the hall, all elbowing toward the front. In the crush, one of Vera's beautiful curls caught on a button on the waistcoat of a man behind her and she couldn't get free. As he pushed his child to the front of the pack, he dragged Vera with him. He was so tall and she was so small her efforts to reach up to tug at his tie were futile. Charles, momentarily pushed back out of range, could only watch helplessly as Vera was hauled along by her hair. She began to cry. Charles battled his way to within reaching distance and grabbed the man by the elbow. The man, turned slightly and became aware of Vera's plight. As people pushed past the ensnarled trio the two men set her free.

Completely unnerved and distraught, Vera began worming her way back through the mob, sans toy, sans candy, sans anything. All she wanted was escape! Charles let her pull him along into the bitter cold outside. To make up to her for the toy she didn't get, Charles led Vera to a warm shop nearby to regain her composure and to browse. She shouldn't go home empty-handed to face the family. The shop sold books as well as trinkets. Not a large collection, but most of the standard works of good literature were there. After she calmed down, Vera began to finger the books, not the trinkets. Charles reached out a hand and smoothed her hair.

"What would you like, Tina?" he asked, using the old pet name she'd abandoned when Gen came back to Tonopah to live.

She looked up at him shyly and asked, "Have you ever read *In Memoriam* by Alfred Lloyd Tennyson?"

Startled, Charles stared down at her in amazement. "No," he said. "Have you?"

"Yes," she sighed, "but I didn't understand it very much. I wish I could have it for my own, and then when I'm a better reader, I'll understand it."

Astounded by her desire for a book she couldn't understand, awed that she preferred a work by Tennyson to a bauble that would have delighted any other child, Charles reached up, took the book off the shelf and handed it to the clerk. "Wrap this up like a fine present," he huskily told the woman. "We're going to put this under our Christmas tree." The clerk, as touched by Vera's choice as Charles, wrapped the book in the prettiest paper she had and tied a big satin ribbon around it. "Here," she said, handing the book to Vera, "and a very Merry Christmas to you." Vera went home clutching her new book in all its Christmas glory with more pleasure than if she'd gotten something out of Santa's pack at the party. She had that book still when she died.

MOUNT AIREY SCHOOL

The day after she was fired from the Mill Valley-Sausalito School district, the day after she cleared out her cabinets at Old Mill School, Vera marched down to Mount Airey School on the corner of Molino Avenue and Mirabel, to see Miss Flagg about a job. Mount Airey was a private school established by the elderly spinster more than a score of years before. Miss Flagg had taken the name for the school from a poem in the fourth grade reader that began, "Up the airey mountain, down the rushing glen, we dare not go ahunting for fear of little men..." Mount Airey's children entered at the nursery school level and continued through the fourth grade. Vera asked for a job as a kindergarten teacher. She had learned to love that age group while working at Old Mill School. All their innocent charms and eager enthusiasms captivated her. The job paid peanuts but it paid something, enough to give her a little pin money of her own. Mount Airey School was a winsome place to work: the classes were small, the children were tutored more than taught, and everything was very informal. Miss Flagg hired Roy Huffman's ex right-hand on the spot. It was an idyllic situation for Vera.

Idyllic rarely lasts long. No sooner did Vera go on staff than, without warning, Miss Flagg abruptly died. It was a shock. Was the school to close? Vera couldn't think of an ending like that to something she'd begun to love. As soon as decency allowed, she and Katie Robson, another teacher at Mount Airey, went to Miss Flagg's brother who had inherited the house. They negotiated a lease giving them permission to take over the school. As head mistress, Vera was plunged back into administration. Ignoring the clause in their rental agreement that gave Miss Flagg's brother the right to sell the property any time he chose, the two women jumped into their new challenge.

For two wonderful years Vera and her staff of four immersed themselves in the children's wonderland they had inherited. Then the other shoe dropped. Miss Flagg's brother decided to put the house on the market and threw them out with only 30 days notice. They'd known it could happen, but they'd lulled themselves into complacency as the days since the death of Miss Flagg went on. Now, confronted with a 30-day notice for which they'd made no preparation, they were shaken. In a panic, Vera and Katie went hat in hand to Zetta to ask for shelter until they could work out some other arrangement to keep a roof over their heads.

At Zetta's, everything was makeshift and awkward and unproductive. Katie, Vera and the three other teachers tried to hang on but the stress level in the new situation was too great. Mount Airey School closed its doors and quietly died. When she stored all her teaching materials in Zetta's basement, Vera didn't know she would never use them again. While it lasted though, while Mount Airey School was Vera's whole life, she made another impact on education that would contribute to her lifetime membership in the PTA awarded at the Meadow Club over 20 years later. Vera ardently loved children as did her mother and her siblings, though they had few of them.

"THE BRIDGE AND THE BUILDING"

I met Vera Schultz one bright spring day in 1971 when I descended the steps that led to her front door from the street above. I had read about Vera in the *Marin Independent Journal.* This woman had wielded extraordinary power in the battle to engage Frank Lloyd Wright as architect for the Marin County Civic Center. Political battles had erupted, at first over the choice of an architect, and later over completion of the building. The background of those battles would make good material for a doctoral dissertation. Wright had ideas about the "impact of art on government" and this building was to be his signature piece. Many people in Marin were far more interested in the impact of an architectural wonder on their pocketbooks than on their form of government. That much I knew but I needed to know much more. I had a dissertation to write and this woman could prove to be the key to the wealth of information I needed.

I had taken on the task of asking, "How could an affluent county commission a building by America's foremost architect and then become embroiled in a major political battle over its completion?" Such a battle had to stem from an unusual social mix. I presented the question to my doctoral committee and they agreed it was a question worth pursuing. The roots of the battle would be virgin territory for original research. I began my work in the archives of the largest newspaper in the county, the *Independent Journal.* The name Vera Schultz dominated all accounts of the enterprise from its beginning.

The lady supervisor struggled with fellow Supervisor William Fusselman and George Jones, seemingly the biggest roosters in the political barnyard of rural Marin County, over every wrinkle in the unfolding drama. Fusselman was partner (or pawn) of George Jones. Jones cast a longer shadow than any county clerk outside the deep South. Outsiders saw that Fusselman crowed loudest while Jones stalked the county and kept his flock under tight surveillance. These were the major characters but what about the plot and setting? Newspaper accounts were not enough. For background, depth, and perspective, Vera Schultz, whose brainchild it had been to bring Wright to Marin in the first place, was the essential source. I asked for an interview and thus began a quarter of a century of dialog.

Vera guided me to all the major players on both sides of the net and helped me gain access to hard-to-reach quarries. She saved me limitless hours of discovering the underlying issues and steered me away from existing quagmires. She never let me take her word for anything but insisted I also hear out the opposition. In 1971-1972, most of the players were still alive and available for interview, all but Mr. Fusselman who refused to see me. He said his papers were going to a nephew who would write the truth someday. I finished the manuscript in the spring of 1972, sent it to the committee and received the degree in August. Vera came out to Hawaii for commencement exercises. The dissertation was accepted, bound, and might have remained on a shelf in the University of Hawaii Library, except both Vera and I wanted it published. So, the dissertation became a book and was published by Carlton Press in 1974 as *The Bridge and the Building*. The book can now be found only in libraries for it has been out of print for over a decade.

The story of Vera's great achievement, in print for all the world to read, is required reading for docents at the Marin Civic Center. Vera said that book rescued her from oblivion. Not so. As long as Vera lived she was never off the public stage for more than short periods. So dynamic a personality could not be repressed for long. So fecund a mind could not be bridled for long. Such devotion to the public good could not be sequestered for long. Vera was a doer! Retirement was a word she never understood. She said: "I think death is the only retirement. How can people 'retire' as long as they have their wits? Too much needs to be done!"

BIBLIOGRAPHY

The Mountain Meadow Massacre - Juanita Brooks, Stanford University Press, 1950

A History of TONOPAH, NEVADA - Robert D. McCracken, Nye County Press, 1992

TONOPAH, The Greatest, the Richest, and the Best Mining Camp in the World - Robert D. McCracken, Nye Country Press, 1990

Vera Lucille Klingensmith Schultz - Bonnie Ryder, Bancroft Library, 1989, "California Women in Politics" Series

The Bridge and the Building - Evelyn M. Radford, Carlton Press, 1974

The Utah and Nevada material came from her memory and from the first three books listed above. In addition to those works, material was taken from Bonnie Ryder's interviews for the "California Women in Politics" project, and from my own book on Marin County. Records of the main events of the public life of Vera Schultz can be found in the Schultz file in the California Room of the Marin County Central Library and in a collection of Vera Schultz materials in the Mill Valley Library's History Room. The *Marin Independent Journal* has its own Vera Schultz file, as does *The Pacific Sun*.

E.R.

LIST OF DONORS

Helen and Stanley Anderson
Jules & Jody Anne Becker
Sally C. Behr
Robert & Yvonne Belton
Brady Bevis
Susan K. Boley
Ed & Joan Boessenecker
Harold C. Brown
Helen L. Brown
Joan L. Brown
Linda Christman
Doug Dawson
Carole Dillon-Knutson
Fred Drexler
Josephine C. Duff
Gloria Duncan
Lynn Duryee
Elva E. Edger
Justin M. Faggioli
Dennis L. Fishwick
Kathleen E. Foote
Joel Freid
Aaron G. Green
James & Sally Hauser
Thomas & Carolyn Horan
Berniece P. Kettenhofen
Leo V. & Dorothy Killion
Steve Kinsey
John Kress
Rosalie Langstein
Harrison M. Leppo
Jacquelyn Mollenkopf
Suzanne & Tobin Mollenkopf
Harry J. Moore
Catherine H. Munson
William & Joanne Murray
Sibyl Ann Otter
Thelma Percy
Rollin & Diane Post

Denis T. Rice
Annette Rose
Robert & Barbara Roumiguiere
Bonny Ruder
Ed Ryken
Ken & Jay Samuelson
Gloria Scott
Elisabeth (Suki) Sennett
Ann & Don Solem
Richard D. Spotswood
William H. Stephens
Richard & Ailene Taylor
Joseph and Anise Turina
Kathleen S. Vote
Rebecca W. Watkin

Contributing Organizations

Marin County Board of Supervisors
Marin Community Foundation
American Association of University Women,
        Southern Marin Branch
League of Women Voters of Marin County
Marin Women's Hall of Fame
Marin Senior Coordinating Council
Mill Valley Historical Society
Raker Architects
U.A.I.C.O. Gen Agency # 18175

INDEX